CHICKEN SOUP FOR THE SOUL® CHRISTMAS COLLECTION

Holiday Stories to Warm the Heart

Jack Canfield
Mark Victor Hansen

Health Communications, Inc.
Deerfield Beach, Florida

www.hcibooks.com
www.chickensoup.com

We would like to acknowledge the many publishers and individuals who granted us permission to reprint the cited material.

The Gift of Grr-Face. Reprinted by permission of Gary B. Swanson. ©1979 Gary B. Swanson. Excerpted from *Christmas in My Heart #6,* compiled and edited by Dr. Joseph Wheeler.

The Christmas Rose. Reprinted by permission of Marlene Chase. ©1997 Marlene Chase.

Christmas Presence. Reprinted by permission of Laura Lagana. ©2000 Laura Lagana.

(Continued on page 389)

**Library of Congress Cataloging-in-Publication Data
is available at Library of Congress**

©2006 Jack Canfield and Mark Victor Hansen
ISBN-13: 978-0-7573-0606-8
ISBN-10: 0-7573-0606-3

Publisher: Health Communications, Inc.
       3201 S.W. 15th Street
       Deerfield Beach, FL 33442-8190

Cover design by Andrea Perrine Brower
Inside formatting by Dawn Von Strolley Grove

Contents

2. THE SPIRIT OF GIVING

CONTENTS vii

Introduction

The Christmas season conjures up memories of cozy fires warming the chill in the air, brightly lit pine trees surrounded by the sparkle of beautifully decorated presents, and wonder on the minds and in the hearts of everyone who believes in the possibilities of cheer and good will. It's been a longstanding tradition at Chicken Soup for the Soul to bring families and friends together in celebration to commemorate the festivities, traditions, and spirituality of this most wonderful time of the year. For this latest Christmas collection, we selected our favorite stories of Christmas from our previous bestselling holiday books, which include *Chicken Soup for the Soul Christmas Treasury*, *Chicken Soup for the Soul Christmas Treasury for Kids*, and *Chicken Soup for the Soul Christmas Virtues* and combined them to create this very best representation of Christmas—Chicken Soup style.

Join us in our celebration of Christmas with endearing stories from readers like you, who have experienced a bit of the wonder, a lot of the love, and a touch of the extraordinary during this magical season.

1

THE TRUE MEANING OF CHRISTMAS

Christmas is not a time or a season, but a state of mind. To cherish peace and goodwill, to be plenteous in mercy, is to have the real spirit of Christmas.

Calvin Coolidge

The Gift of Grr-face

No one has yet realized the wealth of sympathy, the kindness and generosity hidden in the soul of a child. The effort of every true education should be to unlock that treasure.

Emma Goldman

The mother sat on the simulated-leather chair in the doctor's office, picking nervously at her fingernails.

Wrinkles of worry lined her forehead as she watched five-year-old Kenny sitting on the rug before her.

He is small for his age and a little too thin, she thought. His fine blond hair hung down smooth and straight to the top of his ears. White gauze bandages encircled his head, covering his eyes and pinning his ears back.

In his lap he bounced a beaten-up teddy bear. It was the pride of his life, yet one arm was gone and one eye was missing. Twice his mother had tried to throw the bear away to replace it with a new one, but he had fussed so much she had relented. She tipped her head slightly to the side and smiled at him. *It's really about all he has,* she sighed to herself.

A nurse appeared in the doorway. "Kenny Ellis," she announced, and the young mother scooped up the boy and followed the nurse toward the examination room. The hallway smelled of rubbing alcohol and bandages. Children's crayon drawings lined the walls.

"The doctor will be with you in a moment," the nurse said with an efficient smile. "Please be seated."

The mother placed Kenny on the examination table. "Be careful, honey, not to fall off."

"Am I up very high, Mother?"

"No dear, but be careful."

Kenny hugged his teddy bear tighter. "Don't want Grr-face to fall either."

The mother smiled. The smile twisted at the corners into a frown of concern. She brushed the hair out of the boy's face and caressed his cheek, soft as thistledown, with the back of her hand. As the office music drifted into a haunting version of "Silent Night," she remembered the accident for the thousandth time.

She had been cooking things on the back burners for years. But there it was, sitting right out in front, the water almost boiling for oatmeal.

The phone rang in the living room. It was another one of those "free offers" that cost so much. At the very moment she returned the phone to the table, Kenny screamed in the kitchen, the galvanizing cry of pain that frosts a mother's veins.

She winced again at the memory of it and brushed aside a warm tear slipping down her cheek. Six weeks they had waited for this day to come. "We'll be able to take the bandages off the week before Christmas," the doctor had said.

The door to the examination room swept open, and Dr. Harris came in. "Good morning, Mrs. Ellis," he said brightly. "How are you today?"

"Fine, thank you," she said. But she was too apprehensive for small talk.

Dr. Harris bent over the sink and washed his hands carefully. He was cautious with his patients but careless about himself. He could seldom find time to get a haircut, and his straight black hair hung a little long over his collar. His loosened tie allowed his collar to be open at the throat.

"Now then," he said, sitting down on a stool, "let's have a look."

Gently he snipped at the bandage with scissors and unwound it from Kenny's head. The bandage fell away, leaving two flat squares of gauze taped directly over Kenny's eyes. Dr. Harris lifted the edges of the tape slowly, trying not to hurt the boy's tender skin.

Kenny slowly opened his eyes, blinked several times as if the sudden light hurt. Then he looked at his mother and grinned. "Hi, Mom," he said.

Choking and speechless, the mother threw her arms around Kenny's neck. For several minutes, she could say nothing as she hugged the boy and wept in thankfulness. Finally she looked at Dr. Harris with tear-filled eyes. "I don't know how we'll ever be able to pay you," she said.

"We've been over all that before," the doctor interrupted with a wave of his hand. "I know how things are for you and Kenny. I'm glad I could help."

The mother dabbed at her eyes with a well-used handkerchief, stood up and took Kenny's hand. But just as she turned toward the door, Kenny pulled away and stood for a long moment, looking uncertainly at the doctor. Then he held his teddy bear up by its one arm to the doctor.

"Here," he said. "Take my Grr-face. He ought to be worth a lot of money."

Dr. Harris quietly took the broken bear in his two hands. "Thank you, Kenny. This will more than pay for my services."

The last few days before Christmas were especially good for Kenny and his mother. They sat together in the long evenings, watching the Christmas tree lights twinkle on and off. Bandages had covered Kenny's eyes for six weeks, so he seemed reluctant to close them in sleep. The fire dancing in the fireplace, the snowflakes sticking to his bedroom windows, the two small packages under the tree—all the lights and colors of the holiday fascinated him. And then, on Christmas Eve, Kenny's mother answered the doorbell. No one was there, but a large box was on the porch wrapped in shiny gold paper with a broad red ribbon and bow. A tag attached to the bow identified the box as intended for Kenny Ellis.

With a grin, Kenny tore the ribbon off the box, lifted the lid and pulled out a teddy bear—his beloved Grr-face. Only now it had a new arm of brown corduroy and two new button eyes that glittered in the soft Christmas light. Kenny didn't seem to mind that the new arm did not match the other one. He just hugged his teddy bear and laughed.

Among the tissue in the box, the mother found a card. "Dear Kenny," it read, "I can sometimes help put boys and girls back together, but Mrs. Harris had to help me repair Grr-face. She's a better bear doctor than I am. Merry Christmas! Dr. Harris."

"Look, Mother," Kenny smiled, pointing to the button eyes. "Grr-face can see again—just like me!"

Gary Swanson

The Christmas Rose

Christmas—that magic blanket that wraps itself about us, that something so intangible it is like a fragrance. It may weave a spell of nostalgia. Christmas may be a day of feasting, or of prayer, but always it will be a day of remembrance—a day in which we think of everything we have ever loved.

Augusta E. Rundel

A light snow was falling as she turned the key to open Rose's Flower Shop. The name didn't take much imagination, but then it was better than "Rosie's Posies" as Clint had suggested when she had first begun the business.

"Going to the Towers again this year?" asked Cass Gunther, who was opening the European deli next door.

Rose nodded. It was what they did every year. Supper and drinks at the club and Christmas Eve at the posh Park Towers. Swimming. The hot tub. Maybe take in a show. It was a tradition.

She turned on the lights, feeling bone-tired. As usual, people waited until the last minute to place their

Christmas orders. Why did she do this every year? It wasn't the money, though business had gone well. It filled her days, and there was something soothing about working with flowers.

"I'll be home for Christmas . . . ," the sentimental lyric wafted from the radio under the counter. Home was four extravagantly decorated walls, which she welcomed at the end of the day, but when it came down to it, what was really there for her? Perhaps if they'd been able to have children. They'd had a reasonably good marriage, the best house on Carriage Drive, money in the bank and enough friends to keep them from feeling lonely. And goodness knows they were too busy to think about whether or not they were happy. Bills for the mortgage, the car and boat, and a half dozen credit cards never stopped.

Rose sighed. A hollowness plagued her. Even anticipating Clint's surprise when he received the Pendleton sport coat she'd bought held little joy. His gift to her would be something beautiful, expensive . . . but she couldn't remember last year's gift or when they had taken time to really talk to each other.

She felt suddenly at odds, cross. Perhaps if they'd kept up with the family. But family meant Clint's two aunts in Virginia and her stepfather in Wyoming, none of whom seemed famished for their company. Hungry, that was it. She'd forgotten to eat breakfast.

The bell over the door announced a customer, but she kept her back to the counter, consulting the order book.

"Excuse me, Miss," an elderly voice called from behind her.

I haven't been a Miss in fourteen years, thank you. She swallowed the caustic retort and turned slowly to find an old man smiling at her.

He had all his teeth, a look of kind apology and a full head of wavy white hair. He held a plaid cap across his chest and gave her a quaint little bow like an aging Sir

Galahad. "I'm looking for some flowers—for my wife."

At those words, something luminous lit him from within. She wondered if Clint ever looked that way when he spoke about her. "I see," she said slowly, waiting.

He tapped gnarled fingers over his cap in meditation and with warm authority in his raspy voice said, "Not just any flowers. It must be Christmas roses."

"Well, we have roses. American beauty, reds, pink, tea and yellow . . ."

"Oh, no," he said, shifting his weight from one foot to the other. "Christmas roses—white as snow—with some of that feathery fern tucked in. And I'd like a big red bow, too."

"It's Christmas Eve, sir, and I'm afraid we're fresh out. . . ."

"My wife loves white roses," he continued, looking at something she couldn't see. "They remind her of the Babe of Christmas and the purity of his heart. She hasn't seen any roses for such a long time. And now that . . ."

The old man's shoulders drooped ever so slightly, then straightened again. Rose heard the faint tremor and was touched by something beautiful in the old face that made her think of alabaster. No, alabaster was too cold.

"She's ill now. . . ." He paused and tucked his cap under his arm. "We served at a medical clinic in West Africa for more than thirty years. But we've had to return home. Nell has Alzheimer's. We're living at Country Gardens. . . ."

"Oh, I'm sorry," Rose breathed.

The man rushed on without a trace of bitterness. "I have a little room on the floor just below the nursing wing where Nell is. We share meals together—and we have our memories. God has been good to us."

Rose returned his smile, uncomprehending, but unable to deny the man's sincerity. White roses on Christmas Eve? She might be able to get them from Warrensville, but it would be a stretch.

"We'll be spending Christmas Eve in my room—just the two of us—a celebration," he was saying. "Christmas roses for Nell would make it perfect."

"I may be able to get them sent over from Warrensville...."

Rose bit her lip. Was she crazy? It would take a miracle. Then there was the price. "How much do you want to spend?"

The man set his cap on the counter and dug out a faded wallet from his trousers that had seen several winters. He pushed four five-dollar bills toward her with childlike eagerness, then seeing her dismay, hesitated. "I hope it's enough."

"I could give you a nice spray of red roses in a bud vase," Rose began. *White rose centerpieces would start at thirty-five dollars. Then the delivery charge would run another twenty, especially on Christmas Eve. If she could get them!*

"I had hoped for a real special bouquet..." he broke off, and she read his profound disappointment.

"Leave it to me. I'll do my best to get you something nice," she began, astounded by her own words.

"Bless you!" the old man said, reaching across the counter and grasping her hands. "Can they be delivered around four or five? It will be such a surprise! I can't thank you enough." Nearly dancing, he replaced his cap and began backing toward the door. "Arnold Herriman— Room 7! Merry Christmas! God bless you! God bless you!"

What had a tired old man with a sick wife have to be so happy about? She puzzled over that through the next few orders, then placed a call to a supplier in Warrensville. They could get her a dozen white roses at $42.50—but it would be four o'clock before they could be relayed to her shop.

"Okay," she said wearily, realizing that she herself would have to deliver the Christmas roses to Mr. Herriman. No matter. Clint would likely be delayed by a promising client. The flowers arrived at ten minutes to four, and Rose quickly arranged them in a silver bowl, tucking in the feathery greens and sprigs of baby's breath and holly. She secured a lacy red bow into the base and balanced it in one hand while locking the door with the other. Country Gardens hardly resembled its name. Surely a couple who'd spent a lifetime healing the sick in an obscure village deserved better in the sunset of their years.

She found the residential wing and tentatively approached Room 7. Arnold Herriman, in the same old trousers and shirt with a crimson tie, beamed at her. She entered a room with a few pieces of old furniture and walls bursting with pictures and certificates. On the hall table was a crèche. *The Babe of Christmas and the purity of his heart,* Herriman had said.

A diminutive woman sat on the sofa with hands folded over a patchwork quilt on her lap. She had a translucent complexion and vacant blue eyes above two brightly rouged cheeks. A bit of red ribbon had been tucked into her white hair. Her eyes widened, then spilled with tears when she saw the flowers.

"Nell, darling. It's your surprise—Christmas roses," Arnold said, placing an arm around the woman's fragile shoulders.

"Oh, how lovely!" Nell stretched out her arms, her face transformed in radiance. She rubbed one wrinkled cheek against the delicate petals, then turned a watery gaze on Rose. "Do I know you, dear?"

"This is the nice lady from the flower shop who made your bouquet," Arnold said.

"Can you stay for a while, dear?" she asked. "We'll be finished with our patients soon, and we'll take you to our house for tea."

"Oh, no . . ." stammered Rose.

Arnold touched his wife's shoulder. "The patients are all gone, dear. We're home, and it's Christmas Eve."

Rose's throat ached with unshed tears and the sense

that something beautiful lived here from which she was excluded. Could it be that in living their lives for others these two old people who had nothing but each other and a bouquet of white roses had everything that was important?

Suddenly, Nell plucked one of the long-stemmed white roses from the elegant bouquet and held it out to Rose. "Please, I have so many. You must take one for yourself!"

"Yes," Arnold said, taking the stem from his wife and pressing it toward her, "thank you for all your trouble. God bless you."

She wanted to say that he already had, that bringing them the Christmas roses had made her happier than she could remember in a long time, that on this Christmas Eve she had learned something about the meaning of the holiday she had missed until now.

Lt. Colonel Marlene Chase

Christmas Presence

We make a living by what we get; we make a life by what we give.

Duane Hulse

It was the night before Christmas, and all through the evening I reminisced, fondly reliving past Christmases spent with my family. As a second-year nursing student, just nineteen, this was to be my first Christmas away from home. Although I knew that someday I'd be working on Christmas, I never expected to feel this lonely.

Secluded in my room, I yearned for the mouthwatering aromas of Mom's freshly baked cookies, hot chocolate and love. The absence of the usual giggling, slamming doors and ringing telephones made the dormitory seem cold and empty. The unappetizing smell of disinfectant replaced my visions of cookies and cocoa.

Standing in front of the mirror, I conversed with my reflection. "You wanted to be a nurse, didn't you? Well, you're almost a nurse. Here's your chance to find out what Christmas spirit really means." Determined to make the best of it, I turned in early.

"I'll be home for Christmas. You can count on me. . . ." My faithful clock radio announced reveille as I slowly dragged myself out of a toasty-warm bed. I trudged across the snow-filled street and grabbed a quick breakfast in the cafeteria before reporting for duty on the medical-surgical unit.

As I prepared to take vital signs on my first patient, I was startled by a robust voice that came from behind. "Merry Christmas to you. Want anything from the cafeteria? I'm headed that way, Missy."

I took the stethoscope out of my ears and turned around. From the dimly lit room I could see a gigantic, roly-poly elderly gentleman with long, curly hair, all decked out in a bright-red plaid shirt tucked haphazardly into baggy, red trousers. The trousers appeared to be held up by only two wide, fire-engine red suspenders that had long since outlived their elasticity. The only thing missing was the beard. This Santa Claus facsimile was standing in the doorway waiting patiently for an answer to his query.

Looking toward the bright hallway lights from the darkened room, I thought for a moment that I was dreaming. "No, thanks," I responded. "I just came on duty. I'll grab something at lunch."

Before disappearing down the hall he added, "Name's George. Just let me know what I can do for you, Missy. I'll be right back."

As I cared for my patients, George was right alongside. I watched him spread holiday cheer as he became a guest to the patients who had no visitors that day. When trays arrived, he knew who needed assistance and who needed to be fed. He read letters and cards to those whose eyes could no longer see the letters on a printed page. George's powerful body and tender hands were always ready to help, hold, turn, pull up or lift a patient. He was a "gopher" who made countless trips to the supply room for the "needs of the moment."

George also knew when to call for help. While reading a letter to Mr. Jenkins, George noticed that the patient suddenly started to "look funny" and instantly ran to the nurse's station to summon aid. Thanks to George's swift action, we managed to reverse the effects of an impending diabetic coma.

Jovial George clearly enjoyed helping others while he spread cheer and told jokes—the same jokes, over and over again, all day long, one patient at a time. We all enjoyed his presence that Christmas day.

When I finally took my lunch break, I was surprised to find the cafeteria elaborately decorated for the season. I sat down next to one of the staff nurses from the unit. During lunch with Andrea, I had the chance to ask a burning question. "Who is this George fellow? And why is he here on Christmas Day?"

"About ten years ago, George's wife became seriously ill. He spent almost every waking moment by her side. Those two lovebirds were so devoted to one another. There was nothing he wouldn't do for her." Andrea stopped for a few moments, sipping her coffee in silence, before continuing. "George started to visit other patients while his wife was sleeping or having treatments. He was here so much that he seemed to take naturally to helping out wherever he could."

My natural curiosity made me ask, "Does he have any family?"

A serious look came over Andrea's face as she continued, "They never had children, and as far as I know, there are no relatives. But you see, George watched his wife suffer for a very long time. He shared every second of her pain and anguish. On Christmas Eve, after I prepared his wife for sleep, they prayed together. During the prayer,

George promised his wife that if God would take away her misery that night, by taking her 'home,' he would spend the rest of his life as a Christmas volunteer."

Andrea and I finished our lunch in silence.

Laura Lagana

Reptiles Reconciled

I will never forget the Christmas of my seventh year. I was going to sing several carols with my classmates in the Christmas pageant at school. We had been practicing for about a month. A week before the pageant, my mother's family had their Christmas celebration. Mother had been bragging about how I was to sing at school and I was cajoled into singing one of the carols for the Coulter clan gathered there.

Telling my aunt which carol to play, I sang out as sweetly and sincerely as only a seven-year-old can . . . "Hark! Old Harold's angel sings, glory to the newborn King. Peace on earth so mercy smiles, 'cause God and reptiles reconciled . . ."

That is as far as I got because my aunt could no longer play the piano, she was laughing so hard. My uncle laughed so hard he spilled his drink on his lap and when he tried to mop it up, he lost his balance and slid out of his chair.

I was mortified. I had no idea why everyone was laughing at me. I burst into tears and ran upstairs to my bedroom crying. I really was surprised when my oldest and most straitlaced aunt came into my room. (I had always been a little afraid of her.) She tenderly took me in her arms and with loving words told me not to cry. Everyone was laughing because of the wonderful new words I had sung for that Christmas carol. And even though everyone else had learned it a different way, mine was so much better.

She kissed me and then washed my face and told me to come downstairs with her because there was a surprise waiting for me. Hand in hand we took the stairs down to the living room. Just as we got there the music began to play and the whole Coulter clan began to sing my own words. As I stood listening to them sing my misconstrued version of "Hark the Herald Angels Sing," I felt more loved than I ever had in my life.

My lips were still trembling as I stepped forward and began to sing. As my extended family sang carol after carol and arms slipped around each other in a warm familial glow, I realized Christmas wasn't about festive decorations or the Christmas tree or even the gifts under it. Christmas was about love given freely and with joy.

As one of my older cousins gave me a squeeze and a smile, I was sure Hark, old Harold's angel, was singing with us, and I had gotten the words right after all.

Linda C. Raybern

Delayed Delivery

Stella had been prepared for her husband's death. Since the doctor's pronouncement of terminal cancer, they had both faced the inevitable, striving to make the most of their remaining time together. Dave's financial affairs had always been in order. There were no new burdens in her widowed state. It was just the awful aloneness . . . the lack of purpose to her days.

They had been a childless couple. It had been their choice. Their lives had been so full and rich. They had been content with busy careers and with each other. They had many friends. Had. That was the operative word these days. It was bad enough losing the one person you loved with all your heart. But over the past few years, she and Dave repeatedly coped with the deaths of their friends and relations. They were all of an age—an age when human bodies began giving up. Dying. Face it—they were old!

And now, approaching her first Christmas without Dave, Stella was all too aware she was on her own.

With shaky fingers, she lowered the volume of her radio so that the Christmas music faded to a muted background. To her surprise, she saw that the mail had arrived. With the inevitable wince of pain from her arthritis, she bent to retrieve the white envelopes from the floor. She opened them while sitting on the piano bench. They were mostly Christmas cards, and her sad eyes smiled at the familiarity of the traditional scenes and at the loving messages inside. She arranged them among the others on the piano top. In her entire house, they were the only seasonal decoration. The holiday was less than a week away, but she just did not have the heart to put up a silly tree, or even set up the stable that Dave had built with his own hands.

Suddenly engulfed by the loneliness of it all, Stella buried her face in her hands and let the tears come. How would she possibly get through Christmas and the winter beyond it?!

The ring of the doorbell was so unexpected that Stella had to stifle a small scream of surprise. Now who could possibly be calling on her? She opened the wooden door and stared through the window of the storm door with consternation. On her front porch stood a strange young man whose head was barely visible above the large carton in his arms. She peered beyond him to the driveway, but there was nothing about the small car to give a clue as to his identity. Summoning courage, the elderly lady opened the door slightly, and he stepped sideways to speak into the space.

"Mrs. Thornhope?"

She nodded. He continued, "I have a package for you."

Curiosity drove caution from her mind. She pushed the door open, and he entered. Smiling, he placed his burden carefully on the floor and stood to retrieve an envelope that protruded from his pocket. As he handed it to her, a sound came from the box. Stella jumped. The man laughed in apology and bent to straighten up the cardboard flaps, holding them open in an invitation for her to peek inside.

It was a dog! To be more exact, a golden Labrador retriever puppy. As the young gentleman lifted its squirming body up into his arms, he explained, "This is for you, ma'am." The young pup wiggled in happiness at being released from captivity and thrust ecstatic, wet kisses in the direction of the young man's face. "We were supposed to deliver him on Christmas Eve," he continued with some difficulty as he strove to rescue his chin from the wet little tongue, "but the staff at the kennels start their holidays tomorrow. Hope you don't mind an early present."

Shock had stolen Stella's ability to think clearly. Unable to form coherent sentences, she stammered, "But . . . I don't . . . I mean . . . who . . .?"

The young fellow set the animal down on the doormat between them and then reached out a finger to tap the envelope she was still holding.

"There's a letter in there that explains everything, pretty much. The dog was bought while his mother was still pregnant. It was meant to be a Christmas gift."

The stranger turned to go. Desperation forced the words from her lips. "But who . . . who bought it?"

Pausing in the open doorway, he replied, "Your husband, ma'am." And then he was gone.

It was all in the letter. Forgetting the puppy entirely at the sight of the familiar handwriting, Stella walked like a sleepwalker to her chair by the window. She forced her tear-filled eyes to read her husband's words. He had written the letter three weeks before his death and had left it with the kennel owners, to be delivered along with the puppy as his last Christmas gift to her. It was full of love and encouragement and admonishments to be strong. He vowed that he was waiting for the day when she would join him. And he had sent her this young animal to keep her company until then.

Remembering the little creature for the first time, she was surprised to find him quietly looking up at her, his small panting mouth resembling a comic smile. Stella put the pages aside and reached for the bundle of golden fur. She thought that he would be heavier, but he was only the size and weight of a sofa pillow. And so soft and warm. She cradled him in her arms and he licked her jawbone, then cuddled into the hollow of her neck. The tears began anew at this exchange of affection, and the dog endured her crying without moving.

Finally, Stella lowered him to her lap, where she regarded him solemnly. She wiped vaguely at her wet cheeks, then somehow mustered a smile.

"Well, little guy, I guess it's you and me." His pink tongue panted in agreement. Stella's smile strengthened, and her gaze shifted sideways to the window. Dusk had fallen. Through fluffy flakes that were now drifting down, she saw the cheery Christmas lights edging the roof lines of her neighbors' homes. The strains of "Joy to the World" floated in from the kitchen.

Suddenly Stella felt the most amazing sensation of peace and benediction wash over her. It was like being enfolded in a loving embrace. Her heart beat painfully, but it was with joy and wonder, not grief or loneliness. She need never feel alone again.

Returning her attention to the dog, she spoke to him. "You know, fella, I have a box in the basement that I think you'd like. There's a tree in it and some decorations and lights that will impress you like crazy! And I think I can find that old stable down there, too. What d'ya say we go hunt it up?"

The puppy barked happily in agreement, as if he understood every word. Stella got up, placed the puppy on the floor and together they went down to the basement, ready to make a Christmas together.

Cathy Miller

'Twas the Night b4 Christmas

I wish we could put some of the Christmas spirit in jars and open a jar of it every month.

Harlan Miller

Two Decembers ago my dad called wanting to know what I wanted for Christmas. I mentioned a particular book and then interrupted myself and said, "No, what I'd really like is for you to put *The Night Before Christmas* on audiotape."

There was this long pause and then Dad said with familiar stern emphasis in his voice, "Oh for God's sake, Mary. What in Sam Hill do you want that for? You're forty years old!"

I paused, feeling embarrassed yet determined, "Dad, I remember how good it felt when you used to cuddle us all up next to you on the couch when we were little and read *The Night Before Christmas*. I can still remember how strong your voice was, how safe I felt and how well you acted out all the different sounds. I'd really appreciate you doing this, since I live 2,500 miles away and I'm not coming home for Christmas. It would be nice to have you with me."

Dad said, with a little more softness but still incredulously, "You mean you want me to read just like I did when you were kids, with all the bells and whistles and everything?!"

"Yaaaaaah, just like that," I said.

Again, he paused a long time and then said, "I'll get you the book."

I heard the clarity of his decision in his voice and resignedly said, "Okay. Talk to you on Christmas." We said our "I love yous" and hung up. I felt bad but tried to understand. I assumed it was too much sentimentalism for a seventy-six-year-old bear, and that in his mind it was a foolish request for an adult to ask. Maybe. Maybe not. All I knew was that each time I talked to Dad his voice sounded more tired, and I was beginning to accept that it was no longer if, but when, the day would come that I wouldn't hear it anymore.

On Christmas Eve day, a small, brown, heavily recycled padded envelope with lots of staples and tape all over it arrived. My name and address were written out in my dad's memorable architect's lettering with thick black magic marker. Inside was a tape, with a handwritten label, "'Twas the Night b4 Christmas."

I popped the tape in my recorder and heard my father's words come roaring out. "'Twas the niiiiiiiiiiiiight before Christmas when allllllllllllllllllllllll through the howwwwwwse," just like when we were children! When he finished, he went on to say, "And now I'm going to read from *The Little Engine That Could*. I guess Dad had another message in mind when he included one of our favorite childhood bedtime stories. It was the same story we read to my mom when she was dying of cancer three years ago.

He continued with the Mormon Tabernacle Choir singing "Silent Night," our family's favorite Christmas Eve song we sang together before bedtime. And then "Oh Come All Ye Faithful" . . . song after song until the tape ran out. I went to sleep safe and sound Christmas Eve, thanking God for giving me another Christmas miracle with my dad.

The following May, Dad passed away suddenly and unexpectedly. No more phone calls every Sunday morning, no more phone calls asking me, "What was the Gospel about today, Mary?" no more "I love yous." But his voice lives on . . . and continues to remind me that I can do what I put my mind to and that I can stretch myself emotionally for someone else, even when it's difficult. That's the power of love.

For Christmas this year I sent my sisters and brother and their children a copy of the tape, which they weren't expecting. My youngest sister called and left a tearful message on my machine that said, "Mary, I just got the tape. Did you know that on the tape he said it was December 19. That's today! When I put the tape on while I was in the living room, Holden [her two-and-one-half-year-old son], came running out from the kitchen full steam, yelling at the top of his lungs, 'Grampa's here, Grampa's here.' You should have seen him, Mary, looking all around for Dad. Dad *was* here."

His voice lives on.

Mary Marcdante

The Santa Claus on I-40

The wipers struggled to push the heavy, wet snowflakes off the windshield while they kept rhythm to Willie Nelson singing "On the Road Again."

Trint hit the eject button on the tape player. He'd heard that song four times in the last two hours and was sick of it. He shrugged his aching shoulders trying to shake off the miles. It was still a long way to Memphis, a storm was blowing in and Interstate 40 was getting hazardous.

In the distance, Trint spotted the welcome glow of lights at a truck stop and decided to pull off the road and grab a bite to eat while he waited to see if the weather would break or turn into an icy blizzard that would shut down the roads until morning.

He eased his orange Freightliner and fifty-three-foot-long trailer into an empty spot and shut it down. He was hauling a heavy load of tires to Nashville, and after that he was picking up a load in Baltimore and heading to Chicago.

He reached for his jacket and hesitated when he saw the box on the passenger seat. His mother had been worried about him spending Christmas on the road alone and had given him a box filled with presents. He smiled; his mom still treated him like he was a kid. He looked at his watch. It was nearly midnight on Christmas Eve, so he might as well open his gifts now.

Trint tore open the box and found a warm flannel shirt, probably blue. It was hard to tell in the dim light, but his mom knew his favorite color was blue. There were some heavy socks and leather gloves. Mom was always fussing over him and worrying her youngest son would get cold. There were homemade cookies and fudge and a red stocking with Santa Claus on it. He reached into the stocking and pulled out a toy tractor trailer that looked a lot like his rig and wondered how many stores his mother had to go to before she found such a close match.

His eyes stung. Next month he'd be twenty-five years old. He was a man. Men didn't cry over cookies and a toy truck or because they were a thousand miles away from home on Christmas.

He climbed out of his cab and a cold blast of air hit him in the chest like a fist. He pulled his collar up and ran across the parking lot to the all-night cafe. He was tall and thin and without much meat on his bones to protect him from the cold. Inside, it was warm and cozy. A dozen truckers were spread out at the counter and tables. A man and woman and small boy were huddled in a booth, and they looked tired and unhappy.

Trint felt sorry for the boy. He looked like he was around eight years old, and no kid should have to spend Christmas Eve in a truck stop. The parents were loading up on coffee and Trint guessed they'd been driving somewhere to spend the holidays with relatives, and the snow forced them to hole up here. They were drinking coffee hoping to stay awake so they could finish their trip if the weather cleared up.

"It's so cold outside, I was spitting ice cubes," a fat trucker at the counter said, and the others laughed.

A cute waitress with blonde hair offered Trint a menu.
"I'll have biscuits and gravy . . . ," he said.
"And iced tea with lemon," she finished the order for him.
"You're the only trucker around here who doesn't drink coffee." She smiled and didn't seem in a hurry to leave.
"I'm surprised you remember me." Trint returned her smile.
"How could I ever forget those beautiful brown eyes and your country accent?" she asked, hoping he would guess that she watched for him every time a truck pulled in.
"Well, I remember you, too," he grinned. "You want to be a schoolteacher, I think you said first or second grade, you're putting yourself through college by working here at night and your name is Melinda."
"You do remember!" she said, liking the soft way he said her name. Color flushed her cheeks and she hurried off into the kitchen.

Funny how truckers picked up bits and pieces of other people's lives. He looked across the room. Some of the truckers' faces looked familiar but he didn't know any of their names. He might see them again tomorrow at another truck stop, or never see them again. Sometimes the job seemed awfully lonely. Trint liked driving a truck, he liked seeing new places and he liked the good pay, but sometimes, like tonight, he felt lonesome and wondered if this was really the life for him.

He missed his family. His mom raised four kids by herself on a forty-acre farm in Missouri, but no matter how scarce money was, she'd always made sure they had a good Christmas. He thought about his box of gifts in the truck.

He looked at the kid again and knew what he had to do. He forced himself back into the bone-chilling cold outside to walk to his truck. He grabbed the Christmas stocking out of the cab and hurried back to the warmth of the cafe.

He walked to the booth where the family sat in weary silence.

"I think Santa Claus left this for you," Trint said and handed the red stocking to the boy.

The boy looked at his mother. She hesitated just a second and nodded. The boy eagerly reached out and took the stocking and dug inside.

"Wow! Mom, look! A big rig just like the real ones outside!" His crooked grin lit up the whole room.

"Tell Santa . . . well, tell him thanks," the boy's father said and shook Trint's hand long and hard. The mother smiled gratefully.

Trint returned to the counter and ate his biscuits and gravy. He gave the waitress a twenty-dollar tip and told her merry Christmas. She said the money was too much, but he told her to use it to buy some books for school, and she took it and slipped him a piece of paper.

"Take good care of yourself," she said. "And hurry back."

"I will . . . Melinda," he promised and noticed she had the bluest eyes he'd ever seen.

Trint walked outside. It had stopped snowing and a handful of stars sparkled through a break in the clouds.

There was a tap on the window behind him and he turned to look. It was the boy. He was holding up the truck and laughing. Trint waved good-bye, and the boy waved back.

Trint felt good. Somewhere along the road tomorrow he'd call home and talk to his brothers and kid sister. He'd tell his mom about giving the toy to the kid. She'd like that.

Trint reached his truck and stopped. Somebody had written "Merry X-mas," in the snow on his windshield and hung a candy cane on his side mirror. He wondered if it was Melinda or the boy or one of the truckers.

He started up his engine and felt the roar and power as he slowly pulled up to the road. Soon the snowplows would be out and clear the Interstate, but right now the road stretched out like a silver ribbon.

A quiet peace filled Trint's heart. He was a lucky guy. He had a job he loved, Melinda's phone number in his pocket, clear weather and miles of open road ahead.

He wasn't tired anymore, or lonely. He loved this life and he wouldn't change a thing.

Linda Stafford

A Cat Named Christmas

Alan opened the backdoor on Christmas morning to find the yard covered in a beautiful carpet of glittery white snow. But it wasn't beautiful to Alan.

Alan was unhappy, as Alan often was, because he hadn't gotten what he wanted for Christmas. Instead of the BB gun he'd asked for, Alan had received a new bicycle. It was a shiny, red bicycle, with chrome wheels and blue and white tassles streaming from the handlebars. Most children would have been thrilled to find it sitting next to the tree on Christmas morning, but not Alan.

"You're too young for a gun," his mother had explained, trying to comfort him. But it hadn't worked. Alan pouted all of Christmas morning. When Alan was unhappy, he wanted everyone else to be unhappy, too.

Finally, after all the other gifts were opened, his father had asked Alan to take the discarded boxes and crumpled wrapping paper to the trash. As Alan tossed the papers into the barrel, a tiny, shivering kitten popped its head around the fence and greeted him with a timid "meow."

"Scat!" Alan hissed at the kitten, who ignored the command and ran anxiously toward the boy. "You mangy old stray. If I had my gun, I'd shoot you," Alan said. He slammed the lid on the trash can and headed toward the house, the kitten chasing after him.

As Alan climbed the stairs of the back porch, he heard another meow and looked down to find the kitten standing at his feet. "I thought I told you to get lost," he said angrily, and nudged the kitten down the stairs with the toe of his boot. But before Alan could open the door and go inside, there was the kitten, rubbing against his legs and looking up at him hopefully.

"You're sure not much of a cat," Alan said as he sat down on the stoop of the house and rubbed the kitten behind the ears. "And you're about the ugliest thing I've ever seen." The kitten was bone-thin from hunger and its coat was a muddle of colors—brown and black and white and orange and tan—every color a cat could possibly be. "But it is Christmas," Alan said, "and I suppose it couldn't hurt to give you something to eat." So Alan went into the kitchen and returned with a bowl of milk for the little cat.

But the kitten showed little interest in food, even though he obviously was hungry. Instead, he climbed into Alan's lap, rubbed against his jacket and began to purr. "You sure are a friendly little thing," Alan said, petting the happy kitten. And soon, Alan was happy, too. He somehow forgot to be angry about the BB gun, and the skinny little kitten didn't seem so ugly anymore.

With the kitten under his arm, Alan went into the kitchen where his mother was preparing dinner. "Look what I found," Alan beamed as he set the small cat on a rug in front of the stove and fetched another bowl of milk.

"You know you can't keep him," his mother warned, "but I guess it's okay to feed him something. After all, it is Christmas."

Alan's mother had no intention of allowing the cat to stay in the house. The kitten lapped up his milk and had fallen asleep on the rug in front of the warm stove when

Alan's mother knelt down to pick him up and return him to the back porch. The little cat yawned and stretched, nuzzled against her chin and began to purr as he fell back to sleep. "You sure are a sweet little fella," she said quietly, laying him back down on the rug.

Alan's father, too, had said Alan couldn't keep the cat. But later that day, as he sat reading in front of the fire, he felt something pulling at his pant leg. When he looked down, the playful kitten sprang into his lap and knocked his book to the floor.

"Are you still here?" he asked, already heading for the backdoor with the kitten. But the cat scurried up his arm and, sitting on his shoulder, gently bit his chin and began to purr. As Alan's father took the kitten from his shoulder and held him in his hands, the kitten looked up and meowed at the man who smiled down at him. By that evening, the kitten had found a home.

"What shall we call him?" Alan asked as his mother tucked him into bed.

"Well, he's your cat," his mother said. "But since he came today, why don't you call him Christmas?"

And Alan fell asleep with the little kitten named Christmas cozily nestled at his side.

Alan grew to love Christmas very much. He was the best Christmas present any boy could ever receive, Alan thought. The two spent countless hours together during the following summer and when Alan returned to school the next fall, he would come home each afternoon to find Christmas waiting at the backdoor, anxious for his playmate to return.

Christmas would race Alan up the big oak tree in the backyard, or ride in Alan's wagon, or chase the tail of a kite as Alan launched it into the clear, blue sky. Christmas was Alan's best friend, and Alan was no longer an unhappy little boy.

Though it was clear that everyone in Alan's family loved the little cat, and he was always anxious to love them back, Alan knew that Christmas loved him best. But Alan's mother, as Christmas contentedly rubbed against her legs when she prepared a meal, and his father, as he sat reading the newspaper with the cat curled purring in his lap, felt that Christmas must love them best. In fact, anyone who was with Christmas for very long knew he loved them. They felt the little cat must love them better than any cat has ever loved a person. But that's the kind of cat Christmas was.

Then, one afternoon as autumn first began to give way to winter, Christmas wasn't waiting as usual when Alan arrived home from school, and the young boy knew something was wrong. He went to his bedroom to find Christmas huddled on his bed. The small cat was quivering all over and his nose was warm. Alan got his mother, and although she and Alan and his father did all they could to make Christmas well, the little cat grew worse and soon died.

Alan was devastated. And even though days stretched into weeks and soon it was Christmastime once more, nothing seemed to make Alan happy again.

Then one day, as he sat quietly in front of the Christmas tree at his grandparents' house, watching the lights flicker on and off, his grandmother asked, "Why so sad, little man? This is the season of joy."

"I'm sad about Christmas," Alan said. "Why did he come at all?"

Not realizing he was talking about the kitten who had come to Alan's house on Christmas morning, his grandmother took Alan on her lap and said, "Christmas came to show us love. That's why you should be joyful."

"But why did he have to die so young?" Alan asked. "How can I be joyful now?"

"Because the love he brought didn't die. It will always be with you," his grandmother explained.

And when Alan returned home, he was no longer sad when he looked at the tree Christmas used to climb or the wagon they used to play in. Instead, he remembered the love the kitten had brought to him. And he was happy.

And then he knew why Christmas came.

Rand Souden

Blue Christmas

This is a story about Christmas, and about a box under our Christmas tree one year that wasn't big enough, by a long shot, to hold a bicycle. That box, brightly wrapped in blue tissue with a tag "Merry Christmas, Terry—love, Mom and Dad," was the object of my considerable attention, because I knew it held my main gift, and what I really wanted was a bicycle. Not any bicycle, but a particular blue bicycle from Johnston's Hardware Store on the Hill.

On the other side of the tree was another box, wrapped in red, with a tag "Merry Christmas, Steve—love, Mom and Dad." Steve, my nine-year-old brother, wanted an electric train, and he was sure that was what his package held.

It was 1958, my eleventh year, and we were living in Cedar Falls, a town I never really got to know because we moved from there to Iowa City the next fall.

We had a low, ranch-style house, pale green and brand new. It was a new street and a new neighborhood, dotted with expensive new homes.

The Hill was six blocks away and important to us, not only for its small shopping district but also because it was the site of the college my sister, Linda, seventeen, would attend next fall.

The Monday before Christmas, Steve and I headed for the Hill to do our Christmas shopping. Shivering, I plunged my hands as far into my pockets as they would go. The sky was ominously grey, and the cold wind which shook the bare branches of the trees overhead, seemed to cut right through my jacket.

"C'mon, Steve," I called impatiently to my brother. "We'll never get there if we don't hurry."

"Race ya," he cried.

We were off. I was a faster runner than he was, but sometimes with a head start he could beat me. I sprinted behind him, straining to catch up. He stopped at the corner, winded, his face red. "I won," he panted triumphantly.

Any other day I would have called him a cheater. But today was special, so I let him stay the victor. The Hill was in sight. Its lampposts were gaily strung with green cellophane chains and huge plastic candy canes that looked good enough to eat. Steve and I trudged up the hill that gave the small shopping area its name, past the soda shop where we sometimes got ice cream in the summer, past the pet store where we usually admired the parakeets and turtles. We were going to the five-and-dime to do our Christmas shopping—for the first time alone.

My brother had his savings from his piggy bank clutched in his hand, and I had four dollars, some of which I'd earned raking the neighbor's yard, in my pocket.

At the dime store we paused long enough to look in the window. There were a host of wonderful things there—chocolate Santas, dolls with long hair, miniature bright red fire trucks with a hose that sprayed water.

"You could get that for me," I announced to my brother, pointing to a round, blue sliding saucer which sat on a mound of artificial snow. "I'll share it with you."

"I only have sixty-five cents," he reminded me.

Then in we went. Steve stopped by a jar of colored combs and carefully examined one. Then he looked at me. "Don't you have shopping to do?" he demanded.

I headed for the aisle that held envelopes, notebooks and stationery. My sister would need stationery to write to us, I thought. It was a perfect gift. I debated about buying my father a notebook, since he would be going back to college in Iowa City. (At forty-five!) *Too ordinary,* I thought. I wanted to give him something special, not something silly, like the green beanie his friends were planning!

My brother came around the corner and began looking at the pencils. I picked up the stationery I'd chosen and headed for the cash register in front. I had made my mother a set of hot pads, but I wanted to give her something else as well. Suddenly I spotted the perfect gift, a pair of pale blue earrings that would just match her new dress.

I had enough money left to buy baseball cards, bubble gum and a miniature flashlight for Steve. After I paid for my presents I waited for him outside.

Soon he emerged, beaming, a small bag in one hand, a nickel in the other. "Let's go wrap them," he said.

We went home by way of the hardware store, so I could look at my bike. It wasn't my bike actually, but I was saving money to buy it. I wanted it more than anything else in the world. It was a slim blue Italian model; I'd never seen another one like it. I planned to ride it to school, to the ice cream shop, and to see my best friend Cathy, even though she only lived a half block away from me. Next fall, I'd ride it all over Iowa City.

The hardware store was busy, and Mr. Johnston was waiting on a customer. He wouldn't have time to talk today. I would take a quick look at my bike and be on my way. My brother waited by the sporting goods while I went to the back where the bicycles were. There it was, on the end, as blue as the whole sky, just waiting to be ridden. I reached over to touch the blue and white seat, and stopped cold. Hanging from the handlebar was a tag, handwritten in capital letters, SOLD, it said.

It seemed like my heart stopped and time stood still. For three months, ever since the first day I saw it, I'd been saving my money to buy that blue bike.

I ran from the store, fighting back tears. Now somebody else would ride down College Street on my bike, somebody I knew, or, worse yet, a stranger who would carelessly leave it out in the rain and snow to rust and grow old.

On the way home, Steve and I walked slowly. I didn't notice the cold. He wanted to talk, but I was thinking about the bicycle that almost was, the bicycle that wouldn't be. One thing was certain. I could break open my bank. I no longer needed the twelve dollars I'd saved. I started to think of what I would buy with it.

This, our last Christmas in Cedar Falls, would be a truly blue Christmas now, I knew. Next year, we would no longer have the ranch house with its two fireplaces. Instead, we would have a tiny tin barrack left over from World War II, so small it was barely larger than my bedroom in Cedar Falls. Instead of a fireplace it would have an oilstove; instead of a picture window looking out over a spacious green lawn, it would have windows so high you couldn't see out and no lawn at all. My mother said we had to save money, and cut back. She was going to find a job while my father went to school.

I didn't look forward to the prospect of cutting back or moving. I liked Cedar Falls, the shops on the Hill, my school, and my best friend Cathy. But I knew education was important. It had brought us to the new ranch-style with the huge sloping lawn planted with Russian olive trees and weeping willows. That house was miles and miles from the ramshackle houses my father had grown up in; dark, drafty tinderboxes bordering smelly, smoky factories. And it would take us even further—to the university town where my father hoped to get a Ph.D. degree, and then to some other university town where he would become a professor.

If I had my blue bike, I thought brightly, *I wouldn't mind moving so much.* Then, remembering how much my father had gone without as a boy, I decided to put the bicycle out of my mind. There was Christmas to think about, and presents to wrap.

By the time my brother and I got home, my spirits had picked up and we burst excitedly through the door, throwing off our jackets and hats. I heard Bing Crosby on the record player singing "White Christmas." That meant my father had gotten out his Christmas records while we were gone. He was sitting by the fireplace, where a fire was crackling, reading. Occasionally he'd sing a few bars, his off-key tenor voice echoing Crosby's.

My mother was baking, humming as she worked. She was making sugar cookies shaped like bells and reindeer, sprinkled with red and green sugar. My brother and I sat down and had two each, warm from the oven, at the picnic table we ate from in our kitchen. The tempting scent of cookies baking drifted through the warm and cozy house from room to room, as Bing Crosby sang and I wrapped my packages. When I put them under the tree I spotted several small rectangular packages that my brother had wrapped.

One was addressed to me, "Merry Christmas, Terry," the card read, "and no peeking."

A piece of tinsel had fallen off the tree and I put it back on a low branch, then stepped back to admire the tree. Decorating it was a family affair, and each year we dragged out the box of ornaments and happily examined its contents. There were little candle-shaped lights with colored water inside that bubbled when you plugged them in. There was tinsel, which we carefully removed from the tree each year and saved.

At night, when the room was dark and the Christmas tree lights were on, the living room seemed to take on a special glow, a blue glow, as if that tree were the center of the universe and all the promise of the world lay in that room. That tree represented warmth, happiness and security.

"Look," my mother said, "it's snowing."

The sky that had threatened snow all day opened up, and soft flakes fell softly to the ground, piling up around the steps, blanketing the yard, and draping the small pine trees outside. A hush came over the neighborhood and in every picture window, it seemed, the colored lights of Christmas trees twinkled. Even the snow shimmered, catching and reflecting the blue lights strung on trees across the street.

After dinner my father told about Christmas when he was a boy. He told about the time there wasn't enough money for presents, or even food. It was a faraway world that I only knew through his stories, and even though I had seen the rundown houses where he had grown up, I had trouble feeling the reality of going hungry, of going without presents on Christmas day.

Some of his Christmases were happy, and those were the ones I liked to hear about best. I liked to hear about the year he and his brother got a wooden sled, which they found leaning in the snow against their house on a bright Christmas morning. I liked to imagine my father going downhill at top speed, laughing heartily, the snow flying in his face, momentarily blinding him.

But I would always think about going hungry. I secretly hoped I would never know a Christmas without date pinwheel cookies, and the oranges my mother always put in my stocking.

Suddenly I knew what I would give my father for

Christmas—the money I saved for my bicycle. I ran to my room, and on a piece of paper I wrote, "Dear Dad, this is for your education." I carefully folded the paper and in it I put the money I had saved for my bicycle—twelve one-dollar bills. I put the paper in a shoebox. He'd never guess in a million years what a shoebox as light as a feather held. Carefully I wrapped it and put it under the tree.

And then, it was Christmas! Christmas morning, and my brother and I were up at dawn, trying to rouse my parents from their bed. We waited impatiently while my mother made her way slowly to the kitchen and started the coffee in the percolator. My brother and I poked at the presents under the tree, and emptied our stockings of their ribbon candy, oranges, apples and trinkets. Couldn't my mother hurry? Why did they have to have coffee?

Finally the great moment came, as we all assembled around the tree. The anticipation was high. I had come to terms with the fact that there would be no bicycle, but that big box held something else, some wonderful surprise. I knew that. We began to open our presents. My grandmother had sent me pajamas. She had given my sister embroidered pillow cases. My sister had given my father a moustache cup for drinking his coffee. My brother opened a football, and whooped.

Then there was the big box for me, and I shook it to see if it rattled. It didn't.

"Try to guess," my mother said. I couldn't and finally ripped the paper from it. There inside was the big blue saucer from the five-and-dime. It had snowed just in time. My father opened a red flannel shirt my sister had made, and my mother opened the comb from my brother and ran it appreciatively through her hair. "Thank you sweetheart," she said to Steve. My sister opened the stationery and laughed. "I guess this means I'll have to write," she said, giving me a hug.

Finally, my brother picked up his big box. He started to say "A saucer for—" and then something in the box rattled. His eyes opened wide. With my mother cautioning him to save the paper, he gently opened the box. It was an electric train set with a cattle car and a yellow caboose.

"It's just like the Illinois Central," he said.

Then I saw my father holding the shoebox, a puzzled gleam in his eyes. Carefully he untied the ribbon. He reached inside and slowly withdrew the note.

For once he didn't say anything. When he finished reading what I had written, he looked at me, then my mother. His eyes seemed to fill with tears.

Had I ruined Christmas? We all watched him in uneasy silence. Then, as he handed the note to my mother, he stood up, put on his new shirt, tucked his new comb in one pocket and the money in the other. "Looks like I'm all ready for college," he said, laughing.

Then his expression changed and he looked at all of us. "This is the most wonderful Christmas I've ever had. I hope it is for you, too," he said. He winked at my mother.

My mother was smoothing the hot pads I had given her with her hands. She had put on the blue earrings. The way she smiled at me showed how pleased she was.

While my father was pretending to be drinking from his moustache cup, I picked up the coal black locomotive from my brother's train. "It's beautiful," I said.

He whispered, "Maybe you'll get a bike for your birthday."

"Maybe," I acknowledged. My birthday was eleven months off, and the coasting hills would have to do without me for now.

But then a realization came over me, suddenly, as I picked up the blue pencils my brother had given me. Christmas was more than giving presents, or receiving presents.

It was my brother stretching his allowance to buy us

gifts. It was the care I had put into making those hot pads. It was my sister being there, before she went to college. It was my mother bustling in the kitchen, singing "Silent Night," and my father getting out his Bing Crosby record for the umpteenth time. It was carols and cookies and colored lights, a family in a small town on a morning when the snow fell thick and fast. It was love and sharing and being together. It was intangible stuff—memories, tradition, hope—it was catching, for a moment, a glimpse of peace.

My mother interrupted my thoughts. "Terry, could you please see if the coffee is ready?"

Dutifully I hurried to the kitchen, where I could smell a cinnamon coffee cake baking. My mouth watered. "It's ready," I called, and I took out two coffee cups. Then I turned to see if the plates were on the table for breakfast.

I could not believe my eyes. There, parked next to the picnic table, was the bicycle from the hardware store, shinier, sleeker and bluer than it had ever been before, shimmering like a vision. Taking a deep breath, I ran over and touched the gleaming chrome, the leather seat, the tires.

Softly then Bing Crosby began singing "White Christmas" in the living room. I smiled. It might be a white Christmas for everyone else, with plump snow-capped evergreens on soft white lawns. It was a blue Christmas for me. Blue was the color of promise and possibility, of next year and always, of the roads I would follow, on that bike and others. Blue was the top of the hill, the wind at my back, freedom. With a flourish I kicked up the kickstand and wheeled my bike toward the front door.

Terry Andrews

Nickled and Dimed

I was sitting at my desk involved in paperwork one sunny May afternoon when the door opened, and a young boy, about nine or ten, came into the store.

He walked confidently toward me and said he wanted to purchase a gift for his father. His serious countenance made it obvious: This was a mission of importance.

As we wound through the furniture division of Loy's Office Supplies, he expressed dismay at the cost of each chair and lamp. Finally, I suggested a desk-pad set. With eyes glowing, he thoughtfully chose a maroon faux leather unit with matching pencil cup, memo holder and letter opener. His joy nearly matched my own—the whole process ate two hours of my time—and we headed toward my desk to finalize the sale.

"Okay, I'll be in every week to pay on this for my dad," said young Michael Murphy.

"And you'll pick it up just before Father's Day?" I asked.

"Oh, no, ma'am. This is for Christmas."

My mouth gaped as wide as my eyes when he handed me his first payment: a nickel and two dimes. But that day changed all of our lives at Loy's.

As the months passed, neither rain nor snow kept

Michael away. Week after week, he arrived promptly at four o'clock every Friday to make his payment. His mother stood outside during each recorded transaction, and one day I asked to meet her.

From her, I learned that Michael's father was out of work. She took in laundry and ironing to eke out a living for the family of seven. I felt badly, but I respected their pride and refusal of help. But with the approach of winter, all of us at Loy's noticed Michael wore only a thin sweater, no matter how deep the snow. We concocted a story about a stray coat left at the store—that just happened to be his size. It worked.

One day Michael ran in to announce he had a job—bringing in the newspaper and sweeping the front steps for an old lady down the street every day after school. The ten cents she paid each week would bring him closer to his purchase.

As the holiday season drew near, I feared Michael would not have enough money to pay off the gift, but my boss advised me not to worry.

Two days before Christmas, a dejected Michael came into the store. He hadn't earned enough money to make his final payment.

"Could I please take the present for my dad so he'll have it for Christmas?" His eyes bored straight into my own. "I promise I'll be in after Christmas to finish paying it off."

Before I could answer, my boss looked up.

"Why, young man, there's a sale on desk sets today." He glanced at a paper in his hand. "I think it's only fair that you get the sale price, too."

That meant his dad's gift was paid for!

Michael raced outside to tell his mother. Amid teary hugs and broken thank-yous, we sent them on their way, with Michael clasping the precious, gift-wrapped present to his chest. All of us were proud of Michael's commitment to his project and his devotion to the dad he loved so much.

A few weeks after Christmas, a shabbily dressed man came into Loy's and limped directly to my desk.

"Are you the lady my son Michael talks about?" His voice was gruff and as oversized as the man himself.

When I nodded, Mr. Murphy paused. He cleared his throat.

"I've just come to thank you for all your help and patience. We don't have much," he picked at his worn glove, "and I still can't believe that youngster would do this for his old dad. I'm awful proud of him."

Rising from my chair, I walked around the desk to give him a hug. "We think Michael is pretty special, too. As we watched him pay off that desk set, it was clear he loves you very much."

Mr. Murphy smiled in agreement and walked away. But as he approached the door, his head swiveled my way and he blinked back the tears.

"And you know what? I don't even own a desk!"

Barbara "Binkie" Dussault

Charlie's Coat

She'd been on a halfhearted hunt for some misplaced Christmas stockings when she found the coat—warm and soft, brown and dear—in the very back of her bedroom closet, hiding behind a big box of Glenn Miller albums. The sight of it shocked, surprised and saddened her. All three emotions gathered in one scary lump in the space between her throat and her permanently broken heart.

Why hadn't she found it before? Charlie had been gone a year to the day, and she'd been in that closet countless times. She'd pilfered through it like a teary-eyed madwoman looking for bits and pieces of the man she'd loved all of her life, things that were his, things he'd worn. Faded flannel shirts—his second skin from September through every April—broken-in Levi's with permanent white creases sharp enough to slice a loaf of homemade bread and his shoes.

Oh God, the shoes.

Empty shoes, just sitting there all alone. Except for the coat, they were the hardest things to look at. Reebok walkers, white on white, his old standbys. She'd bought them just two weeks before he passed away.

Where was the man who filled those shoes?

Not here. Not sitting with her on the side of the bed, not out in the woodshop, not at the corner take-out, not jawing at the fence with the neighbors, not dangling a grandkid on his knee, not here in this house.

Where he belonged.

Ginny made herself stand, take two small steps, and with eyes closed, reach to the back of the closet. There, she thought. She felt it. See? She could feel that coat and not go to pieces. But could she hold it, asked a small, inner voice. Could she smell it, look at it? And while she wondered, it hit her again . . . how did it get here, and where had it been for a whole, long year?

She'd told the kids she wanted it back. She didn't care which one of them had taken it. She knew it was out of love that they conspired to hide it away, like a piece of hurt she wouldn't have to see. She knew, she knew . . . out of sight, out of mind.

But they had insisted, all three of them, that they did not hide the coat, the chocolate brown barn coat she'd given him their first Christmas, 1962. The one he wore to work every day for the next twenty-five years, the one she'd teasingly threatened to toss away when the pockets wore off and the deep ribs became smooth and dull and the points on the collar curled up. The one he insisted on keeping long after it was presentable.

In less than a breath, she reached up now, on her toes, and tugged at the coat with all the loneliness and despair and gut-wrenching longing that was in her, and just as suddenly, with great care and respect and love, she pulled it to her small, shaking frame and slipped it on, one arm at a time, until she could double the breast, and then held on tight, and remembered.

"A bee-yoo-tee-ful lady I knew bought it for me," he'd said, "and I'm not about to give it up."

She still remembered the pain and the pride she'd felt

when he'd said that, looking at her like she was the best thing he could ever hope to possess, and she'd understood. He most certainly had been the finest thing she had ever known.

And oh, that did it. That single, long-ago moment broke the dam. Just his quiet words, "It was the first time in my life, Ginny, that anyone ever loved me enough to buy me a new coat, a brand-new coat. Thank you for that, for loving me like that."

And after the horrible pangs of his sudden death, she'd searched for it everywhere. She'd torn the house up looking for it and hadn't been able to find it. But now here it was, one year later, wrapped all around her. The snow was falling, the Christmas bells were ringing, it was growing dark, and here it was.

Ginny pulled the coat tighter and bent her face to the collar. She breathed in and found the scent of pine woodchips, English Leather, good, strong coffee . . . and Charlie. She took another deep, deep breath from way, way down and every moment she'd ever shared with him flashed before her mind and her heart, and she snuggled even further into the warmth.

Oh, yes. She'd loved him that Christmas so long ago. And all the Christmases in between. And she loved him still, this Christmas, when there was nothing left of him except the memories.

And his old brown coat.

Robin Clephane Steward

I'm Not Scrooge . . . I'm Just Broke!

*Creativity is inventing, experimenting, growing,
taking risks, breaking rules, making mistakes
and having fun.*

Mary Lou Cook

It's said that you can never have too many friends, but Christmas was just a week away and I had five people left to shop for on my Christmas list and only three dollars to my name. How do you tell your mother, brother and three friends that you can only spend sixty cents on each of them?

"Let's set a price limit on our gifts this year," I suggested to my best friend, Joanie.

"That's a good idea," Joanie agreed. "How about nothing over five dollars?"

"How about nothing over sixty cents?" I felt like the biggest cheapskate in the world.

"I guess this is where I'm supposed to say it's not the gift, it's the thought that counts," Joanie smiled. "But don't blame me if all you get is a stick of gum!"

It is almost impossible to buy anything for under sixty

cents, so it was really going to have to be very small gifts with very big thoughts. I'd never spent so much time or effort trying to come up with the right gift for the right person.

Finally, Christmas day arrived, and I was worried how people would feel about my "cheap" gifts.

I gave my mother a scented candle with a note that said, "You are the brightest light in my life." She almost cried when she read the note.

I gave my brother a wooden ruler. On the back of it I'd painted, "No brother in the world could measure up to you." He gave me a bag of sugar and had written on it, "You're sweet." He'd never said anything like that to me before.

For Joanie, I painted an old pair of shoes gold and stuck dried flowers in them with a note that said, "No one could ever fill your shoes." She gave me a feather and a Band-Aid. She said I always tickled her funny bone and made her laugh until her sides ached.

To my other two friends, I gave one a paper fan and wrote on it, "I'm your biggest fan." To the other, I gave a calculator that cost one dollar and I painted a message on the back, "You can always count on me." They gave me a rusty horseshoe for luck and a bundle of sticks tied with a red ribbon because "friends stick together."

I don't remember all the other gifts that I got from people last Christmas, but I remember every one of the "cheap" gifts.

My brother thinks I'm sweet. My mother knows she is the most important person in my life. Joanie thinks I'm funny and I make her laugh, which is important because her dad moved away last year and she misses him and is sad sometimes.

I was worried I wouldn't have enough money for Christmas gifts, but I gave gifts to five people and still had twenty cents left over. We all still talk about our "cheap" gifts and how much fun it was to come up with a gift that cost pennies but told someone how we really felt about them. On my bookshelf, I still have a bag of sugar, a feather, a horseshoe and a bundle of sticks . . . and they are priceless.

Storm Stafford

Helping Lauren

The joy of brightening other lives, bearing each other's burdens, easing other's loads and supplanting empty hearts and lives with generous gifts becomes for us the magic of Christmas.

W. C. Jones

It would be safe to say that I was definitely not looking forward to my first Christmas after moving to southern Georgia, away from the comforts of my home, friends and family back in Baltimore. Of course, I was looking forward to the presents, but in spite of the joys of the season, I approached Christmas skeptically. I missed the cold weather, the steaming mugs of hot cocoa, my best friends' annual Christmas party, our front hall with its gleaming tree and, most of all, Christmas at Grandma's house.

Our family would tramp into her warm kitchen, all six of us, after a long two-hour drive. The delicious aroma of cookies baking and the turkey roasting in the oven always made my mouth water. Grandma would bustle in with her apron covered in flour, smile and give us each a hug. She would cluck about how cold it was getting, pat us on the head and send us kids off to play. My three sisters and I would wait eagerly for our cousins to arrive. When they finally came, we would all rush down to the basement to discuss Christmas presents in secret. Every Christmas, for as long as I can remember, that's what we did. But now that my family had moved, that Christmas tradition was gone. It was depressing, really; Christmas this year would be different. Yet I learned, with the help of a five-year-old girl named Lauren, that I'm not so unlucky after all.

School was finally out for the holidays, and we were going Christmas shopping—not for us, not even for friends, but for a little girl named Lauren. Lauren is a poverty-stricken five-year-old, and my family and our friends were buying Christmas presents for her that her family could not afford.

I walked into Target thinking, *What kind of toys would a five-year-old little girl like?* But as I gazed down at the list her mother had sent us through Lauren's school, I realized that it didn't have a single toy on it. Lauren had asked Santa for socks, underwear, clothes and shoes—necessities that I had always taken for granted. I can remember many occasions being disappointed by certain presents. I would eagerly grab a box labeled, "To Maddy from Santa" and rip off the shining paper to find . . . clothes. I would toss it aside. It never dawned on me that some people really don't have these luxuries. Lauren wanted as gifts the things that most kids her age would classify as a waste of wrapping paper.

My sisters and I delighted in picking out little outfits for her and choosing pajamas that had to be warm because, as my sister pointed out, "They probably don't have heat."

The real shock came, however, when we went to deliver the packages. We arrived early, at seven o'clock, to spare the little girl's mother possible embarrassment. The whole street was asleep; not even a dog barked as we approached. We drove past the dark windows of abandoned shops, tumbledown houses and trailers. Many of the houses did not have street numbers, and it was difficult to find Lauren's. Her tiny, rusty trailer sat in what seemed to be a random plot of land. They didn't have a driveway, not even a mailbox. Their ancient, dilapidated van was parked in the middle of the muddy yard among trash and broken furniture. The yard was so small that we could barely fit our car into it. The rickety wooden steps leading up to the door looked as if they would collapse under the weight of our bags, and the windows were taped over with black trash bags. Our bright red and green presents stood out against the dark, gloomy landscape.

My mother cautiously picked her way across the grassless yard and approached the steps. Slowly, she laid the bags down and knocked. She returned to the car and was about to drive away when the rusty trailer door slammed open. A woman stepped out, looking angry and confused.

"This is for Lauren," my mother explained through the car window, smiling. The lady appeared not to have heard and continued staring blankly at my mother. She hadn't noticed the bright bags at her feet. I quickly reached over and shut off the ignition. My mother got out and once again explained, "We've left something for Lauren—it's for Christmas." The lady's dark eyes softened, and she smiled. She seemed too stunned for words. Offering a simple, "Merry Christmas," we drove off, leaving the woman still standing in her doorway, smiling.

That Christmas, as I sat looking at my brightly wrapped presents, the shining tree and my happy family, I remembered Lauren. I hoped that she was having just as wonderful a Christmas with her family. I felt like we had helped to keep a little girl's belief in Santa Claus alive.

Without realizing it, little Lauren helped me learn how truly lucky I am. She taught me a lot about giving and love, and the true meaning of Christmas. That Christmas truly was a memorable holiday. Wherever Lauren is, I hope she felt the same way.

Maddy Lincoln, thirteen

Many Times Over

The wise man does not lay up treasure. The more he gives to others, the more he has for his own.

Lao-Tse

It was a cold day in early December. I was pretty bored just sitting around the house. There was nothing on TV, my friends weren't around, and I'd read every magazine I had on skateboarding, snowboarding and every other hobby of mine. I was about to go stir-crazy when my Aunt Mary, who had stopped by to visit, asked me if I'd like to go grocery shopping with her.

Perfect opportunity to get a new magazine, I thought. There was one problem, though. I'd run out of allowance money. So I decided to ask my mom, in the nicest, sweetest voice I could, if I could have five dollars from my upcoming allowance to buy a magazine that I had been wanting really badly. To my relief, Mom agreed to the deal, and my aunt and I took off shopping.

As we were walking into the grocery store, a poor, homeless woman sat outside the doors asking customers for money donations. *Wow,* I thought. *And I was having a bad day because I was bored.* I checked on the five dollars in my pocket as I thought about the magazine that was waiting inside the store. My aunt went to do her shopping, and I headed for the magazine racks. As I flipped through the new magazines, looking for the one with the article my friend had told me about, I kept flashing on the woman sitting out in the cold without a home to keep her warm. Before I knew it, I had put the magazines back and was heading in the direction of the homeless woman. I realized that she needed the money a lot more than I needed a new magazine.

As I passed the produce section, I saw my aunt picking out vegetables, so I stopped to tell her that I'd meet her at the checkout counter. Before she could question me about where I was going, I was off and running toward the store entrance.

I stepped out into the cold air and looked to my right. Sure enough, the woman was still where she had been when we came in. I reached into my pocket, pulled out the five dollars and handed it to the woman. The look of appreciation on her face was worth more than five dollars. She was so grateful that she stood up and gave me a big hug. "Thank you, young man," she said with a shaky voice. "I can't believe that you ran all the way back here to give me your money."

"No problem," I assured her. "And, hey—Merry Christmas," I said, as I smiled and turned to go find my aunt.

When I arrived back at my house, my mom said there was some mail for me. Much to my surprise, my uncle had sent me a Christmas card—with a twenty-dollar bill inside!

I've heard it said that if you give from the heart, unselfishly and unconditionally, it will be returned to you many times over. On that cold December day, I realized how that isn't just a saying. Good deeds do come back to you.

Nick Montavon, thirteen

A Warm Bed for Christmas

Can I see another's woe and not be in sorrow, too? Can I see another's grief and not seek for kind relief?

William Blake

Police officers know that crime never stops and the police department never closes. For the third straight year, I'd drawn midnight-shift duty for the holidays. In a state of self-pity, I patrolled the silent streets, unaware that the true spirit of Christmas would touch me that night.

Christmas Eve turned bitterly cold and windy that year. An arctic air mass settled over North Carolina, plunging us into a state of paralysis. Icy blasts dropped temperatures well below zero.

It had been a slow night with few calls for service and scarce radio traffic. Even the car-to-car channel remained unusually quiet. Nothing moved on the streets, and the crisp, crystalline quality of the night air lent an edge of sharpness to the landscape.

The dispatcher's voice reverberated through the car,

shattering the silence. "Charlie 182, suspicious person in front of the Radio Shack, 2364 Main Street. Described as a white male wearing a dark-colored shirt and blue jeans."

I headed toward the business district several blocks away. On arrival, I recognized the man as a local transient. He was crouched in the doorway of the business, trying to take advantage of what little wind protection it offered. His ragged flannel shirt, threadbare blue jeans and well-worn tennis shoes provided no protection from the elements, and he was obviously very cold.

Pulling up to the curb, I got out of the car and approached him.

"Frank," I said, "what are you doing out here on a night like this? Why aren't you at the Salvation Army or somewhere you can stay warm?"

He looked at me and smiled wistfully. "It's Christmas, ain't it? Well, there ain't no room at the inn. They're all full up, and I got no place to go. 'Sides, ain't you got nothing better to do than bother with me?"

"No, Frank, actually I don't," I said. "Tell you what. It's warm in my car. How about sitting in the back while I check with dispatch and see if they can find a place for you tonight?"

"Okay," he replied, "but I'm telling ya, everywhere's full up. You ain't gonna have no better luck than I did. But I wouldn't mind warming up while you try."

Frank painfully stood and hobbled toward my car, his arms still hugging his body. I patted him down and, finding no weapons, opened the back door of the car for him. I got in the front and slammed the door in the face of a renewed blast of arctic air. Again I silently cursed my luck at having to work another Christmas Eve, especially this cold and miserable one.

I called dispatch to ask the local shelters if anyone could take Frank for the night. Ten minutes stretched into fifteen. It could only mean they were having trouble locating a place. Then my thoughts were interrupted by dispatch.

"Charlie 182, I've contacted all the local shelters and churches that are taking people, and all advised they were full."

A knowing voice from behind me said, "See? I told ya it was a waste of time. Now let me outta here, and I'll be on my way. I'll find something."

He wasn't under arrest, so I had no legal right to detain him. I opened the back door of the patrol car to let him out and watched as he shuffled back to the sidewalk. Then a sudden movement caught my attention, followed almost immediately by the sound of shattering glass. Frank had thrown a rock through the plate glass window of the Radio Shack.

Frank shuffled toward me. "Look what I just went and done. I broke that window so I guess you have to arrest me and take me to jail."

"Yeah, you're right," I said. "Come on, let's go."

During the drive to the jail, Frank lapsed into his usual apologetic state following one of his petty crimes. "I'm sorry for breaking that window back there," he said, "but I didn't have no choice. It's warm in jail, and they feed you."

It was close to midnight. I knew the jail had already served dinner and Frank wouldn't get fed until morning.

No restaurants stayed open this late on Christmas Eve, but I knew a convenience store that did. It wasn't much of a dinner, but I bought him two hot dogs, a large bag of potato chips and a large cup of coffee.

Frank ate like a man possessed. As I sipped my cup of hot coffee, he devoured his meal. The combination of food and warmth worked their magic, and Frank's peaceful snores accompanied me for the remainder of the drive.

On arrival at the jail, I escorted Frank inside, completed

the booking process and left him. On my way out, I approached Frank and the jailer escorting him to his holding cell. Frank extended his hand and said, "Merry Christmas, Officer Smothers. Thank ya for everything ya done."

I smiled and said, "Merry Christmas, Frank. You're welcome."

Thoughts of Frank rode shotgun with me for the rest of the night. There were six hours remaining on my shift—six hours before I could go home to a hot breakfast, warm bed and loving family.

The next morning, I celebrated Christmas with my loved ones. Wrapping paper littered the floor, carols resounded throughout the house, and a warm fire blazed in the hearth. Yet, I couldn't stop thinking about Frank. He had been willing to commit a crime just so he could get warm for the night, and I had been feeling sorry for myself because I had to work. I experienced a wave of guilt over my feelings of self-pity the night before. And silently I thanked Frank for what he'd unknowingly given me—the gift of gratitude for all that I've been blessed with.

It was the best gift I received that year.

Elaine C. Smothers

Love Cannot Be Measured

The best of all gifts around any Christmas tree: the presence of a happy family all wrapped up in each other.

Burton Hillis

Two! Only two weeks before Christmas and there were no presents under the tree. I guess my family couldn't afford to get any this year. I knew that all our money went to pay the bills and rent and buy food for our family. I understood how important that was. But it was Christmas!

Thinking that maybe I could do something about it, I looked all over my room in every hiding place I had to see if I had any money left. Then I went into the living room and dug under all of the sofa cushions. I searched the pockets of my pants and jackets. Expecting to find at least ten dollars after all my efforts, I only found seven. I thought to myself, *Ah man! How am I going to afford to get five presents for my family with only seven dollars?* Buying cheap ones at the Ninety-Nine-Cent Store was out of the question.

A week went by, and there was still not one single present under the tree. One day during lunch, I thought about asking my parents if they had forgotten about the upcoming holiday, but I decided not to. I know how it feels not to have enough money.

That night, I prayed that someday my family could give me a very special present and that we could all live a better life—one without struggles over money.

As the days passed, I began to get depressed. To get my mind off Christmas presents, I decided to go play with my friend, San. While we were playing and talking, San asked me if I had any presents. I felt embarrassed to say no, so I told her that I didn't know for sure. Perhaps soon presents with my name would be under the tree.

I asked San, "What about you?"

San responded excitedly, "There are over ten gifts under the tree with my name on them!"

I was surprised that she had that many. Luckily, at that moment, I had to go in for dinner, so I didn't have to suffer through any more of that conversation.

During dinner, I remembered Santa. I thought that surely he would bring lots of presents for my family and me. There were only four more days 'til Christmas, so I had to be extra good, I decided. I had to give Santa a wonderful last impression!

The next morning, I made a list of presents that I wanted. The rest of the time I kept busy by helping out and being good. As long as I believed in Santa, I knew he would show.

That night, before going to sleep, I prayed again for presents for my family and me. Pretty soon, I started to feel ashamed of my selfishness. So instead, I began to pray for love and happiness and that I would continue to have such a wonderful family.

When I woke up the next morning, it was Christmas! I was so excited that I jumped out of bed and went right to the tree.

There were no presents at all!

At first I felt really sad, but then I looked around and saw my family's faces full of love and happiness as they worked together to make a special Christmas breakfast. At that moment I realized how much we loved each other.

I began to realize that Santa *did* bring me the best present I could ever have—love. Hearing the words, "I love you," and knowing that there is always someone who is there for you, no matter what, is the greatest gift anyone can ever have.

At age eight, I realized that love cannot be measured by how many presents are under the tree. Love is strong. Love is special. Love is ageless and timeless. It doesn't matter if we are rich or poor, sick or healthy. As long as we have love, we have Christmas every day.

Quynh Thuc Tran, ten

Mason's Sacrifice

The manner of giving is worth more than the gift.

Pierre Corneille

It was Christmas morning the year that my only son, Mason, was thirteen years old. I had been raising him alone for ten years now. My husband had been diagnosed with cancer when Mason was two, and he passed away when Mason was only three. The years had been tough, but my son and I had a very special bond. We were best friends, and my son was the most thoughtful and caring person I knew.

At thirteen, Mason got a weekly allowance of five dollars for keeping his room clean and doing odd chores around the house. Each payday, Mason would jump on his bike and ride to the nearby drug store to buy some candy or the latest magazine. He just couldn't seem to save his money, and so by the time Christmas rolled around, he had nothing to spend on gifts for others. I had never gotten a gift from him that was not homemade, so this year I expected nothing different.

After Mason finished opening all his gifts, he thanked me, kissed me and then slid off into his room. I wondered why he didn't seem to want to spend any time playing with the new stuff he had gotten. Caught in my thoughts, I was startled by Mason, who was now standing in front of me holding a nicely wrapped gift. I assumed that it was a project he had made at school, and I was looking forward to seeing what he had created this time. I cherished all of his gifts, just as I cherished him.

Inside the box was a brand-new pair of expensive black leather gloves, price tag still attached. The shock on my face was very apparent. As tears welled in my eyes, I asked him where he had gotten them. "At the store, Mom, where else?" he simply said.

I looked confused, as I knew that he didn't have that much money. I asked if someone had helped him purchase them, and he shook his head, held it high and said he had bought them all by himself.

After figuring out just the right questions to ask, I got him to reveal to me how he was able to buy the beautiful gloves. He had sold his brand-new bike to a friend at school, the one he had just gotten for his birthday two months earlier.

I cried just thinking about his sacrifice. Through my tears I told him that this was the most thoughtful thing he's ever done for me, but that I wanted to get his bike back for him.

He simply said, "No, Mom, please don't. Because Dad isn't here anymore, you never get a nice gift at Christmas, and you never buy yourself nice things. I wanted to get this for you. My old bike is still perfectly fine, really. Please, Mom, keep the gloves and know I love you every time you wear them."

We hung out for hours that morning, and I never removed the gloves. From that day on, I put them on so often that, eventually, I wore holes in them. But I still have them, tucked in a drawer in my closet. Once in a while, I come across them and am reminded of Mason's sacrifice. I immediately become filled with the gift of love that they represented that Christmas morning—the kind of gift that can never wear out.

Veneta Leonard

2

THE SPIRIT OF GIVING

Christmas gift suggestions:
To your enemy, forgiveness.
To an opponent, tolerance.
To a friend, your heart.
To a customer, service.
To all, charity.
To every child, a good example.
To yourself, respect.

Oren Arnold

An Inch of Kindness

*Kindness is in our power, even when fondness
is not.*

Samuel Johnson

It was the Sunday after Christmas and the seven o'clock mass was beginning. Chilled latecomers hurried up the side steps, and the rear seats were filling up with stragglers, who welcomed the warmth of the radiators that backed the last pews.

The assistant pastor had begun the age-old celebration and the parishioners were very quiet, hardly participating. Each was in his or her own world. Christmas was two days ago, and it had taken its toll. Even the children were still. It was a time of rest from the season's whirl, and all were inclined to sit back and rest. As Father John began his sermon, he looked over a most subdued crowd. He began with a pleasant introduction about the holiday time and its true meaning. Then he carried his sermon a little further and talked about charity and love and being good to others all the time. He said we couldn't go wrong by being nice. It was a talk we had all heard before, and we each felt smugly that we had done our part. Then there was a pause, and Father John added a new thought for his flock to contemplate, and we were startled and roused from our reveries.

He talked about the vagrants, the "trolls," the bums and the homeless that were walking the streets of the city and giving testimony to the new poverty. In quiet tones, he said that they needed care most of all. Some of us squirmed in our seats and exchanged glances. It was obvious we had some reservations about his statements. Most of us were thinking about the influx of wanderers into the city. Vagrants inhabited the parks, the shopping malls and the downtown area. Most of the petty crime seemed to be blamed on them, and they certainly weren't viewed with charity.

Mrs. Scupp was terrified by their looks and grimy appearance. Last week a dingy stubble-faced man with a blanket wrapped around him had asked her for money. Startled and scared, she dropped all her packages as she squealed, "No!" He stooped and helped her pick up her gifts. Then she did find some money in her purse and gave it to him. The experience had unnerved her, and now she shuddered at the thought of repeating it.

Joe Walden's puffy face twisted with a grimace. *Yeah, sure,* he thought. *Show these people an inch of kindness and they'll ruin your business.* At first he hadn't complained about the groups playing violins and guitars in front of his store and asking for donations for their entertainment. But prospective buyers were uncomfortable and passed the shop by. His sales had dropped, and he blamed the street people. *What was this priest suggesting?* He snorted to himself.

Margaret was so horrified by the ragged-looking bunch down in the grocery store parking lot that she hated to go shopping there, and she cringed at the thought of even being near the homeless. But the store was the closest place to home, so she went at noon when there were plenty of other shoppers.

Al sat back in his pew and was lost in this part of the message. He was deeply involved in reviewing his career as a cop and how it applied. It was his job to round up those that disturbed the peace or interfered with others. The terrible antagonism aroused between the citizens and these wanderers had led to many arrests and "move on" orders. Were they justified? One thought came to mind. *Is there a little extra I could do?* Al pulled his head into the warmth of his coat, stuck his hands into his pockets and dismissed the thoughts.

The priest continued with the sermon, touching on many sore spots. He ended by asking people to be kinder to the less fortunate, to be fair and to treat everybody the way Christ would treat them. He left the pulpit to continue Mass, leaving everybody in a ruffled mood.

The Mass continued, but at the same time a noise assaulted the solemnity. A cross between a groan and a whistle, it sounded again and again. A snicker ran through the church. It was a snore . . . a mighty one. Anxious looks at the altar proved that Father was unaffected by the noise, but others were. A lady in front with a big red hat was turning one way and then the other, seeking its originator. Three children were giggling. Their father tried to quiet them and at the same time scan the congregation. Halfway up the middle aisle, to the right, was a hunched-up figure covered with a blanket—the source of the noise. Each time a chord was struck, the gray covering vibrated as the snore escaped its confines.

The snorer was obviously not a member of the church. Maybe he was one of those wanderers on his way south, or somebody who came in from the cold. Maybe he was a bum. One thing was certain: His snoring was offensive.

People coughed nervously and then waited for the next sound.

"Do you think he had a nice Christmas, too, Mommy?" Whispers and hugs identified a little girl in a new pink jacket.

"God loves him, too, doesn't he?" Another flurry followed as her father, nodding, picked her up in his arms. She rested her chin over his shoulder and was looking at the inert man. The people moved in their seats. This was a member of the poor that the sermon was about. What an uncomfortable thought!

Father John was saying the final prayers when the little girl spoke to her father in a stage whisper that carried from one end of the church to the other. "Daddy, can't we share our Christmas with him? Can I have some money? I won't wake him up. Promise." There was quiet rustling and movement as she crossed the aisle and laid some bills on the blanket. Al rose to his feet and did the same. Joe Walden strode up with his offering. As Father John finished the Mass, other bills were dropped on the sleeping figure. He watched Mrs. Scupp gingerly place a five-dollar bill on the gray blanket that was now heaped with money. Margaret met Father John's grin as she left her offering.

It was a strange crowd who greeted Father John after services. The man in the blanket had made an impression, and while few words were said, everyone greeted the priest with a special heartiness. *It comes with the satisfaction of giving,* he thought.

When Father John returned to the empty church and walked up the aisle to the man, he saw the green bills nestled in the folds of the gray blanket. There was more money on the floor around the man. Father John gently shook him. The snoring man raised his head and looked vacantly at the priest for a moment. "Oh, I fell asleep, I guess. What's this?" The money cascaded around him as he rose and dropped the blanket. The priest looked with surprise into the face of Chris Gregory, a fireman and paramedic he had known for years. "Gee, Father John, I'm awfully sorry." As Chris gently scooped up and counted the wealth, Father John explained what had happened. Then Chris told his story.

His department had received three calls for fires down in the lagoon and along the railroad tracks. He had been out all night. The last call included a girl who was about to give birth. She was one of those who had sought the warmth of a fire that got out of hand. Before she could be taken to the hospital, he delivered her baby, a boy. Chris went to the hospital and stayed longer than he expected. It had been a long night, and he had stopped to make early morning mass before going home to sleep.

There was $600.60 altogether. Father John said, "Suppose we divide it. I'll use my share for the soup kitchen, and you take the rest for the new mother. She's going to need it. Now, let's get some breakfast. And fold up that blanket—I don't really think the parishioners want to know who the man in the gray blanket was."

Jeanne Williams Carey

Simple Wooden Boxes

It is the heart that makes a man rich. He is rich according to what he is, not according to what he has.

Henry Ward Beecher

I suppose everyone has a particular childhood Christmas that stands out more than any other. For me, it was the year that the Burlington factory in Scottsboro closed down. I was only a small child. I could not name for you the precise year; it is an insignificant blur in my mind, but the events of that Christmas will live forever in my heart.

My father, who had been employed at Burlington, never let on to us that we were having financial difficulties. After all, children live in a naive world in which money and jobs are nothing more than jabberwocky; and for us, the excitement of Christmas could never be squelched. We knew only that our daddy, who usually worked long, difficult hours, was now home more than we had ever remembered; each day seemed to be a holiday.

Mama, a homemaker, now sought work in the local textile mills, but jobs were scarce. Time after time, she was told no openings were available before Christmas, and it was on the way home from one such distressing interview that she wrecked our only car. Daddy's meager unemployment check would now be our family's only source of income. For my parents, the Christmas season brought mounds of worries, crowds of sighs and tears, and cascades of prayers.

I can only imagine what transpired between my parents during that time. I don't know for sure how they managed, but somehow they did. They made sure they scraped together enough money to buy each of us a Barbie doll. For the rest of our presents, they would rely on their talents, using scraps of materials they already had.

While dark, calloused hands sawed, hammered and painted, nimble fingers fed dress after dress after dress into the sewing machine. Barbie-sized bridal gowns, evening gowns . . . miniature clothes for every imaginable occasion pushed forward from the rattling old machine. Where we were while all of this was taking place, I have no idea. But somehow my parents found time to pour themselves into our gifts, and the excitement of Christmas was once again born for the entire family.

That Christmas Eve, the sun was just setting over the distant horizon when I heard the roar of an unexpected motor in the driveway. Looking outside, I could hardly believe my eyes. Aunt Charlene and Uncle Buck, Mama's sister and her husband, had driven all the way from Georgia to surprise us. Packed tightly in their car, as though no air was needed, sat my three cousins, my Aunt Dean, who refused to be called "Aunt," and both my grandparents. I also couldn't help but notice innumerable gifts for all of us, all neatly packaged and tied with beautiful bows. They had known that it would be a difficult Christmas, and they had come to help.

The next morning we awoke to more gifts than I ever could have imagined. And, though I don't have one specific memory of what any of the toys were, I know that there were mountains of them.

And it was there, amidst all that jubilation, that Daddy decided not to give us his gifts. With all the toys we had gotten, there was no reason to give us the dollhouses that he had made. They were rustic and simple red boxes, after all. Certainly not as good as the store-bought gifts that Mama's family had brought. The music of laughter filled the morning, and we never suspected that, hidden somewhere, we each had another gift.

When Mama asked Daddy about the gifts, he confided his feelings, but she insisted he give us our gifts. And so, late that afternoon, after all of the guests had gone, Daddy reluctantly brought his gifts of love to the living room.

Wooden boxes. Wooden boxes painted red, with hinged lids, so that each side could be opened and used as a house. On either side was a compartment just big enough to store a Barbie doll, and all the way across, a rack on which to hang our Barbie clothes. On the outside was a handle, so that when it was closed, held by a magnet that looked remarkably like an equal sign, the house could be carried suitcase style. And, though I don't really remember any of the other gifts I got that day, those boxes are indelibly etched into my mind. I remember the texture of the wood, the exact shade of red paint, the way the pull of the magnet felt when I closed the lid, the time-darkened handles and hinges. I remember how the clothes hung delicately on the hangers inside, and how I had to be careful not to pull Barbie's hair when I closed the lid. I remember everything that is possibly rememberable, because we kept and cherished those boxes long after our Barbie doll days were over.

I have lived and loved twenty-nine Christmases, each new and fresh with an air of excitement all its own. Each filled with love and hope. Each bringing gifts, cherished and longed for. But few of those gifts compare with those simple wooden boxes. So it is no wonder that I get teary-eyed when I think of my father, standing there on that cold Christmas morning, wondering if his gift was good enough.

Love, Daddy, is always good enough.

Martha Pendergrass Templeton

Christmas in the Sticks

Real generosity toward the future consists in giving all to what is present.

Albert Camus

The year I moved to Alaska, I lived with my husband's family while he stayed in Montana and worked. I had never been around a huge family before, and he was the oldest of ten children, most of them married with kids of their own. They all lived within a forty-mile radius and used any excuse for a family gathering.

No one had any money. Kids were small, families were young, and many of the parents worked more than one job just to pay the bills.

But that first year, the Christmas of 1981, they showed me what giving was all about.

I had only been there for about six months and was still in awe of the strength and power that the love of a big family can generate. What they did that year was a long-standing tradition for them, but I had never seen anything like it.

Two days before Christmas, the entire family gathered

at Mom's house. Each couple threw one hundred dollars into a pot; singles tossed in fifty dollars if they could; kids pitched in allowances or baby-sitting money.

Then the church assigned us a name and an address, and we got "our family." We were all eager to help once we knew the situation: Dad's been out of work; the baby's been sick; Mom didn't want to put up a Christmas tree because she didn't want the children to be disappointed when Santa didn't come; the power company had shut the gas off once, but the church had paid the bill.

First we went to the grocery store. Ten adults, a dozen or more kids, we took the store by storm. Stomping snow off our boots and shedding hats and gloves, we worked up and down the aisles with five carts, soon full of turkey, dressing, potatoes, pies and Christmas candy. Someone thought of simple stuff, how about toilet paper? Did anyone get butter? What about orange juice and eggs for breakfast?

Then the kids got to work. I watched, amazed, as a six-year-old gave up her two-dollar allowance so another little girl could have new mittens. I saw a ten-year-old's eyes light up when he found the illuminated sword he'd wanted, and then put it in the cart for a little boy he didn't even know. A warm, fuzzy blanket for the baby was my four-year-old nephew's choice.

Back to Mom's to wrap the gifts. There were two separate boxes of hand-me-down clothes, sized, pressed and folded. Soon ten grocery-store boxes, overflowing with holiday food, joined them.

The kids created an assembly line to wrap gifts: big gifts, little gifts, special mugs and warm driving gloves. Paper and ribbon were everywhere. Laughter was woven in and out of satiny bows; love was taped to every tag.

Colorful plastic sleds were shoved in the back of the Bronco and stashed in the available trunk space of warm cars idling in the sub-zero Christmas chill. The moon was out, and the trees were covered with hoar frost, glittering like a snow globe in a happy child's hand.

The favorite uncle got to play Santa. Dressed in a dapper red suit, he led the caravan to the trailer stuck back in the scrubby alder woods. Once we had to stop because the ruts in the snow got too deep, and someone's car bottomed out. We transferred gifts and people, and we carried on.

There were no other houses around the frosty mobile home, but the lights were on and a dog on a long rope barked from the wooden porch when we pulled up. Most of us stayed out on the main road, but we loaded the boxes on the sleds, tied them together and sent "Santa" and a few of the older kids to the door. We hung back and sang "Silent Night."

Santa and his helpers knocked and went right in when the door opened. The young family had, after all, decided to put up a tree, and they were stringing lights when we got there. They stood, stunned, as the Santa's helpers unloaded box after box, piled gifts upon gifts. It wasn't long before the tree was dwarfed by a mountain of presents.

Santa said the mom didn't start crying until she pulled the wool coat out of the clothing box. She only said, "Where did you come from?" and then, softly, "Thank you so much."

With the standard "ho, ho, ho" and lots of "merry Christmases!" the delivery crew sprinted back to the car.

We sang one last verse of "We Wish You a Merry Christmas," jumped in our magic sleighs and disappeared into the night.

Debby Mongeau

The Sharing Season

As a California tourist unaccustomed to single digits, the bitter cold of that December day in Washington, D.C., was dampening my holiday mood. Accounting for the windchill factor, the temperature was below zero. When I ducked into Union Station, I hoped only to get warm. What I got was a lesson in the real meaning of the season—from a homeless person.

Warmth was slowly being restored to my hands and feet as I settled onto one of the public benches with a gleaming cup of coffee. Now I was ready to relax and do some serious people-watching. I noticed a homeless man seated nearby and several tables of diners spilling out into the great hall from the upscale America Restaurant. Heavenly aromas from gourmet treats were tempting me to consider an early dinner. From the longing look in my neighbor's eye it was obvious that he, too, had not failed to notice the banquet taking place around us. I wondered how long it had been since he had eaten anything. Expecting he would approach me for a handout, I welcomed such a plea on his part. He never did. The more I took in this scene, the crueler his plight seemed. My head and heart were battling it out: the former telling me to mind my own business, and the latter urging me to make an immediate trip to the food court on his behalf.

While this internal debate was raging, a well-dressed young couple suddenly approached. "Excuse me, sir," began the husband. "My wife and I just finished eating and our appetite wasn't as big as we thought. We hate to waste good food. Can you help us out and put this to good use?" The kind stranger handed a large styrofoam container overflowing with goodies. "God bless you both. Merry Christmas," came the grateful reply. Feeling good about what I had seen, but dismayed by my own lack of action, I observed my neighbor's response to his sudden good fortune. First he scrutinized his newfound bounty, arranging the soup crackers, inspecting the club sandwich and stirring the salad dressing. Then he slowly lifted the lid off the soup, inhaling the aroma and cupping his hands around the steaming bowl. It was obvious that he was going to prolong the enjoyment of this miracle meal. Finally, he appeared ready for that long-dreamed-of first taste. Meticulously unwrapping the plastic spoon, he filled it to overflowing, lifted it towards his mouth and—with a suddenness that stunned me—stopped dead in his tracks.

The reason for this unexpected behavior soon became clear. Entering the hall and shuffling in our direction was a new arrival. In his seventies (or so he appeared), hatless and gloveless, he was clad in lightweight pants, a threadbare jacket and open shoes. His hands were raw and his face had a bluish tint. I wasn't alone in gasping aloud at this sad sight, but my neighbor was the only one doing anything about it. Quickly pulling aside his treasure, he leaped up and guided the elderly man to an adjacent seat. He took the old man's hands and rubbed them in his own. He tenderly draped his down jacket over the older man's shoulders. Finally, he spoke. "Pop, my name's Jack, and one of God's angels brought me this meal. I just finished eating, and I hate to waste good food. Can you help me out?" Placing the steaming cup of soup in the stranger's hands, he didn't wait for an answer. But he got one. "Sure, Son, but only if you go halfway with me on that sandwich. It's too much for a man my age."

It wasn't easy making my way to the food court with tears blurring my vision, but I soon returned with the largest containers of coffee and the biggest assortment of pastries possible. "Excuse me, gentlemen, but. . . ."

My parents, like yours, taught me to share, but it wasn't until that day in Union Station that I truly learned the meaning of that word. I left the hall feeling warmer than I had ever thought possible.

Marion Brenish

Our "Family"

My daughter Gina was in Mrs. Melton's fourth-grade class. After only a month in school, she began to come home on a regular basis asking for pencils, crayons, paper, etc. At first I just dutifully provided whatever she needed, never questioning her.

After ongoing requests for items that should have easily lasted a mere six weeks of fourth grade, I became concerned and asked her, "Gina, what are you doing with your school supplies?" She would always respond with an answer that satisfied me.

One day, after supplying the same thing only a week earlier, I became irritated with her pleading for more and sternly asked her once more, "Gina! what is going on with your school supplies?" Knowing her excuses would no longer work, she bent her head and began to cry. I lifted her tiny chin and looked into those big brown eyes, filled now with tears. "What?! What is wrong?" My mind was racing with all sorts of ideas. Had she been bullied by another child? Was she giving her supplies to him or her to keep from being hurt, or to gain their approval? I couldn't imagine what was going on, but I knew it was something serious for her to cry. I waited for what seemed like an eternity for her to answer.

"Mom," she began, "there is a boy in my class; he doesn't have any of the supplies he needs to do his work. The other kids make fun of him because his papers are messy and he only has two crayons to color with. I have been putting the new supplies you bought me in his desk before the others come in, so he doesn't know it's me. Please don't get mad at me, Mom. I didn't mean to tell you a lie, but I didn't want anyone to know it was me."

My heart sank as I stood there in disbelief. She had taken on the role of an adult and tried to hide it like a child. I knelt down and hugged her to me, not wanting her to see my own tears. When I pulled myself together, I stood up and said, "Gina, I would never get mad at you for wanting to help someone, but why didn't you just come and tell me?" I didn't have to wait for her to answer.

The next day I visited Mrs. Melton. I told her what Gina had said. She knew John's situation all too well. The oldest of four boys, their parents had just moved here and when the school presented them with the school supply list for all four grades they were overwhelmed. When the boys came to school the next week, they barely had the necessities—a few sheets of paper and a pencil each.

I asked Mrs. Melton for the list from all four grades and told her I would take care of it the next day. She smiled and gave me the lists.

The next day, we brought the supplies in and gave them to the office with instructions to give them to the boys.

As Christmas neared, the thought of John, his brothers and family weighed heavily on my mind. What would they do? Surely they would not have money for gifts.

I asked Mrs. Melton if she could get me their address. At first she refused, reminding me that there was a policy that protected the privacy of the students, but because she knew me from my work at the school and involvement on the PTA board, she slipped a piece of paper into my hand and whispered, "Don't tell anyone I gave it to you."

When my family began to set the stage for our traditional Christmas Eve, which was usually held at my house, I simply told them all that my husband, the kids and I did not want gifts, but instead we would prefer to have groceries and gifts for our "family."

As the girls and I shopped throughout the holiday season, they delighted in picking things out for the four boys. Gina was especially interested in things for John.

Christmas Eve came and my family began to arrive. Each of them had bags of food and gifts wrapped for the children. My living room was full and the excitement was contagious.

Finally at 9:00 we decided it was time to take our treasures to them. My brothers, dad, uncles and nephews loaded up their trucks and set out for the apartment complex address that Mrs. Melton gave us.

They knocked on the door and a little boy appeared. They asked for his mother or dad and he ran away. The guys waited until a young man, hardly more than a child himself, came to the door. He looked at the men standing there, with arms full of gifts and bags full of groceries, and couldn't say a word. The men pushed past him and went straight to the kitchen counter to set the bags down.

There was no furniture. It was an empty one-bedroom apartment with a few blankets on the floor and a small TV where they obviously spent their time. A Christmas tree was the result of the kids bringing in a bush they had found in the field behind the complex. A few paper decorations made in their classrooms made it look like a real Christmas tree. Nothing was underneath.

The boys and their parents stood without speaking as the men sat down bag after bag. They finally asked who had sent them, how did they know them and so on. But the men just left them with shouts of "Merry Christmas!"

When the guys got back to my house they didn't say a word. They couldn't.

To break the silence, my aunt stood up and began to sing "Silent Night," and we all joined in.

When school resumed, Gina came home daily telling of John's new clothes and how the other children now played with him and treated him like the rest of the children.

She never told a soul at school about what we did, but every Christmas since that one she will say to me, "Mom, I wonder what happened to John and his family? While I'm not quite sure of the answer, I'd like to think that John and his family were somehow helped by my daughter's gift.

Linda Snelson

Patches

It was such an exciting time of the year, for me especially. Christmas was just around the corner, the signs of which were already appearing at the malls, and my baby shower was just a week away. Mom was worried about how many people would actually come, considering Christmas was so close. She had worked so hard on planning the perfect baby shower for her first grandchild. She was so tickled, I laughed just watching her trip all over herself planning it.

She had really hoped I would find out the gender of the baby so she could have a pink or blue shower, whichever was applicable. She also wanted to include that tidbit of information within the invitations; at both of her showers she had received a lot of boy items, and of course, she had had two girls.

I knew Mom had gone over her budget on the shower, especially with Christmas right around the corner. I made her promise that she would not buy a shower gift in addition to all she had done. I was worried about the money, but I also had another reason. I had not found out if it would be a boy or a girl, and I wanted Mom to be the one to pick out the special "coming-home outfit" for my child.

December nineteenth, what a day it had been! I will never forget that day or that date. I felt like I had been opening presents for hours, and what wonderful presents I had received. The generosity of my family and friends overwhelmed me. As I replaced the top of the box on what I thought was the last gift, I was handed one more. *I hadn't seen that one. Where had it been?* It wasn't wrapped with traditional baby shower paper; it was wrapped with beautiful Christmas paper adorned with angels singing hymns, the words written in gold so delicately on the paper. There was no gift tag attached, but there was a Christmas card. "To my daughter . . . ," it read. Mom had promised not to buy a shower gift, but I had said nothing about a Christmas gift! I gave her one of those "I'm going to kill you" looks, and she just sat there, smugly smiling.

"This one is from my mom," I announced as I opened the gift. Inside was a quilt. I tried to smile as I held it up for all to see, hoping Mom couldn't see my face. She would know my smile wasn't genuine; she could read me like a good book, cover to cover. The quilt was not very pretty, you see. It was not a "baby quilt." It wasn't made of pink, blue and yellow materials; it didn't have bunnies or bears. It was just a patchwork quilt sewn of materials that were of all different colors and patterns. Holding the quilt up, I noticed a note tucked in the bottom of the box.

Not realizing the note was intended to be private, I set the quilt aside, picked up the note and began reading it. Mom had made the quilt for me. The unmatched materials were remnants of my life she had saved over the years. She had cut swatches of material from items dating back to my first Christmas dress and as current as the shirt I wore to the doctor the day I found out I was finally pregnant. She had accumulated "patches" of my life for all those years to make this quilt for my child.

By the time I finished reading Mom's letter telling of the

"patch" of her old robe—I remembered it well; it was fleece and I used to insist she wear it so I could lay my head on it when she rocked me—and the "patch" of Dad's flannel shirt I used to put on after my bath, and each and every other "patch" and its meaning, there was not a dry eye in the dining room. I picked up the quilt and held it against me and I cried. To think, just seconds before I had thought it ugly. It was beautiful. It was the most beautiful quilt I had ever seen. This quilt was made of my life and with my mother's love. She had sewn her love into every stitch. To think my mom could sew!

The quilt now hangs on my son's wall. It is a reminder of my life, my mother's love and the wonderful Christmas present I received at my baby shower.

Cathy Novakovich

The Student's Mite

The situation seemed hopeless.

From the first day he entered my seventh-grade class-room, Willard P. Franklin had existed in his own world, shutting out his classmates and me, his teacher. My attempts at establishing a friendly relationship were met with complete indifference. Even a "Good morning, Willard" received only a grunt. His classmates fared no better. Willard was strictly a loner, finding no desire or need to lower the barrier of silence he had erected. His clothes were clean—but definitely not on the cutting edge of style. He could have been a trendsetter because his outfits possessed a "hand-me-down" look before such a look was in.

Shortly after the Thanksgiving holidays, we received an announcement regarding the annual Christmas collection.

"Christmas is a season of giving," I told my students. "There are a few students in the school who might not have a happy holiday season. By contributing to our Christmas collection, you will help to buy food, clothing and toys for these needy people. You may bring your money tomorrow."

When I called for the contributions the next day, I discovered every one had forgotten—everyone except

Willard P. Franklin. The boy dug deep into his pants pockets as he strolled up to my desk. Carefully he dropped a nickel into the small container.

"I don't need no milk for lunch," he mumbled. For a moment, just a moment, he smiled. I watched him turn and walk back to his desk.

That night, after school, I took our meager contribution—one lone nickel—to the school principal. I couldn't help telling him the giver's identity and sharing with him the incident.

"I may be wrong, but I believe Willard may be ready to become a part of the world around him," I told the principal.

"Yes, I believe it sounds hopeful," he nodded. "And I have a hunch we might profit from him letting us share a bit of his world. I just received a list of the poor families of our school who most need help through the Christmas collection. Here, look at it."

And as I gazed down to read, I discovered Willard P. Franklin and his family were the top names on the list.

David R. Collins

Santa D. (for David) Claus

"Ho, ho, ho! And what would you like for Christmas this year, young man?" Eyebrows raised in anticipation, Santa readjusted his cotton beard as he waited for the answer to his question.

"Well, Santa," Mr. Cassady answered, "there's not a whole lot I need right now." He glanced around his room in the nursing home and shrugged his shoulders. "Maybe some candy would be nice."

Santa reached deep into his pack and pulled out a candy cane, paused, then reached back in and pulled out another. "Here, take two and have a merry Christmas!" Then, with another set of "Ho-ho-ho's," he picked up his bag, jingled his sleigh bells and left Mr. Cassady licking one of his candy canes.

Once in the hallway, I, being the helper elf, consulted the list of nursing home residents we were to visit. "Mrs. Stone's room is down the next hall, Room 223. She is blind and is sometimes confused and forgetful," I told Santa. On our way to Mrs. Stone's room, nurses brought residents out of their rooms and into the hallways to see Santa as he passed by.

When we reached Room 223, we knocked on the door.

The jingling sleigh bells and the familiar "ho, ho, ho's" alerted Mrs. Stone as to our identity.

"Santa, is that really you?" she asked. "Oh, come closer so I can hold your hand." Santa obliged. "Are your reindeer with you?"

Santa paused only a moment before he answered. "No, they had to stay up at the North Pole to rest up for Christmas Eve. Pulling the sleigh full of toys is pretty hard on them, you know."

"Yes, I suppose so," Mrs. Stone replied. "Who else is here with you?"

"Aunt, uh, Elf. Aunt Elf is here."

"Merry Christmas, Mrs. Stone," I said, taking her hand.

"I brought you a candy cane," Santa said as he placed it in her hand.

"Oh, thank you, Santa. I wish I could see you; I am so glad you came."

As we stepped back into the hallway, a nurse came over to us and whispered, "Santa, there's someone who could use a visit from you. Mr. Hansen is new here and is very angry. I think that he's also very frightened, but he won't talk to anyone and keeps his blinds closed like he's shutting out the whole world. He may not welcome you, but it's worth a try." Santa nodded and we followed the nurse to Mr. Hansen's room and knocked. There was no answer. We knocked again and the nurse called out, "Mr. Hansen, there's someone here to see you. May we come in?"

Finally, a gruff "okay" came through the door. Santa stepped past the nurse as she opened the door and entered the darkened room shouting, "Ho, ho, ho, and Merry Christmas, Mr. Hansen. I brought you a candy cane." Mr. Hansen, unsmiling, looked Santa up and down and then reached for the candy cane. Another long, unsmiling stare was aimed at me. He then looked back at Santa. "She's pretty big for an elf, isn't she?" I smiled nervously, but Santa replied, "Well, we feed them pretty well up there at the North Pole."

A smile started to tug at the corner of Mr. Hansen's mouth. "And I somehow remember you, Santa, as being quite a bit taller."

A brief moment passed and Santa responded, "Well, you were quite a bit smaller, just a kid, when I saw you last, so I guess I look different to you, that's all."

"I believe you're right, Santa," Mr. Hansen said softly as he unwrapped the candy cane. A boyish smile spread across his eighty-five-year-old face. "Thanks for the candy and thanks for coming by, Santa."

"No problem," Santa grunted as he hoisted his bag over his shoulders. "Have a merry Christmas."

The nurse was still standing by the doorway as we left the room. "It was pure Christmas magic," she said. "This is the first time I have seen him smile."

We visited other residents until all of the candy canes were handed out. It was time to leave. Shouts of "Goodbye, Santa, thanks so much for coming" followed us down the hall and out the door.

Santa waited until we were in the car before he took off his beard. I gave him a hug. "You were great, David," I told him. "This was a wonderful idea you had; you were a terrific Santa."

"Thanks, Aunt Karen, you weren't a bad elf, yourself," David told me. I beamed. It was high praise from an eight-year-old Santa.

Karen M. Sackett

The Unexpected Gift

First the snow came lightly. I watched it out of the window, the flakes flying in the wind the bus made as it sped from Cincinnati, where we lived, to Canton, Ohio, where we were going to spend Christmas with my uncle and cousins. My brother and I were traveling alone because our parents were on the way from Pittsburgh, where they had gone to take care of things after my grandmother died. It was a family emergency and though my mother did not like the idea of leaving us with her best friend, or having us travel alone, she did not have much choice.

Soon we would all be together in my uncle's house playing the rowdy games and eating too many sugar cookies, which my Aunt Alice made in the shape of snowmen. They always had little stubby hands and feet too. For some reason I liked to eat the feet first. My brother always ate the cherry nose.

I had the window seat for this leg of the trip. My mother always made us trade off to avoid fighting about it and we did that even when we were by ourselves. There was a very big woman sitting across from us who talked to us at the last stop. She thought we were young to be traveling alone and she bought us each a doughnut even though she seemed poor. Her name, she said, was Mrs. Margaret Mills and her husband was dead. I don't know why she told us that.

Before long the snow got heavier and heavier and the bus began to slow down. It slowed and slowed and before long it was just kind of crawling along and the world outside had turned completely white. I heard the driver talking on his radio about what we should do. So I woke up my brother in case we were about to hit a snowdrift and be boarded by bandits. He always hoped for some big adventure that just never seemed to come our way. *Now might be his chance,* I thought.

The other passengers began to stir about and go stand in line for the bathroom and make each other nervous. I gave my brother my seat and he kept his face plastered to the glass.

"Look, look," he would say every once in awhile. "More snow. More snow."

It was about an hour later that we eased into a gas station that had a little restaurant shaped like a railroad car attached to it. We all bundled up as best we could, pulled our hats down over our ears and ran for shelter. The wind was making a very weird sound . . . like a bird screeching. Finally we were all inside and the bus driver told us we were likely to have to spend the night here and might make it out in the morning if the storm stopped and the plows came through.

Now I was frightened and my brother was crying. I told him we would be all right and the weird woman took us to the counter and ordered hot chocolate. My mother had pinned a card inside my coat pocket—she pinned it there because I was always losing things I needed, like mittens—with my uncle's name, address and phone number.

While we were having hot chocolate, the bus driver

asked us if we had a phone number for whoever was going to meet us and I gave him the card.

People were very upset. After all, we were about to spend Christmas with a handful of strangers and no one wanted to do that. All the joy and anticipation of being with family and friends was replaced by disappointment and sadness. We were a sorry lot. Some people drank coffee and some ate chicken salad sandwiches and some just sat staring at their folded hands.

I wanted to talk to my parents, and just as I had that thought, the bus driver called me and I went to the phone. He had my aunt on the line. My parents were out at church with my cousins and Aunt Alice was very calm about our situation. She said we would be all right and that we should do what the bus driver said. And that we should not leave the place where we were because my family would come get us in the morning when the roads were plowed.

That made me feel a lot better. But my brother was hard to console. He wanted to be home, to be singing carols while Aunt Alice played the piano, to be having the kind of Christmas Eve we loved. I didn't know what to do to help him and it was beginning to make me mad that he was crying all the time.

Then a strange thing happened. People began to talk to each other and to us. And then they began to laugh and tell stories about their families and where they'd been and where they were going. The man who owned the restaurant turned on the lights of the Christmas tree he had in the corner of the room. They were shaped like candles. And together with the colored lights that bordered the big front window, the room began to seem a little festive. I hoped it all would cheer my brother up, but it did not.

"What are we going to do? I want to see Mama, I want to have cookies, I want to sing the manger song with Aunt

Alice, I . . . I . . ." and then he would lean against me and cry some more.

The weird woman watched us from time to time. I thought she disliked his sniveling as much as I did, but finally she came to the booth were we were sitting by ourselves and said, "I believe I'll just join you, if you don't mind."

She sat down before I could say anything and she took up quite a lot of space doing it, too.

Then one of the strangest things I have ever seen happened. Her face, which I thought was a little scary—she had a very big nose and this huge neck—softened and gentled as she looked at my brother. And then she began to sing. Out of her strange body came one of the loveliest sounds I've ever heard. She put her arm around my brother and pulled him close to her. And softly, very softly, she sang as though singing just for us, "Away in a manger, no crib for a bed, the little Lord Jesus laid down his sweet head."

He looked up at her. I think he was startled at first to hear his favorite carol sung to him by a strange woman in a snowbound bus stop. But soon the sadness left his face. Soon he put his hand in hers. And then they sang together, louder now, "The stars in the bright sky looked down where he lay, the little Lord Jesus asleep on the hay."

After that a young man unpacked his guitar and the bus driver pulled out a harmonica, and before long, everyone was singing just about every Christmas carol you ever heard in your life. We sang and drank hot cocoa with marshmallows and ate cupcakes until people finally settled down for the evening, huddled in the booths, sitting on the floor, leaning against each other for comfort and support. And so we spent Christmas Eve.

The roads were cleared by eleven the next morning and we said good-bye to everyone on the bus. Our parents had called the restaurant and were on their way to pick us up. The last person we saw was Mrs. Mills. She hugged us and I thanked her. Then she bent over and kissed us both on the forehead. "I'll never forget you two boys. You were my Christmas present. That's the way I'll always think of you." Then she got on the bus and I never saw her again.

Later that night, when we were all comfortable and warm before the fire at Aunt Alice's, I asked my dad what the strange woman could have meant. I'd told him the whole story, of course, except for the part about getting mad at my brother for crying so much.

He said, "That's the thing about a true gift. You can only give it. You never know how much it means to another person."

"But what was our gift, dad? We didn't give her a present or anything."

"I don't have any way of knowing that. It might have been your cute faces. It might have been that you liked her, or weren't afraid of her because of the way she looked. Or it might have been that you sang along with her in a strange place she never planned to be in. Just be grateful that you had something to give that woman, something she treasured and would remember. Make that a part of who you are and that will be your gift to me."

And then Aunt Alice went to the piano and we, all of us, began our annual caroling, the singing of songs together that I liked better than almost anything in the world. But what I was thinking about most that evening was Mrs. Margaret Mills and what a wonderful voice she had. And as I thought about her, I missed her. Truly missed her. And I hoped that wherever she was, she was singing for someone who liked her as much as I did.

W. W. Meade

Chords of Love

She lay prostrate on the wooden floor, unable to lift her head or move her body. Five minutes passed. Ten. Fifteen. All because she'd reached for a Christmas ornament and fallen out of her wheelchair.

What a day for John to be late, she thought, as her immovable position grew more and more uncomfortable.

The wedding photo on the table had tipped over with her. Out of the corner of her eye, she saw a beautiful bride and a handsome groom, each with Irish blue eyes and dark hair. Friends told her that raising three children hadn't aged either of them one bit.

John's car crunched in the snowy driveway. Her heart pounded as she heard him leap the stairs of their split-level home two at a time, eager to see his wife. Stunned to find her on the floor, John dropped to his knees—and wept with her.

Not out of sympathy. Peg's quips disarmed any of that maudlin stuff. Out of love—the deepest kind.

At that almost sacred moment, I intruded. "Oh I'm sorry," I said.

According to my custom as Peg's physical therapist, I had knocked and let myself in. Her husband dried his tears, scooped up her thin body, paralyzed from multiple sclerosis, and carried her to the bathroom. This was his habit every lunch hour.

"I'd do the same for you if things were reversed," Peg told him, her pluck restored.

"No you wouldn't. I'm too big for you," he said with a broad smile as he placed her back in her electric wheelchair, flipped on the Christmas tree lights and left for work.

"Do you hurt today after the fall?" I took off my hooded coat and red scarf.

"No, go ahead and do the routine," Peg said, then added, "I went to the counselor yesterday."

"How did that go?" I stretched her arm.

"Okay, until he asked, 'How's your intimate life?' I answered him, 'Fine, how's yours?' That quieted him right down."

No one tampered with this lady's love life or, for that matter, with her willingness to persevere. When therapy was over, she asked me to place a nativity set on her lap tray so she could arrange it. She knew her fingers were useless, but hey, why not give it a try? It was the holidays.

I shook my head with wonder.

Eager to show my love for this special couple, that very evening I gathered a group of carolers outside their family room window. I saw Peg seated in her wheelchair before the fireplace and John behind her like a tall, protective sentinel.

One, two, three. We struck the first chords, "Deck the halls with boughs of holly . . ." Trombone lifted, bells ringing, we sang a festive medley.

They invited us in for our grand finale, "We Wish You a Merry Christmas." The oven smelled of John's pumpkin bread. A little shy of strangers, they retreated to the back of the garland-strewn room.

When we strolled away, I glanced through the frosty window at Peg's forever smile. Her husband had resumed his attentive stance—her guardian, lover, friend for life. Oh, sure, Peg and John were pleased we had serenaded them. But their happiness came not from others. It came from an unbreakable cord of love, the kind that binds.

Once upon a time I had skimmed through a photographic album about couples. The artist prefaced his work with the words, "We two form a multitude." Surely, he must have known Peg and John.

Margaret Lang

Drawn to the Warmth

Factoring in the windchill, I knew the temperature was below zero. The bitter cold cut through my Californian sensibilities, as well as my enthusiasm as a tourist, so I ducked through the nearest door for warmth . . . and found myself in Washington, D.C.'s Union Station.

I settled onto one of the public benches with a steaming cup of coffee—waiting for feeling to return to my fingers and toes—and relaxed to engage in some serious people-watching.

Several tables of diners spilled out into the great hall from the upscale American Restaurant, and heavenly aromas tempted me to consider an early dinner. I observed a man seated nearby and, from the longing in his eyes, realized that he, too, noticed the tantalizing food. His gaunt body, wind-chapped hands and tattered clothes nearly shouted, "Homeless, homeless!"

How long has it been since he's eaten? I wondered.

Half expecting him to approach me for a handout, I almost welcomed such a plea. He never did. The longer I took in the scene, the crueler his plight seemed. My head and heart waged a silent war, the one telling me to mind my own business, the other urging a trip to the food court on his behalf.

While my internal debate raged on, a well-dressed young couple approached him. "Excuse me, sir," the husband began. "My wife and I just finished eating, and our appetites weren't as big as we thought. We hate to waste good food. Can you help us out and put this to use?" He extended a large Styrofoam container.

"God bless you both. Merry Christmas," came the grateful reply.

Pleased, yet dismayed by my own lack of action, I continued to watch. The man scrutinized his newfound bounty, rearranged the soup crackers, inspected the club sandwich and stirred the salad dressing—obviously prolonging this miracle meal. Then, with a slow deliberateness, he lifted the soup lid and, cupping his hands around the steaming warm bowl, inhaled. At last, he unwrapped the plastic spoon, filled it to overflowing, lifted it toward his mouth and—with a suddenness that stunned me—stopped short.

I turned my head to follow his narrow-eyed gaze.

Entering the hall and shuffling in our direction was a new arrival. Hatless and gloveless, the elderly man was clad in lightweight pants, a threadbare jacket and open shoes. His hands were raw, and his face had a bluish tint. I wasn't alone in gasping aloud at this sad sight, but my needy neighbor was the only one doing anything about it.

Setting aside his meal, he leaped up and guided the elderly man to an adjacent seat. He took his icy hands and rubbed them briskly in his own. With a final tenderness, he draped his worn jacket over the older man's shoulders.

"Pop, my name's Jack," he said, "and one of God's angels brought me this meal. I just finished eating and hate to waste good food. Can you help me out?"

He placed the still-warm bowl of soup in the stranger's hands without waiting for an answer. But he got one.

"Sure, son, but only if you go halfway with me on that

sandwich. It's too much for a man my age."

It wasn't easy making my way to the food court with tears blurring my vision, but I soon returned with large containers of coffee and a big assortment of pastries. "Excuse me, gentlemen, but . . ."

I left Union Station that day feeling warmer than I had ever thought possible.

Marion Smith

School of "Hire" Learning

I wrinkled my nose and sniffed the air as I closed the classroom windows; still, I couldn't identify the faint odor. But it was Friday afternoon, my first week of teaching, and—although already in love with my hardworking students—I was exhausted and ready to leave the building.

For the most part, my twenty-four fifth-graders were the children of seasonal agricultural workers on Long Island. Their parents were employed at the local duck farm, many on welfare. They lived in converted duck shacks, with outside privies, cold-water hand pumps and potbellied, wood-burning stoves.

So odors weren't that unusual.

However, by Monday morning the foul smell overpowered the hot room. Like a dog scenting its prey, I sniffed until I found it: a rotting sandwich in Jimmy Miller's desk, the bread smeared with rancid butter and the meat green. I rewrapped the sandwich, put it back in his desk and threw open all the windows before my students filed in.

At noon, the children got their lunch bags and fled to the playground picnic table. I saw Jimmy unwrap his sandwich and pretend to eat. Making certain the kids didn't see, he wrapped it again, put it in his pocket and slipped it back into his desk when the class returned.

My stomach knotted in empathy over Jimmy's poverty . . . and his pride.

After a private discussion, another teacher and I "hired" Jimmy for classroom chores like cleaning the chalkboards. As payment, we treated Jimmy to lunch with us each day. We also encouraged him to study and provided him with after-school tutoring. Before long, Jimmy took pride in his special lunches and earned top grades in all his subjects. As word traveled through the faculty grapevine, Jimmy was "rehired" by each year's succeeding teacher.

After a time, however, I accepted another teaching position and moved away.

It was on a trip back eleven years later that my friend Chris asked if I remembered Jimmy. "He's attending college now and is home for Christmas break. When I mentioned that you were coming, he asked to see you. "

"Really? He was just a little shaver when I knew him."

"He's grown some since then." Chris tried to hide a smile. "Says he has a Christmas present for you."

"A gift? For me?"

Jimmy drove up a bit later, and I walked out to meet him. At 6'6" and pushing 280 pounds, he certainly was no longer a little shaver.

"Happy holidays." Jimmy stuck out an oversized paw. "I hear you got your doctorate. Congratulations! Do you mind if I call you Doc?"

"It's all right with me, Jimmy." I tilted my head and looked up the full length of him. "What have you been doing?"

"Well, I got a four-year football scholarship, and I've made the dean's list every semester. I graduate in June."

"Great work. I bet you've signed a pro contract already. Big bucks, you know."

"Yeah, I've had a few offers, but I'm not goin' into the pros."

"No kidding. Why not, Jimmy?"

"I have other plans."

"Oh?"

"I finished my student teaching last week, Doc." He smiled when I registered surprise. "I've decided to be a teacher—just like you." For a quiet moment, Jimmy gazed over my shoulder . . . and into the past. "I know you fellas invented those classroom jobs for me." He cleared his throat. "You helped me keep my dignity, and I've never forgotten."

I felt a lump in my own throat as Jimmy looked me full in the face.

"When teachers really care, students know it," Jimmy said. "That's why I want to teach. I want to be there for my students the way you were there for me."

What a Christmas gift, I thought. And, a little teary eyed, we shook hands.

No longer teacher and pupil, we were now two men with the same hopes—and the same goals.

Edmund W. Ostrander

Surprise Santa

A few days before Christmas, a devout Christian couple held the hands of their young son and walked briskly to their nearby church. But the boy pulled back a bit, slowed and came to an abrupt halt.

"Santa," he whispered. "Santa!"

The four-year-old broke free of his parents' grasp and ran toward an elderly gentleman with a long, flowing white beard.

Tugging on the stranger's coattail, the youngster begged, "Santa, will you bring me a teddy bear for Christmas?"

Embarrassed, the couple started to apologize, but the man merely waved them aside. Instead, he patted their son on the head, nodded once, winked wryly at the youngster and—without a word—went on his way.

On Christmas morning, a knock interrupted the family's festivities. In the doorway stood the old man holding out a large bear with a plaid bow around its neck.

"I didn't want the little fellow to be disappointed on his holiday," he explained with an awkward grimace and turned to leave.

Uncomfortable and stunned, the parents could only

stutter a weak, "Uh, th-thanks. And M-merry Christmas to you . . . Rabbi."

Henry Boye

Stroke by Stroke

I pushed through the crowd huddled in winter coats. There lay Blackie in the snowy street. I fell at my collie's feet and spread my arms around her as if to protect her from further injury. Not a car stirred that cold Sunday morning—nothing moved at all except her soft tricolor fur and my tears.

"Why don't they come?" I looked at the sad faces above me. "Why don't they hurry?" I was sure *they* would save her life . . . unfortunately there was nothing left to save.

My parents led me away, while, hand stretched back to my beloved pet, I called out to her for the last time, "Blackie, oh, Blackie."

Christmas joy extinguished as fast as the hit-and-run vehicle had skidded along the icy road. Tinsel on the tree lost its sparkle, stockings by the fireplace their promise, red and green chocolate kisses their sweetness. Without a collie curled up on the Oriental rug, gray became the holiday color.

Mom lost interest in her baking. My cousins no longer pinned sequins on Styrofoam balls. My brother abandoned his ice skates. Worst of all, the carols on the stereo could not be heard above my relentless wail. The crying jag took on a life all its own. Even Dad's lap, usually the solution for all problems, held no answers at this time.

Until Grandfather got involved. "Can't someone stop that noise?"

Startled, I held my breath . . . not certain it was safe to sob anymore.

My Aunt Veramina's gentle words softened the atmosphere. "Come with me to your room, Margaret, so I can brush your hair."

My hand in hers, we followed the garland-wrapped banister up to the second floor of the big colonial house. She sat me down in a pink frilly chair and took my brush from the grooming set on the dresser top.

"Now, doesn't that feel better?" she asked as she loosened my long braids and with her competent hands, pulled the bristle brush through my thick auburn tresses.

The spasms of crying relaxed. A sniffle sputtered out. A whimper crept away. Finally, I filled my grief-weary lungs with one long restorative breath.

Under my aunt's soothing strokes of kindness, my head tilted back and forth. The rhythm, much like that of a rocking chair, changed the sadness of the day into the peace of the moment.

Sometime later, my braids and I bounced down the stairs. At my appearance in the living room, I heard a combined breath drawn. I leaned over the box of ornaments and, by coincidence, chose the large glass teardrop. This tear wasn't sad; it was merry, very merry—shocking pink with gold embroidered trim. When I hung it on the fragrant spruce, I felt a combined sigh of relief around me.

"Here," said Grandfather, as he handed me his peace offering of fresh pecans. With aged fingers around a silver nutcracker and pick, he had labored to extract the meat of six unbroken pieces for his granddaughter.

"Thanks, they're my favorite." I popped one into my mouth.

It seemed like someone suddenly flipped a power switch. The stereo hummed "Winter Wonderland." Sequins whizzed onto Styrofoam balls, powdered sugar onto cookies. And my brother zoomed toward the door, skates over his shoulder, "Anyone wanna join me at the park?"

Funny how on that tragic day, all the season's colorful trimmings and trappings combined had not been able to restore Christmas joy like one plain bristle brush in my aunt's hands. To be sure, I never forgot Blackie. But within a few days, a new collie dog had curled up beside me on the Oriental rug.

Margaret Lang

A Slice of Life

Jean heaved another world-weary sigh. Tucking a strand of shiny black hair behind her ear, she frowned at the teetering tower of Christmas cards waiting to be signed. What was the point? How could she sign only one name? That was half a couple, not a whole.

The legal separation from Don left her feeling vacant and incomplete. Maybe she could skip the cards this year. And the holiday decorating. Truthfully, even a tree felt like more than she could manage. She had cancelled out of the caroling party and the church nativity pageant. After all, Christmas was supposed to be shared, and she had no one to share it with.

The doorbell's insistent ring startled her. Padding across the floor in her thick socks, Jean cracked the door open against the frigid December night. She peered into empty darkness. Instead of a friendly face—something she could use about now—she found only a jaunty green gift bag perched on the porch railing. From whom, she wondered, and why?

Under the bright kitchen light, she pulled out handfuls of shredded gold tinsel, feeling for a gift. Instead, her fingers plucked an envelope from the bottom. Tucked inside was a typed letter. No, it was a . . . story?

The little boy was new to the overpopulated orphanage, and Christmas was drawing near, Jean read. Caught up in the tale, she settled into a kitchen chair.

> *From the other children, he heard tales of a wondrous tree to appear in the hall on Christmas Eve. Of scores of candles that would light its branches. Of the mysterious benefactor who made it possible each year.*
>
> *The little boy's eyes opened wide at the mere thought. The only Christmas trees he'd seen were through the fogged windows of other people's homes. There was even more, the children insisted. More? Oh, yes! Instead of the orphanage's regular fare of gruel, they would be served fragrant stew and crusty hot bread that special night.*
>
> *Last and best of all, the little boy learned, each of them would receive a holiday treat. He would join the line of children to get his very own . . .*

Jean turned the page. Instead of a continuation, she was startled to read: "Everyone needs to celebrate Christmas, wouldn't you agree? Watch for Part II." She refolded the paper while a faint smile teased the corner of her mouth.

The next evening, Jean rushed home from work. If she hurried there was probably enough time to decorate the mantle. She pulled out the box of garland but dropped it to race for the door when the bell rang. This time, she opened a red bag.

. . . to get his very own orange, Jean read. An orange? That's a treat?

> *An orange! Of his very own? Yes, the others assured him. One for each child. The boy closed his eyes against the wonder of it all. A tree. Candles. A filling meal. And—last and best of all—an orange of his very own.*
>
> *He knew the smell, tangy sweet, but only the smell.*

He'd sniffed them at the merchant's stall in the market-place. Once he'd even dared to rub a single finger over the brilliant, pocked skin. He fancied for days that his hand still smelled of orange. But taste one, eat one?

The story ended abruptly, yet Jean didn't mind. She knew more would follow.

The next evening, her pile of unaddressed Christmas cards was shrinking when the doorbell rang. Jean wasn't disappointed. However, the embossed gold bag was heavier than the others had been. She tore into the envelope resting on top of the tissue paper.

Christmas Eve was all—and more—than the children had promised. The piney scent of fir competed with the aroma of lamb stew and homey yeast bread. Scores of candles diffused the room with golden haloes. The timid boy, at the very back of the line, watched in amazement as each child in turn eagerly claimed an orange and politely said, "Thank you."

The line moved quickly, and he found himself in front of the towering tree and the equally imposing headmaster. "Too bad, young man, too bad. The head count was in before you arrived. It seems there are no more oranges. Next year. Yes, next year you will receive an orange." Brokenhearted, the empty-handed orphan raced up the stairs to bury both his face and his tears beneath his pillow.

Wait! This wasn't how she wanted the story to go. Jean felt the boy's pain, his aloneness.

The boy felt a gentle tap on his back. He tried to still his sobs. The tap was more insistent until, at last, he pulled his head from under the pillow. He smelled it before he saw it. A cloth napkin rested on the mattress. Tucked inside was a peeled orange, tangy sweet. It was made of segments saved—last and best of all—from the others. A slice donated from each of his new friends. Together the pieces made one whole, complete fruit.

An orange of his very own.

Jean swiped at the tears trickling down her cheeks. From the bottom of the gift bag she pulled out an orange— a foil-covered, chocolate orange—already separated into segments. And, for the first time in weeks, she smiled. Really smiled.

She set about making copies of the story, segmenting and wrapping individual slices of the chocolate orange. After all, she had visits to make. There was Mrs. Potter across the street, spending her first Christmas alone in fifty-eight years. There was Melanie down the block, facing her second round of radiation. Her running partner, Jan, single-parenting a difficult teen. Lonely Mr. Bradford losing his eyesight, and Sue, sole caregiver to an aging mother . . .

Perhaps, just perhaps, a piece from her might help make one whole.

Carol McAdoo Rehme

Mother to Mother

I sit in the audience with the other parents, beaming at our children filing into their seats. My little ones' black hair and sienna skin make exclamation points among the other, pastel angels forming the pageant choir.

The chorister raises her arm, and the pianist comes in with the downbeat. So do some of the kids—a bit early. In cherubic fervor, their words spill out, "I am a child of God ..."

Oh, how I wish both of you could see this. They're perfect. Just perfect.

I often send this silent message to my children's birth mothers. I long to comfort and reassure them, to share with them the unspeakable joy their babies have brought into my life. I long to tell them their precious ones are beautiful and bright, healthy and strong.

"... and he has sent me here ..." I can almost distinguish Shyloh's sweet voice in the choir.

Just the other day, she asked, "Mommy, why is my hair black? Yours isn't."

The answer came easily to me. "To make you look beautiful, Shyloh, just like your mother in China." And typically Tiggerlike, she bounced away, grinning in satisfaction.

I hope you find peace in your decision to share this happy girl with me.

"... has given me an earthly home, with parents kind and dear ..." I catch the eye of my Samoan daughter, Whitney, whose hair is a shining cape flung across her shoulders and whose voice rings loudest of all the angels. She's singing with all her young heart.

She's adjusting, Mama. I grin through my burning eyes. *Your daughter's finally joining in. So is little Luke.*

My grateful tears plop down to bless the slumbering head of Whitney's contented baby brother, asleep on my lap.

What sacrifices these women made for their children, their difficult choices possible only because their powerful mother-love transcended all else. And what joy their decisions continue to bring into my life.

Whoever you are, wherever you are and whatever your circumstances, I hope your intuition calms you and tells you all is well.

Mother to mother, I wish I could wrap my arms around them this holiday season—those selfless birth moms—and assure them of my appreciation for these beautiful children of ours. More than anything, I wish I knew *how* to express the gratitude in my heart.

"... I am a child of God, and so my needs are great ..." Their angelic voices supplicate and saturate the auditorium and reach into the depths of my consciousness.

And—with sudden, deep conviction—I *do* know how, the only way that makes sense: I'll continue to love and cherish their little ones with all my being.

That will be thanks enough.

Annette Seaver

Chilly Today, Hot Tamale

"It's my own fault." Carl Fenter tugged his jacket closer against the abnormal bite of cold morning wind. "The rest of the family is home, where it's warm."

Just another one of his brilliant ideas—a big tamale feast after tonight's Christmas Eve service at church—and look where it landed him: waiting in a line fifty people deep.

Who would've guessed that every tamale shop in the city would be sold out the day before Christmas? But they were, as Carl knew. He'd been driving all over El Paso that morning. Determined to bring home the tamales, Carl tried one last *tienda*, an old favorite out in Canutillo.

When he arrived, a fresh batch was due off the steamer in forty-five minutes. Taking his place at the end of the snaking line of tamale-seekers, he watched the woman in front of him remove her jacket to drape around her shivering youngster. It wasn't long before she, too, shuddered in the chilly wind. After only a moment's hesitation, Carl shed his own jacket and offered it to the grateful mother.

Together, they cheered when the line crept forward at last, and smiling people exited the shop toting steamy bags. Finally, Carl got inside the door and inched his way closer to the counter, the woman now first in line.

"Sorry folks," the clerk announced, "that's the last of the tamales."

"No way!" Carl groaned with everyone else lined up behind him.

"But," stressed the man at the counter, "we'll have a final batch ready in, oh, about two hours."

Defeated, Carl backed away, but the young mother grabbed his arm.

"You're leaving?"

"I have to," Carl glanced at his watch. "I promised to put up luminarias at my church."

"I'll get your order of tamales and bring them to your house."

Carl's brow furrowed. "I couldn't ask you to do that."

"But it's the least I can do. You lent me your coat." Her smile overrode his objections. "Just give me your address." She and her little girl settled in for the long wait.

And at exactly noon on Christmas Eve, they delivered four dozen fragrant tamales—along with Carl's brown jacket—to his home.

Ellen Fenter
Submitted by Pat Phillips

A Piece of Themselves

Some see a group of women, twenty-three strong. Others see a group of twenty-three strong women. Everyone sees that their fingers are flying nearly as fast as their mouths.

Going to Pieces, the quilting guild at the Fort Drum, New York, army base, is at it again: their monthly sewing spree. It's a time each woman anticipates. A time to share patterns and platitudes. A time to trade ideas and intimacies. A time to join quilt blocks—and lives.

With many of their husbands deployed to the Middle East, the women seek relief in this regular gathering. Finding strength in numbers, they learn to emphasize life over loss, joy over loneliness and victory over defeat. In part, they achieve this closeness by telling stories—mostly about their children. They laugh over the latest toddler's antics, cringe over an adolescent's angst, roll their eyes over an update on teen fads and fashion. And the telling and sharing bind them into a sort of extended military family.

Even while war's dark cloud hovers over them, they choose to meet and mingle—especially with the holidays creeping nearer.

But tonight's mood is somber.

Something is obviously absent: There are no Christmas patterns in sight. No button-eyed snowmen, beaded holly or smiling nutcracker appliqués in hoops. No splashes of seasonal snowflakes, gingerbread men or angel prints on tables.

There's no casual chatter about old favorites like Log Cabin, Irish Chair or Tumbling Blocks. Neither do any of the women introduce new patterns, show a quilt they've recently completed or suggest working on a sampler.

Tonight a reverence blankets the room. Rather than creating individual blocks to join, they know this particular quilt requires more—a personal piece of each of them to make the whole. The project they've chosen echoes that faraway place always so near in their minds: Iraq.

The pieces they cut with such precision come from a young man's clothes. His desert-sand camouflage—fatigues and battle dress uniforms that will never be worn again, never be needed again. The template they pick is Lover's Knot—the pattern they see as most symbolic of the quilt's purpose, as well as their own feelings. The pieces will fit together like a complex jigsaw puzzle.

And the women wish they could as easily fit together the fragments of their compassion, their unspoken grief, their empathetic heartbreak.

Each snip and stitch is done with the knowledge that this quilt will go to one of their own. The family of the oh-too-young soldier who paid the ultimate sacrifice for his country.

When memories dim—until there is nothing more than a feeling, a taste, a smell to remind him of the Daddy he'll never know—it will wrap a lonely child.

When night presses in—to remind her of the husband whose death left a jagged hole in the fabric of her life—it will swaddle a sobbing widow.

With this purpose in mind, these stoic women hold in

tears of their own to cut and piece, quilt and bind. And, when their work is completed, they will bestow the quilt with love rather than pomp . . . with gratitude rather than ceremony.

Why?

Because these sorrowful sisters, above all others, under-stand the sacrifice involved, and this is how they choose to express their appreciation.

Carol McAdoo Rehme

Ho, Ho, Hope

My decision in the 1960s to run away from a newly divorced life in California and move to the safety of Canada was a big one—one I had to think over for nearly five minutes.

Hooking a battered trailer to my ancient Chevy, I gathered my five young children and headed for parts unknown. Along with my little brood, I took a month's worth of rent money, a pocketful of dreams, some hope for our future and a heart filled with faith.

Vulnerable and haggard after the long drive, I slowed my rickety rig when I saw the sign ahead. With five tousled heads bobbing in the windows, the startled border guard's mouth flew open.

My seven-year-old tossed him her cheekiest smile. One six-year-old twin looked tremulous and wide-eyed at the large man brandishing a gun on his hip; the other glared in defiance. My two- and three-year-old toddlers babbled to capture his attention and interest him in their toy cars and stuffed animals.

Obviously, we'd caught the bewildered guard . . . *off guard.*

Warning that I'd better have a job (I did) and threatening

immediate deportation if I attempted to go on welfare, he waved us through.

Shortly after we settled in a small apartment, my old car sputtered to a quick death. I found a sitter for the children and began hitchhiking to work, but because I was sometimes late, I lost the job. My last check went for another month's rent, and there was nothing left for food. As Christmas approached, desperation dogged every waking minute and even disturbed my sleep.

So did the kids' concerns.

"Is Santa *real*, Momma?"

"Will he find us, Momma?"

"Do you believe in him, Momma?"

With painstaking care, I explained that Santa didn't know where we'd moved and would miss us this year, but we had each other, and we would make do and . . . sing Christmas songs and . . . try making gifts and . . . and . . . well, everything would work out.

So, even without a tree, we glued colored paper garlands and strung popcorn to make the apartment festive and ourselves cheerful.

But the day before Christmas, my desperation reached a new low: We had nothing in the cupboard for supper. Reluctantly, I approached our neighbor and asked to borrow a can or two of soup to feed my children. After a curt "No," the door slammed in my face.

Humiliation and shame were my new companions.

And, for the first time in my life, I felt utter fear, despair and hopelessness.

Christmas Eve, I drew my little ones near—the boys on my lap, the girls nestled at my sides. In our meagerly decorated room, we told stories, played games and sang seasonal songs. I smiled at my wee darlings, but inside I was crying. And praying, again and again.

Please, God, oh please, God, send us help.

A sudden, loud *THUMP* at the door startled us all.

"Ho, ho, ho!" A hearty voice accompanied a loud knock.

And there in our doorway stood the jolly old man himself!

With a full sack slung over his back and three merry elves crowding his sides, Santa Claus brought the excitement of Christmas into our small home. He came bearing all kinds of wonderful gifts, something special for each child. Plus, an assortment of toys, games and books—even a gift for me—appeared from the depths of his deep pack! Christmas dinner (courtesy of the Vancouver Fire Department) was included, as well: turkey and the trimmings, enough to last several days.

Laughing and crying, I gazed around the joy-filled room at the satisfied faces of Santa and his helpers and the gleeful abandonment of my little family.

"Momma, Momma, he's real!" they chorused. "Santa found us!"

Yes, indeed he found us . . . in answer to my prayer. And that made a believer out of me.

Angela Hall

The Family Tree

"Mr. Zimmerman's sons are returning home to take over the farm."

The adult conversation around the kitchen table worried me. At seven years old, I was big enough to understand what that meant: My father and brother would no longer be working for the German farmer, and that spelled disaster.

The Great Depression had hit our rural Idaho community, and money was scarce that Christmas. Most of Father's income from Mr. Zimmerman was in trade for food and a place to live. This place. The only home I'd ever known. The home I loved.

The two-story farmhouse had one large sleeping room upstairs. It opened to a balcony overlooking the backyard and my favorite oak tree. During the spring and summer, soft, warm breezes blew through the room, and Jimmy, Eddie, Iris and I played for hours on end.

Now it was too cold. We had closed off the upstairs for everything but sleeping. Most of our winter living was done downstairs next to the warm fireplace, or in the kitchen where Mother was always baking yeasty breads and fragrant pies.

I was sitting on the floor playing with Harley, who was learning to crawl, when mother came in from the pump and set the bucket on the large woodstove. Water sloshed onto the hot stovetop, sizzling and filling the air with steam.

"Mother, will we really have to leave here?" My question was blunt. It was the worry foremost in my mind.

She looked down at me, sympathy and understanding etching her kind face. "Yes, Carol, we will."

I frowned. "But what about Christmas?"

"It will be the last holiday we'll celebrate in this house." Mother verbalized my darkest fear.

"And a tree? Will we have a tree?"

"Child, we have no means to get a tree this year."

But I couldn't—I wouldn't—accept her calm answer. Somehow we *must* have a tree for our last family Christmas in this wonderful old farmhouse.

That night I prayed for a very, very long time.

The next morning I hurried downstairs fully expecting to see the answer to my prayers, but there was no tree. I put on my warm sweater and mittens and headed to the outhouse. As the cold air hit my face, I became even more determined.

When Father left to walk the four miles into town, I decided to wait outside until he returned—even if it took all day. I settled beneath my favorite oak on the cold, hard ground, certain he'd bring home a tree.

It seemed like I'd been sitting for hours when I felt the ground start to rumble and heard a dull, distant roar that grew louder and louder. I jumped to my feet and ran to the fence. A large truck—full of Christmas trees—was headed for delivery in the city. My heart pounded as it drew up beside our house.

And then, like a hand tossing them from heaven, two large branches flew right off the truck and bounced into our front yard. My prayers had been answered. My tree had arrived!

I raced inside and, my words tripping over each other, babbled to Mother about how badly I wanted a tree for our last Christmas here and how hard I had prayed for it and how I was hoping Father would bring one home and how I just *knew* we'd get one in time for Christmas and now . . . and *now!*

Mother took my hand and walked me outside where Iris, Jimmy and Eddie stood gawking at the miracle in our yard. She smiled and pulled us together in a hug. "And to think, children, it was Carol's faith that brought us our tree."

We tied the bushy limbs together, then decorated them with wallpaper scraps and garlands of popcorn. I admired the tree as it stood in our big farmhouse home and knew it was the most beautiful tree I'd ever seen.

That year I also received the only doll I would ever have as a child. But my greatest gift was the discovery that—with faith—miracles happen.

Carol Keim
As told to (daughter) Tamara Chilla
Submitted by (niece) Laura Linares

Christmas Derailed

Boxes, ribbons and wrappings cluttered the entire room, evidence of a rowdy but generous Christmas morning for five-year-old Christopher and his three-year-old brother, David. But Christopher was far too withdrawn and quiet for a little boy who had just received his first electric train set. A bit concerned, I kept watch from the corner of my maternal eye while I scrambled eggs, maintained a running conversation with Grandma and periodically hauled Blossom, our bumbling sheepdog, away from the now listing tree.

What could be wrong? I wondered. Tummy ache? Christopher wasn't complaining. Disappointment? Not likely, considering his ecstatic response when he saw the train set. Annoyed by the toddling interference of his little brother? No, David played across the room, chattering incessantly to his grandpa and daddy.

Yet I knew a mysterious, dark cloud hung over Christopher's mood this Christmas morning and carved a furrow of deep thought across his forehead. What in the world was making him so sad and dejected? Unable to find a moment alone with him in all the holiday chaos, I worried as he periodically retreated to his room, only to reappear with the same gloomy look.

When the breakfast dishes were finally put away, and the rest of the family had settled into the quiet hum of conversation and coffee, I took my cup of tea and slid to the floor next to Christopher, where he distractedly spun a wheel on one of his new trucks.

"Hey, honey," I whispered quietly in his ear, "I noticed that you seem a little sad this morning. What's wrong?"

"Well, Mommy," he said in a melancholy little voice, "remember that ring I got in the gumball machine? I gave it to the Tooth Fairy for Christmas."

Oh no, I groaned inwardly.

"How did you do that?" I asked, with a foreboding sense of what I was about to hear.

"Oh, I put it under my pillow where she always looks. But she didn't take it. I been checking all morning, and it's still there. And I really wanted to give her a present. How come she didn't want it?" he asked plaintively, looking up at me for an answer.

Rejected by the Tooth Fairy! How could she have been so thoughtless? And how could I explain without completely deflating the faith and kind heart of this little boy?

"Hmmm," I stalled. "Do you think she's busy collecting teeth this morning? Maybe she'll come later."

He considered the possibility thoughtfully, but shook his head. "No, I don't think so. She comes at night when kids are asleep."

I had to make this right. But how? Moments passed while I groped for another idea—any idea. Then, quite unexpectedly, Christopher's entire being erupted with eureka joy.

"Mommy, I bet I know why she didn't take it!" he blurted. "I bet she's Jewish!" And with that resolved, off he ran, smiling broadly, to engineer his new electric train.

Armené Humber

My Christmas Wish

Hope deferred makes the heart sick, but when dreams come true, there is life and joy.

Proverbs 13:11–13

It became a very sad Christmas for us when we found out why Grandpa had been so sick lately. The doctors called my family to tell us that Grandpa had cancer. If that wasn't bad enough news, we learned that we wouldn't be able to have Christmas at home with him because he would be in the hospital getting treatment. We went to visit him on Christmas day, but he was too weak to really enjoy celebrating with us.

Over the next nine months, he was admitted to many hospitals and was continually moved from room to room: from ICU to private room, etc. I could hardly keep up with where he was.

One day, while Grandpa was watching TV in the hospital, he saw a commercial with a Jack Russell terrier that was shown flying through the air to the slogan, "Life's a journey—enjoy the ride." Grandpa fell in love. When my Uncle Shane went to visit him, Grandpa wouldn't stop talking about "that cute little dog on the commercial." To humor him, Uncle Shane found a picture of a Jack Russell terrier just like the one in the commercial. He brought it to the hospital and hung it on the wall of my grandfather's room. Whenever Grandpa moved to another room, he brought the picture with him.

By September, Grandpa wasn't improving like the doctors expected he would, so they told him he should see a special doctor in Dallas. Everyone agreed, and Grandpa was flown by air ambulance to another hospital in Texas.

One day, as we were chatting with him on the phone, Grandpa told us, "I want a Jack Russell terrier, and I am going to get one when I get well." We realized then that the thought of getting a little terrier was encouraging him to keep going and was giving him hope.

Months passed and Grandpa had several surgeries to help him beat the cancer. He was still very weak, so I wondered if he would be home for Christmas. As December arrived, having Grandpa home with us on Christmas became the only thing I wished for. Every night, I prayed that my wish would come true.

Then right before Christmas, the doctors said he could go home. With some help from Uncle Shane, my grandpa would be able to leave the hospital and begin his journey back home.

My whole family was excited to get the news. It had been a long, hard year for all of us. Since Grandpa would be coming home on Christmas Eve, everyone wanted to do something extra special for him this year. As soon as a Jack Russell terrier was mentioned, we knew that it was the surprise that would really make Grandpa happy. It was the kind of dog that Grandpa had looked at every day on his hospital wall, the dog that kept my grandpa hoping to get well. So, for days, my mom, uncles and aunts searched the ads in the papers looking for a real Jack Russell terrier puppy to give to Grandpa.

Finally, the day before Christmas Eve, we found a home that had Jack Russell terrier puppies for sale. I helped pick out just the right one that I knew would make my grandpa very happy.

The following evening, as we were sitting by the fire playing with the puppy, we got a phone call from Uncle Shane saying that he and Grandpa were stuck in New York City because of a storm. They wouldn't be making it home that night. We were all so disappointed. Before I fell asleep, I prayed once again that Grandpa would make it home for Christmas. He was so close!

I woke up Christmas morning to wonderful presents under the tree. But even though they were all things that I liked, they didn't make up for not having Grandpa home. Throughout the day, my family waited anxiously to hear from Uncle Shane again. Finally, we couldn't take it anymore and decided to just go over to Grandpa's house and wait there. We played games, did jigsaw puzzles and tried to enjoy the day, but by late in the afternoon, we were getting sadder by the minute.

Then suddenly, we heard someone coming up the front stairs. I peeked out the front door to see my uncle holding my grandpa in his arms. He had to carry him because he was so weak from the long trip.

We all screamed when they came through the door. They were finally home! Suddenly, the puppy began barking from all of the excitement. You should have seen the look on my grandpa's face. I can't remember seeing him smile that big in my life. He was so happy! All night long, the puppy, which he named Tara, and Grandpa, snuggled together in Grandpa's favorite chair.

Before Christmas day had ended, the only thing I had wished for had come true.

Grandpa was home.

Megan McKeown, twelve

An Unlikely Angel

Kindness is the golden chain by which society is bound together.

Johann von Goethe

It was just before Christmas. An angry middle-aged man stood at the counter of the animal shelter, gripping the leash of an aging German shepherd. "Why won't you take him?" he shouted. "I need to get him off my hands!"

The adoption counselor tried once more to explain. "At fourteen, Samson is too old to be a good adoption candidate," she said.

"Well, then just take him and put him down," the man yelled. "I want to be rid of him."

"We don't take animals just to put them down," the counselor explained. "May I ask why you no longer wish to keep the dog?"

"I just can't stand the sight of him," the man hissed, "and if you won't put him down, I'll shoot him myself."

Trying not to show her horror, the counselor pointed out that shooting an animal was illegal. She urged the man to consult with his veterinarian for other options.

"I'm not spending any more money on this animal," the man grumbled and, yanking the leash, he stalked out.

Concerned, the counselor wrote down the license plate of the man's truck and offered up a quick prayer for Samson.

A few days later, a German shepherd was found abandoned. He was brought to the shelter, and the staff recognized him as Samson. The town where he had been abandoned was where his owner lived. The man was contacted by the police and, under questioning, admitted that distraught over his recent divorce, he had sought revenge through the shepherd. He hadn't even wanted the dog, but he fought to keep him to spite his wife. Once his wife was gone, he couldn't bear to see the animal. The man was charged with abandonment, and Samson came to stay at the shelter.

The wife and the couple's son were located in Pennsylvania. They were horrified to hear what had happened to their dog and agreed immediately to have him come live with them.

There was just one problem: The wife was nearly broke after the divorce and their initial move. She could take no time off from work to drive to New Hampshire and get the dog, and she couldn't afford any other method of getting him to her. She hated to have Samson in the shelter any longer but didn't know what to do. "We'll come up with something," the staff assured her, but in their hearts they didn't know what. They were concerned, as well. Samson had lived with his family all his life. Within a few weeks, his whole world had been turned upside down. He was beginning to mope, and the staff could tell by his eyes that if he wasn't back with his family soon, he would give up.

Christmas was only two weeks away when the angel arrived. He came by pickup truck in the form of a man in his mid-thirties. Through a friend of a shelter staffer, he had heard about Samson's plight. He was willing to drive Samson to Pennsylvania, and he would do it before Christmas.

The staff was thrilled with the offer, but cautious. Why would a stranger drive hundreds of miles out of his way to deliver a dog to people he didn't know? They had to make sure he was legitimate and that Samson wouldn't be sold to meat dealers or dumped along the interstate.

The man understood their concerns and, thankfully, checked out to be an upstanding citizen. In the course of the conversation, he explained why he had come forward.

"Last year, I left my dog in my van while I went to do some grocery shopping," he explained. "While I was inside, the van caught fire. I heard people hollering and rushed out to see my van engulfed in flames. My dog meant everything to me, and he was trapped. I tried to get to the van, but people restrained me. Then I heard someone shouting, 'The dog is safe! The dog is safe!' I looked over, and there was this man I'd never seen before, holding my dog. He had risked his own life to get my dog out. I'll forever be in his debt. Just when you don't think there are heroes any more, one comes along.

"I vowed then and there that if I ever had the chance to do someone a good turn when it came to a beloved pet, that I would. When I heard about Samson and his family, I knew this was my chance, so here I am."

The shelter staff was amazed. They all knew about the van rescue story. It had been in all the papers, and the shelter had even given the rescuer a reward, but they had never dreamed that Samson's angel was connected to this earlier good deed.

A few days later, Samson and his angel were on their way. The dog seemed to know he was going home, because his ears perked up and his eyes were brighter than they had been in some time.

Just before Christmas, the mail brought one of the best cards the shelter had ever received. Along with a thank-you note were photos of a deliriously happy Samson romping with his family in the snow and snuggling with them by their Christmas tree. Samson was truly where he belonged, and the staff knew he would live out his days happily there.

They also knew that Samson's journey home was a true Christmas miracle, and that angels—and heroes—may still appear when you need them, even in the most unlikely forms.

Crystal Ward Kent

Double Angels

Nothing is ever lost by courtesy. It is the cheapest of pleasures, costs nothing and conveys much. It pleases him who gives and receives and thus, like mercy, is twice blessed.

Erastus Wiman

Waking up to the sound of my alarm, I smiled at the joy of only having to wait one more day. I got out of bed and threw some clothes on. Digging around the kitchen for some breakfast, I settled on a bowl of Cheerios and some leftover pizza from the night before. After watching cartoons, playing some video games and chatting on-line with some friends, it suddenly hit me that I hadn't bought a present for my mom. It was Christmas Eve, and the stores were going to be closing pretty soon. So I threw some shoes on, grabbed my skateboard and set off to the mall.

I swung open the heavy glass door into the mall only to see an incredible sight. People were running and panicking everywhere, trying to find the perfect gift for their loved ones. It was total madness. I decided to begin trying to make my way through the crowds when a guy in a black coat came up to me and told me with desperation in his voice that he had lost his brown leather wallet. Before I could say a word, he shoved his gray business card into my hand.

"Please call me at the number on the card if you happen to find it," he said. I looked at him, shrugged my shoulders and replied, "Yeah, no problem. I'll do that."

He turned to stop another person, and I continued to make my way through the unending stream of shoppers to look for a gift for my mom. I searched everywhere, up and down the mall in every store, with no luck. Finally, toward the very end of the mall, I spotted a small antique and glass-art store. It looked like it might have some interesting stuff—not the same as I'd seen in every other store. I figured I had nothing to lose so I went in.

Papers and boxes had been thrown everywhere from all the greedy Christmas shoppers digging around for the perfect gifts. It was pretty bad. It looked like a dirty bedroom with smelly clothes scattered around in it. As I tried to make my way through the pile of stuff, I tripped over a box in the aisle and fell flat on my face. I was so frustrated and worn out from shopping that I stood up, screamed and kicked the box. It flew through the air and hit a big, high-priced clay statue, almost knocking it over. My anger had gotten the best of me, but luckily no harm was done.

As I picked up the box to put it back on the shelf, I noticed a flat, green box hidden under some wrapping paper. I opened it up to find an amazing glass plate with a Nativity scene on it. There it was, the perfect gift, just lying in some trash waiting for me to find it. It felt like one of those moments when you hear angels singing hallelujah and beams of light stream down right over the place where you're standing. I smiled broadly, gathered it up and headed for the cash register. As the cashier was ringing up my purchase, I reached into my pocket to get my money. But my pocket was empty! I began to scramble around searching every pocket when I realized I had left my wallet at home. This was my last chance to get my mom a gift since the mall would be closing in ten minutes and it was Christmas Eve. It would take me twenty minutes to skate home and back. That's when I started to panic. *Now what do I do?* I silently asked myself.

So I did the only thing I could think of at that moment: I ran outside the store and started to beg people for money. Some looked at me like I was crazy; others just ignored me. Finally, giving up, I slumped down on a cold bench feeling totally defeated. I really had no idea what to do next. With my head hanging down, I noticed that one of my shoes was untied. *Great,* I thought. *All I'd need now is to trip over my shoelace and break my neck. That'd be the perfect ending to this useless trip.*

I reached down to tie my shoe when I spotted a brown wallet lying next to the front leg of the bench. I wondered if it could be the wallet that the man in the black coat had lost. I opened it and read the name on the driver's license inside. Yep. It was his. Then my mouth dropped in awe when I discovered three hundred dollars inside.

I never even questioned what I should do. I knew that I had to do the right thing, so I found a nearby pay phone and made a collect call to the number on the gray business card. The man answered and said that he was still in the mall. He sounded really happy and relieved. He asked me if I would meet him at the shoe store, which happened to be right next to the antique and glass store. When I got there, the man was so excited that he thanked me over and over while he checked to see if his money and credit cards were still there.

I turned to drag myself out of the mall and back home when I felt the man grab my shoulder. Turning to face him,

I let him know that I hadn't taken anything. "I can see that," he replied. "I don't think I've ever met a kid like you who would return all that money when he could have taken it without anybody knowing." Then he opened up the wallet and handed me four twenty-dollar bills, thanking me again.

In great excitement, I leaped into the air and shouted, "Yes!" I thanked *him* this time and told him I had to hurry and go get my mom a present before the mall closed. I made it to the store just as they were getting ready to lock up. The lady was really nice about it and let me in.

I bought the glass plate and started skating home, grateful that everything had worked out. I found myself whistling Christmas carols as I replayed the evening over in my head. Suddenly, it hit me. I realized that I had been sort of a Christmas angel for the man who had lost his wallet, and that he had been the same for me when I'd forgotten mine. *Double angels!* I thought. It was another one of those moments when choirs of angels begin to sing and beams of light shine down on you. I knew that I'd never forget this Christmas Eve for as long as I lived.

The next morning, my mom opened my "miracle present." The look on her face assured me that she really loved it. Then I told her all about what happened when I was trying to get her gift. The story made the plate even more special to her.

Still, to this day, she keeps that green glass plate on our main shelf as a centerpiece. It reminds her of me, of course, but it continues to remind me that amazing things can happen when you least expect them. Especially during that magical time called Christmas.

David Scott, sixteen

An Angel Among Us

Do all the good you can, by all the means you can, in all the ways you can . . . as long as ever you can.

John Wesley

I come from a large family of nine brothers and sisters, and all of us have kids of our own. On each Christmas night, our entire family gathers at my oldest sister's home, exchanging gifts, watching the nativity skit put on by the smaller children, eating, singing and enjoying a visit from Santa himself.

The Christmas of 1988, my husband Bob and I had four children. Peter was eleven, Leigh-Ann was nine, Laura was six and Matthew was two. When Santa arrived, Matthew parked himself on Santa's lap and pretty much remained dazzled by him for the rest of the evening. Anyone who had their picture taken with Santa that Christmas also had their picture taken with little Matthew.

Little did any of us know how precious those photos with Santa and Matthew would become. Five days after

Christmas, our sweet little Matthew died in an accident at home. We were devastated. We were lucky to have strong support from our families and friends to help us through. I learned that the first year after a death is the hardest, as there are so many firsts to get through without your loved one. Birthdays and special occasions become sad, instead of joyous.

When our first Christmas without Matthew approached, it was hard for me to get into the holiday spirit. Bob and I could hardly face putting up the decorations or shopping for special gifts for everyone. But we went through the motions for Peter, Leigh-Ann and Laura. Then, on December 13, something extraordinary happened to raise our spirits when we didn't think it was possible.

We were just finishing dinner when we heard a knock on the front door. When we went to answer it, no one was there. However, on the front porch was a card and gift. We opened the card and read that the gift-giver wanted to remain anonymous; he or she just wanted to help us get through a rough time by cheering us up.

In the gift bag was a cassette of favorite Christmas music, which was in a little cardboard Christmas tree. The card described it as being "a cartridge in a pine tree," a twist on the "partridge in a pear tree" verse in the song, "The Twelve Days of Christmas." We thought that it was a very clever gift, and the thoughtfulness of our "elf" touched our hearts. We put the cassette in our player and, song by song, the spirit of Christmas began to warm our hearts.

That was the beginning of a series of gifts from the clever giver, one for each day until Christmas. Each gift followed the theme of "The Twelve Days of Christmas" in a creative way. The kids especially liked "seven swans a-swimming," which was a basket of swan-shaped soaps plus passes to the local swimming pool, giving the kids something to look forward to when the warm days of spring arrived. "Eight maids a-milking" included eight bottles of chocolate milk, eggnog and regular milk in glass bottles with paper faces, handmade aprons and caps. Every day was something very special. The "five golden rings" came one morning just in time for breakfast—five glazed doughnuts just waiting to be eaten.

We would get calls from our family, neighbors and friends who would want to know what we had received that day. Together, we would chuckle at the ingenuity and marvel at the thoughtfulness as we enjoyed each surprise. We were so caught up in the excitement and curiosity of what would possibly come next, that our grief didn't have much of a chance to rob us of the spirit of Christmas. What our elf did was absolutely miraculous.

Each year since then, as we decorate our Christmas tree, we place on it the decorations we received that Christmas while we play the song "The Twelve Days of Christmas." We give thanks for our elf who was, we finally realized, our very own Christmas angel. We never did find out who it was, although we have our suspicions. We actually prefer to keep it that way. It remains a wondrous and magical experience—as mysterious and blessed as the very first Christmas.

Rita Hampton

From the Heart

From home to home, and heart to heart, from one place to another . . .
The warmth and joy of Christmas brings us closer to each other.

Emily Matthews

Dear Dad,

I didn't know what to get you for Christmas. Actually, I don't know what you ever want for any holiday, even on your birthday. I mean, I could always get you a "#1 Dad" shirt or mug, but what dad doesn't have enough of that stuff sitting around collecting dust?

I have been concentrating extremely hard on thinking about what you would possibly want. I know you love NASCAR, but I have always gotten you racing stuff for Christmas. I tried to think of what you do for fun, hoping that might spark an idea, but I don't know what you do for fun. You are always working, Monday through Friday, and then coming home to find just more stuff that needs to be done around the house. I don't think you ever get a break to have time to do the fun activities that other people enjoy (except for Sunday afternoons, which are totally dedicated to watching cars go round and round a track for hours on end). If you are not outside taking care of the dog or mowing the lawn, you might be found inside painting or even preparing meals.

I don't know how you accomplish everything every day, working nine-hour days, completing the things needing to be done around the house, paying the bills and still having time for your family, church and going to almost all of the sporting events that we kids are involved in.

I was at the mall, looking for gifts with one of my friends, when it finally hit me. I knew what I wanted to give you for Christmas. All you have ever asked for on any holiday, including your birthday, is for everyone to get along. You don't want gifts that are purchased at the mall.

I returned home, went straight to my room and prepared the present I have decided on. I spent the whole night working on it.

Dad, I didn't get you a store-bought present this year. Here it is, the perfect Christmas gift from me to you . . . that truly came from my heart.

DAD

Mr. Fix-It,
Trying to repair it all.
Mr. Yard Keeper,
Raking the leaves in Fall.
Mr. Homework Helper,
Helping me prepare for tests.
Mr. Encourager,
Telling me to do my best.
Mr. Punisher,
Grounding me when I do wrong.

Mr. Worker,
Laboring all day long.
Mr. Cook,
Making his famous food.
Mr. Holiday Helper,
To Santa, the Tooth Fairy and the Easter Bunny, too!
However you want to say it,
In good times and in bad,
He is all these things wrapped up in one,
And to me . . . he is my DAD.

Love, Jessica

Jessica Lamb, fifteen

A Timeless Gift

The greatness of a man can nearly always be measured by his willingness to be kind.

G. Young

Shopping for a Christmas gift can be the most nerve-wracking event of the year. Shopping for my wife can be a special challenge. Vacuum cleaners are too impersonal, football tickets are too impractical, and kitchen gadgets are downright impossible. I was at a loss, with Christmas fast approaching. In desperation, I asked my secretary, Sally, to help me pick out a present.

We walked side by side in a fast-paced walk, two blocks to the jewelry store. Working in the downtown business district had its advantages; being close to a lot of shopping places was one of them. However, there were disadvantages as well. On the way, our path crossed a couple of homeless men, huddled together by a vent from one of the nearby buildings.

I started to cross the street to avoid them, but traffic was too thick. Just before we approached, I switched sides with Sally to keep them from confronting her. They were surely going to beg for money, pretending to buy food, but any donation would surely end up as beer or wine.

As we got closer, I could see that one was probably in his mid-thirties and the other was a boy of school age— around thirteen or fourteen. Both were dressed shabbily, the older with a too-tight sport coat ripped at the sleeve, while the boy was without a coat at all, only a tattered shirt separating him from the blowing wind. *A quarter or two and they'll leave us alone,* I thought. "I'll handle this," I said with my best male bravado.

But Sally seemed undisturbed by the sight of the two beggars. In fact, she seemed comfortable in their presence. Before they asked, she offered.

"Is there anything I can do for you?" she directed her question to the two homeless men. I was in shock, waiting to pull Sally away from a dangerous situation, but she stood firm.

The two men looked at her with surprise until the older one spoke up. "Yes, ma'am. We do need something."

Here it comes—the hook, the gouge, I thought. *The two panhandlers are looking for a handout, an easy mark.* As I watched, I could tell the younger boy was shivering in the winter breeze, but what could I do?

"Could you tell us the time?" asked the older man. Sally glanced at her watch and replied, "Twelve-fifteen." He nodded his thanks and didn't say another word. We continued on our way to the jewelry store, and I had to ask Sally about the encounter.

"Why did you ask if you could help that man?"

"He was cold and in need, that's why," she replied in a matter-of-fact tone.

"But he's a bum. He could have tried to rob you or something."

"I take care of myself. But sometimes you have to take a chance on someone."

We arrived at the jewelry store, and Sally quickly found the perfect gift for my wife—a pair of diamond earrings. While she was there, she bought a man's watch, not an expensive one, but she was always thrifty. *Probably a gift for her husband,* I thought.

As we walked back to our building, the two vagabonds were still hovering around the sidewalk grate. Once again, I tried to come between Sally and the two, but she wouldn't let me. To my surprise, when we got next to them, she pulled the watch out of the bag and handed it to the older man.

"Here, I'm sure you know how to use it."

He was as shocked as I was. "Thank you, much obliged, ma'am," he said, trying the watch on his wrist. As we walked away, Sally had a gleam in her eyes, proud of what she had done.

"Why on Earth did you do that?"

Sally shrugged and said, "God has been so good to me, and I decided to do something good for him."

"But he didn't deserve it."

"Even the poor want something special, and besides, God's done things for me that I don't deserve—but He did them anyway."

"He's probably going to buy beer with that watch."

Sally just smiled at me and said, "Well, so what if he does? That's not my concern. I did something for good and that's all that matters. What he does with the watch is his challenge."

We arrived back at our building and went into our separate offices. I wondered about the encounter, and I thought about the two men. *Surely they were at the pawnshop, getting ready for a hot time at Sally's expense.*

The next day, I was going to lunch alone at a hamburger stand outside our building. As I walked down the street, I noticed the same two men that Sally and I had encountered. They were both still hovering around the heater vent. The older man recognized me and said, "Excuse me, sir. Could you give me the time?"

Aha! I had caught him. Sally's watch was nowhere to be found. Exactly what I thought.

"Where is the watch my secretary gave you yesterday?" I asked, hoping to stir his heart.

He hung his head down and admitted his guilt. "Sir, I'm sorry but I had to do something." It was then I noticed the new parka around the shoulders of his young companion. "Wouldn't you do something for one of your own?"

Speechless, I handed him a quarter and continued on my way. As I walked, I started thinking about the incident. He had sold the watch all right, but he bought a coat, not beer, with the money. Sally's act of kindness did have meaning. So did her words: The challenge was answered.

As I arrived at the hamburger stand, I suddenly lost my appetite. I turned around and headed back to the office. The two men were still by the grate. I tapped the older man on the shoulder and he looked up at me, obviously freezing. I took my long, gray overcoat off and draped it over his shoulders without saying a word. As I walked away, I knew that my own challenge had been met. The few steps back to my office made my teeth chatter. But, you know . . . it was one of the warmest trips I have ever made in my life.

Harrison Kelly

The Christmas Cookie Can

There is no surprise more magical than the surprise of being loved: It is God's finger on man's shoulder.

Charles Morgan

It was almost Christmas again, and I was in my father's home . . . one last time. My dad had died a few months before, and the home that we had grown up in had been sold. My sister and I were cleaning out the attic.

I picked up an old Christmas cookie can that my dad had used to store extra Christmas lightbulbs. As I stood there, holding the can, the memory of a past Christmas swirled through my mind like the snowflakes outside the attic window swirling towards the ground.

I was eleven years old, and with Christmas only a week away, I woke up one morning to a perfect day for sledding.

It had snowed all night, and my friends would be hurtling down the sledding hill at the end of our street. It wasn't what you would call a great challenge, but we all had fun, and I couldn't wait to try out the fresh layer of snow on the runs.

Before I could go anywhere, my mom reminded me that I had to shovel the walkways around the house. It seemed like forever, but after about an hour and a half I was finally finished. I went into the house to get a glass of water and my sled. Just as I got to the front door to leave, the phone rang.

"Joey will be right over," my mom said in reply to someone.

Geez, not now, I thought. *The guys are waiting for me.* I opened the front door, but there just wasn't enough time to get away.

"Joey, Mrs. Bergensen wants you to shovel her sidewalk," my mother stated.

"Mom," I groaned, "tell her I'll do it this afternoon." I started to walk out the door.

"No, you'll do it now. This afternoon you'll be too tired or too cold. I told her you would be right over, so get going."

My mother sure is free with my time, I thought to myself, as I walked around the corner to the old lady's house. I knocked on her door.

The door opened, and there was Mrs. Bergensen with this bright smile on her old face.

"Joey, thanks for coming over. I was hoping someone would come by, but no one did."

I didn't reply, just shook my head and started shoveling. I was pretty mad and wanted to take it out on Mrs. Bergensen. *Sure, you were hoping someone would come by. Why would they? You're just an old lady,* I fumed in my mind. At first, my anger helped me work pretty fast, but the snow was heavy.

Then I started thinking about Mrs. Bergensen and how her husband had died years ago. I figured she must feel lonely living all by herself. I wondered how long it had taken her to get that old. Then I started wondering if she was going to pay me anything for my work, and if she did, how much she was going to give me. *Let's see, maybe $2.50, with a fifty-cent tip thrown in. She likes me. She could have called Jerry, the kid across the street, but she called me. Yep, I'll be getting some bucks!* I started to work hard again.

It took me about another hour to finish. Finally, it was done. *Okay, time for some money!* I knocked on her door.

"Well, Joey, you did an outstanding job and so fast!" I started to grin. "Could you just shovel a path to my garbage cans?"

"Oh . . . sure," I said. My grin faded. "I'll have it done in a few minutes." Those few minutes lasted another half-hour. *This has to be worth another buck at least,* I thought. *Maybe more. Maybe I'll get five bucks altogether.* I knocked on her door again.

"I guess you want to get paid?"

"Yes, ma'am," I replied.

"Well, how much do I owe you?" she asked. Suddenly, I was tongue-tied.

"Well, here. Here's a dollar and a fifty-cent tip. How's that?"

"Oh, that's fine," I replied. I left, dragging my shovel behind me. *Yeah, right, that's fine. All that work for a buck fifty. What a lousy cheapskate.* My feet were freezing, and my cheeks and ears were stinging from the icy weather.

I went home. The thought of being out in the cold no longer appealed to me.

"Aren't you going sledding?" my mom asked as I dragged in the front door.

"No, I'm too tired." I sat down in front of the TV and spent the rest of the day watching some dumb movie.

Later in the week, Mrs. Bergensen came over and told my mom what a good job I had done for her. She asked if I would come over to shovel her sidewalks every time it snowed. She brought with her a can loaded with homemade Christmas cookies. They were all for me.

As I sat holding that can in my lap and munching the cookies, I figured that shoveling her sidewalk had been a way for me to give her a Christmas gift, one that she could really use. It couldn't be easy for her being all alone with no one to help her. It was what Christmas was really all about . . . giving what you could. Mrs. Bergensen gave me the cookies she made, and I gave her my time. *And hard work!* I started to feel better about the whole thing, including Mrs. Bergensen.

That summer, Mrs. Bergensen died, and it ended up that I never had to shovel her sidewalk again.

Now, years later, standing in my family's attic and holding that Christmas can, I could almost see Mrs. Bergensen's face and how she had been so glad to see me. I decided to keep the can to remind myself of what I had figured out so many years ago, about the true meaning of Christmas. I dumped the old lightbulbs that were in it into the trash. As I did so, the piece of paper that had been used as the layer between the cookies and the bottom of the can floated into the trash as well. It was then that I saw something taped to the inside of the can.

It was an envelope that said, "Dear Joe, thank you and have a Merry Christmas!" I opened the yellowed envelope to find a twenty-dollar bill . . . a gift to me, with love, from Mrs. Bergensen . . . the cheapskate.

Joseph J. Gurneak

The Unusual Package

Do not judge according to appearance, but judge with righteous judgment.

Jesus of Nazareth

The glow of the large colored lights illuminated the long strands of silvery tinsel and pinecone angels that decorated the huge tree in our classroom. Desks had been shoved to the back and replaced by rows of brown folding chairs. We had just finished our wonderful Christmas pageant. Now restless family members and friends wanted to head for home on this snowy Wisconsin evening, but they sat waiting. To them it was time to leave, but to each of us it was finally time to exchange the brightly wrapped presents piled under the tree.

Earlier in December, each of us students had pulled a slip of paper with a name on it out of an old coffee can. Then it was our job to buy a Christmas present for that person. All of us hoped that we would pull the name of our crush, or at least the name of our best friend.

The moment had finally come. One by one, our teacher handed Santa the presents, and he called out each name.

Some of the kids hurried up to the front and then sat down to tear off the paper right away. Others took their time to receive their gift, carefully removing the bow and then trying to take off the paper without ripping even one corner. Soon, all kinds of gifts, from board games, candy, scarves and mittens to small toys and stuffed animals had been opened.

I stood off to one side with my two best friends, Carrie and Megan. Patiently, I oohed and aahed as they each opened their gifts. Carrie's gift was from Kevin. This was no surprise. Everyone in school knew how Kevin had held his brother's head in a snowbank until he finally agreed to give up Carrie's name. Kevin had given her a two-pound box of chocolates, which she generously shared with Megan and me. I think Carrie was secretly hoping for something a little more personal like a bracelet or a ring, but I'm sure Kevin's mother had something to say about what he was allowed to give Carrie.

Megan's package contained a book of 365 crossword puzzles and word searches, "One for Every Day of the Year," the bright red print on the cover proclaimed. This was perfect for Megan, who happened to be the brains of our group. She rushed over to thank Shelby.

As Carrie flirted with Kevin and Megan pored over her book, I stuffed chocolate after chocolate in my mouth. I tried to appear calm and disinterested while, one by one, the pile of presents shrank.

Finally, the last brightly wrapped present was gone from under the tree, and I began to silently panic. I quickly put what I hoped was a brave smile on my face, which wasn't particularly easy to do, because I was thirsty after eating six chocolates and my mouth was already dry from anxiety.

Santa was about ready to get up and distribute candy bags to the kids in the crowd when our teacher handed

Santa one more gift. He called out my name, and I hustled to the front of the room, too relieved to even pretend to be disinterested. Santa handed me an old, sort of dirty-looking envelope. *That's weird,* I thought. *What an unusual package. Who would wrap something like this?* I vaguely remember mumbling "thank you" as someone in the crowd giggled. Red-faced, I hurried back to my friends.

"Who's it from?" asked Carrie.

I turned over the envelope and revealed, "To Barbie from Sarah," written in pencil. My heart dropped down to my toenails when I saw it.

Sarah was the middle child of eleven. Her family had moved here about two years ago. They lived in a house that would have been too small, no matter how few kids would have been in the family. Their yard was strewn with cars that no longer worked and parts of broken toys; a bicycle wheel there, a wagon handle here, a stuffed bear that their dog had probably chewed the legs off of. Sarah was nice enough but terribly shy. She wore strange combinations of clothes and had trouble with her schoolwork, especially reading. Sometimes our teacher asked me to help her.

My mother had instilled in me that I should always be polite and act as if I like a gift (even the time that I got a black and white shirt from my sister that made me look like an escaped convict).

"Feelings are more important than things," she always said. "There is nothing in the world worth hurting someone else's feelings over." So with my mother—and the entire roomful of people looking on—I was ready to act as if I had just been given the best present I had ever received.

"Maybe it's money," whispered Carrie.

"I think it's probably a poem," chimed in Megan.

But when I tore open the envelope and reached my

fingers in, I knew they were both wrong. I felt something hard in the corner. I pulled out a long silver chain. Dangling from the chain was a teardrop-shaped blue iridescent pendant with a scalloped silver border. It was truly beautiful.

I looked up and saw Sarah's anxious face across the room. I flashed her a big smile and mouthed, "Thank you." She smiled back, revealing pink candy cane–stained teeth.

That night, I received more than the gift Sarah gave me, which I still have. Even more valuable than that pretty necklace were the lessons that I learned that Christmas. I learned not to prejudge others, and that sometimes my turn will come last. And finally, that nice presents and kind hearts can come in unusual packages.

Barbara King

The Christmas Care Bear

May no gift be too small to give, nor too simple to receive, which is wrapped in thoughtfulness and tied with love.

L. O. Baird

I began to lose hope. The most treasured person in my life was slowly slipping away. My blind, ninety-four-year-old great-grandmother was sleeping soundly in the hospital bed. As I sat quietly with my family, I listened to the constant buzzing of the machines that kept her alive. Her face was pale and empty. No longer was she the cheerful and jubilant person I had always known.

Thoughts flooded my head. *It seems like every day she gets worse. She might not make it through Christmas.* I tried to think of a present to give to her. Since she was blind, I would have to get her a gift that she didn't have to see to appreciate, but that she could feel with her hands.

I remembered that when she lived with us she always wanted to touch and play with my stuffed animals. Her favorites were my unique collection of bears. I knew right then what to get. *She's always wanted one for herself!* I would have a teddy bear made especially for her.

"Grandma's Bear" is what I named the brown, furry animal . . . "Bear" for short. He was quite charming with his tiny black button nose and his big chocolate eyes. I looked forward to visiting her on Christmas morning and seeing the look on her face when I gave Bear to her.

The day came quicker than I thought. I clutched Bear in my arms as I walked to room 208 with my family. There was Grandma, propped up in her bed. Her eyes were wide open. I think she was sensing that we were coming. A grin grew on her face as we sat on her bed, close to her frail body hidden under the covers.

"Merry Christmas!" my dad said. Our family chatted for a while with Grandma until it was time at last to give her the gifts we had brought. My mother gave her fresh-smelling baby powder because she could never have enough of it. My father brought her favorite caramel candies, and my brother brought her a new nightgown. Now it was my turn. I placed the fuzzy bear in her gentle, skinny hands. Her face was suddenly filled with joy. The last time I had seen her that happy was many months earlier.

She cooed and hugged the stuffed animal the whole time we were there. She absolutely loved Bear, and she didn't want anyone to take Bear from her because she feared they'd lose him. Before we left, she thanked me numerous times. She said that it would never leave her side. From that day on, she gradually started to heal. Everyone said it was a miracle.

One month later, my great-grandmother moved back into the nursing home where she had lived before she was sent to the hospital. The nurse said that she slept with Bear every single night and never forgot him. One day when I visited the nursing home, the nurse informed me that my great-grandmother was one of the funniest and happiest residents in the nursing home. She also said that she's taking very good care of Bear. I replied, "No, *he's* taking good care of her."

Ever since my great-grandmother got Bear, her health improved. Bear was the perfect gift. She made it through Christmas when all of us believed she wouldn't.

Months later, when I turned eleven, my great-grandmother passed away peacefully in her sleep. The nurse said that she found her in the morning, still hugging Bear. It might not have been the bear that was the miracle that prolonged her life and helped her to live the rest of her life in joy . . . but I believe it was.

Molly Walden, thirteen

Truly Cool

Maturity begins to grow when you can sense your concern for others outweighing your concern for yourself.

John MacNaughton

My heart was in my throat. As mom and I entered the store, I had only one thought in my mind, *I hope my pretty pink bike is still there.* It would be my first bike ever. But since it was about a week before Christmas and the stores were in total chaos, Mom gently reminded me that it was possible that the bike I wanted would be sold out.

I could feel the excitement in my stomach, and my hands were jittery. I was so anxious to get the bike. I crossed my fingers as we came around the corner to the bike section. My stomach did somersaults when I finally spotted it near the end of a long row. There it was, my big, shiny pink bike! I thought it was too clean and pretty to touch, so I stuck my hands in my pockets to keep from smudging it.

The week went by really slowly. The only thing that we were looking forward to, besides school letting out, was a charity drive that our school was doing for a homeless children's shelter. We had made little toys for the kids who were living there. I was surprised to see how many were on the list—so many who didn't have a real home where they could spend Christmas.

Still, I didn't think as much about helping them as I was thinking about my bike. I couldn't wait for winter break to get over so that I could ride my bike to school for everyone to see. I would be the cool kid for once.

While we waited in the classroom for the bus to come and take us to the children's shelter to deliver our presents, I sat at my desk writing my mom a thank-you letter. I explained how I had never wanted anything as badly as I did that bike. Just as I finished, the bus driver came into our room to let us start getting on the bus. I ended up sitting next to a guy who was getting a skateboard for Christmas. We talked about how excited we were about our big gifts.

We chatted all the way there and were still talking as we came through the shelter doors. Suddenly, my mouth dropped, and I stopped in mid-sentence. I was in shock seeing kids wearing torn-up and worn-out ragged clothes. I felt sad as I looked around the place.

Our teacher encouraged us to find a kid who was staying in the shelter and visit with him or her. I noticed a little girl sitting in a corner by herself. When I walked up, it seemed like she didn't want to say "hi" or anything, but I felt like I should say something to her. So I started out by asking her if she was excited about Christmas coming. I told her about how I was getting a bike. Suddenly, her eyes lit up, and a huge smile came across her face. She told me that she would be the happiest kid in the world if she could ever get one.

Then she explained to me what her life had been like. To say the least, she didn't have a normal childhood. She had never known what it was like to live in a real home of her own with pets and everything. Her parents had been alcoholics and constantly had money problems. They moved around often because they either couldn't pay the rent or would be thrown out for some reason. Things got so bad with them that they finally abandoned her, and she ended up in this shelter.

She no longer had anyone to call family.

I realized that her getting a bike anytime soon was out of the question. I mean, who would buy it? Her parents were gone, and she was alone in the world, other than for the people who ran the shelter. My heart just ached for her.

We got so involved in our conversation that my teacher had to come and tap me on the shoulder to tell me that it was time to leave. I grabbed my bag and told her that I hoped she'd have a merry Christmas and get everything she wanted. Before leaving the room, I looked back and gave her a little smile.

Later that night, I lay in bed remembering what the girl had told me about what it was like to live at the shelter. I thought about her life and about mine as well. All I had ever done was want and want and think that I never get enough. Now I'd met a girl my age who had barely enough to get by and took nothing for granted. I never understood when people would tell me how lucky I was. Now I finally understood.

Over the next three days, I kept thinking about ways that I could help make this girl's life better. Then on Christmas Eve, while sitting in church listening to the preacher speak, it dawned on me. I wanted to give her my new bike (which I had not yet received)!

When I explained everything to my mom, she gave me a smile that I could never fully describe—one like I have never seen before. My mom found the paper that told what children's shelter I had gone to and, on Christmas morning, we headed for the shelter with my new bike in the trunk of my mom's car.

I walked in feeling somewhat sorry that I would not be the one getting the bike, but I also felt really good inside. When I finally found her, she was sitting in the corner where I had first met her. Her head was down, and she seemed to be sad. I walked over and said, "Merry Christmas." Then I told her that I had something for her.

Her face brightened, and she smiled as she looked up at me. She looked happier than I have ever seen a kid look before. I grabbed her hand and walked her over to the door. Parked outside was my bright pink bike with a big red bow on it. I was expecting a bigger smile than what I had seen moments before, but instead I saw a tear running down her cheek. She was so happy that she was crying. She thanked me over and over again. I knew then that what I had done was truly cool. I knew I had made her the happiest kid in the world.

What I didn't know was that giving away the only bike I'd ever had would change the way I thought about things. But over time, I found that I wasn't as greedy as I was before.

I now realized that receiving a great gift gives you a good feeling, but giving from the heart gives you a feeling that's even better.

I also realized that I had been counting on that bike to make me cool. Although I never got to show up at school riding it, my mom was proud of me and so was everybody else. In the long run, that meant more to me than the bike, or looking cool, ever could have.

Brittany Anne Reese, fifteen

3

YULETIDE MEMORIES

Life brings simple pleasures to us every day. It is up to us to make them wonderful memories.

Cathy Allen

Christmas Mother

Within every adversity lies a slumbering possibility.

Robert H. Schuller

As a kid growing up in Chicago, the winter weather was cause enough to remember a few Noels with a twinge of discomfort. My brother and I, however, had other things working against us as well way back in 1925.

Our dad had died three years before, leaving our mom with only her pride and a strong back.

My brother, Ned, was four years older than I, and he went to school. It was necessary for my mom to take me with her to the only job she could find—as a cleaning lady. In those days, work was scarce and money was scarcer. I remember watching Mom hour after hour scrubbing floors and walls, on her hands and knees or sitting on the outside of a window sill washing windows, four stories off the ground, in freezing weather—all for twenty-five cents an hour!

It was the Christmas Eve of 1925 that I shall never forget. Mom had just finished working on the near Northside, and we headed home on one of the big, red, noisy and cold Chicago streetcars. Mom had earned her $2.25 for nine hours of work, plus a jar of tomato jam as a Christmas present. After she lifted me onto the rear platform of the streetcar, I remember how she searched through her precious few coins for five pennies and a nickel. Her fare was seven cents and mine was three cents. As we sat together on the cold seats, we held hands. The roughness of her hands almost scratched my cold hands as she held them tightly in hers.

I knew it was Christmas Eve, and even though I was only five, the past few Christmases had conditioned me not to expect anything more than some extra food, a visit to Marshall Fields' window display of animated toys and snow, and other kids' excitement.

With Mom's hand in mine and the knowledge that our Christmas basket had been delivered by Big Brothers, a charitable organization, I felt a warm sense of security as we headed home.

We had just passed a major intersection where Wieboldts, a large department store, was letting out the last of its shoppers before closing for Christmas Eve. Their feelings of holiday cheer, cries of joy and happiness could be felt and heard through the cold, steel walls and noise of the traveling streetcar. I was insensitive to the joy, but as I looked up at Mom I could feel her body racked with pain. Tears streamed down her weathered face. She squeezed my hand as she released it to wipe away her tears with her chapped and cracking hands. I will always remember her hands with the swollen knuckles, enlarged veins and coarse surface that somehow reflected her sacrifices, her honesty and her love.

The bitter cold struck our faces like a slap as we stepped down from the streetcar and onto the icy, snow-covered street.

I walked close to Mom to stay warm and looked into the

front-room windows that framed brightly lit Christmas trees. Mom walked straight ahead without a side glance, one of her ungloved hands holding mine, the other holding a paper shopping bag that contained her soiled white uniform and the jar of tomato jam.

Our flat was a corner unit in the middle of the block. Each Christmas, Nick, the barber, sold Christmas trees on an empty lot next to his shop. In those days, tree lots were sold out long before Christmas Eve, leaving only broken or dead brown branches covering the ground. As we passed the quiet, emptied lot, Mom dropped my hand and picked up a bundle of broken, discarded pine-needle branches.

Our second-story flat was without heat except for a small pot-bellied stove in the kitchen. Ned and I fed the stove with coal that dropped from railroad cars a couple of blocks away and wooden fruit boxes that we found in the alley next to our house. It was natural for each of us to bring home anything that would burn.

As we climbed the dingy, uncarpeted, wooden stairs to our flat, I'm sure my relief was only minimal compared with Mom's. We opened the door to the front room that felt like a refrigerator. The still air actually made it colder than it was outside.

The front bedroom and Ned's bedroom, next to the kitchen, were no warmer. The door to the kitchen was kept closed to trap what little heat there was in the bathless bathroom, the rear bedroom and the worn linoleum-covered kitchen. Other than two beds and a lion-clawed wood table with four chairs, there was no other furniture or floor covering in the entire flat.

Ned had started a fire and pulled up close to the stove to absorb what little heat it afforded. Fortunately, he was absorbed in an old issue of *Boy's Life*. Mom unbundled me and sat me next to the stove, then prepared the table for our Christmas feast.

Few words were spoken because the season was about joy, giving, receiving and love. With the exception of love, there was an obvious void in the remaining Christmas features. We sat facing the little wood stove as we ate canned ham, vegetables and bread. Our faces flushed with the heat as the cold attacked our backs.

I remember that my only concerns that evening were having to go to bed early because of no heat and the shock of cold sheets.

As usual, we washed our hands and faces in cold water, brushed our teeth and made a charge to our respective deep freezes. I curled up in a fetal position between the two sheets of ice with my socks and Ace cap still on. A cold draft of air attacked my behind because one button was missing from my thin, secondhand long underwear. There was no great anticipation about what I would or would not receive for Christmas, so I fell asleep fast and soundly.

Because the streetlight was directly opposite my bedroom window and the Oscar Meyer slaughterhouses were only half a block away, it was common for large trucks to wake me several times a night. But at my age and with the cold, it was no challenge to escape back to my dreams.

During the twilight before dawn, I awoke. The streetlight clearly illuminated Mom's ticking tin clock (with one missing foot). I hadn't heard the milkman rattling bottles or his horses' hoofs in the alley, so I knew I could sleep at least a few hours longer.

However, when I looked over to see my mother sleeping beside me, I realized that she hadn't been to bed yet. Suddenly I was wide awake in a state of panic, wondering if Mom was sick or if she possibly and finally had endured enough and left.

The trucks had passed but my panic had not as I lay there staring at the streetlight with my wool cap over my eyebrows and flannel blankets up to my eyes. I couldn't imagine life without Mom.

I lay in the icy stillness, afraid to get up and confirm my fears, but totally incapable of going back to sleep. Then, I heard a grinding, twisting sound coming from the kitchen. It was as constant as a machine: It would stop for a few seconds, then continue, then pause again.

As best as I could tell time at that age, I figured it was about 5:00 A.M. With the darkness of winter there was no assurance of what time it really was, other than it was long past the time Mom should have been to bed.

As much as I feared the truth, I knew I had to find it. I rolled under the covers to the edge of the bed and dropped my stocking-covered feet to the cold, bare wood floor. With the streetlight illuminating the bedroom, I could see my breath as clear as if I were out in the street.

Once into the darkness of the front room, I was guided to the kitchen by a light glowing from under the door, which was ajar. The grinding and twisting sound became louder as I approached. The stove had been out for hours, and I could see Mom's breath as well as my own. Her back was towards me. She had wrapped a blanket over her head and back for some small insulation against the cold.

On the floor to the right was her favorite broom, but the handle had been whittled off just above the sweeping portion. She was working at the old wood table I had never seen such total concentration and dedication in my life. In front of her was what appeared to be some sort of disfigured Christmas tree. As I stared in awe her effort became apparent to me. She was using her broken kitchen knife to drill holes in her broom handle, into which she had inserted the branches from Nick's empty tree lot. Suddenly it became the most beautiful Christmas tree I had ever seen in my life. Many of the irregular holes had not been effective in supporting the branches, which were held in place with butcher's string.

As she continued to twist and dig another slot for the remaining branches, my eyes dropped to her feet, where a small can of red paint was still open. A wet brush lay next to it. On the other side of her chair there were two towels on the floor that were almost covered with red toys: a fire engine with two wheels missing off of the back; an old steel train with a number of wheels missing and the caboose's roof bent in half; a jack, out-of-the-box, with no head; and a doll's head with no body. I felt no cold, no fears, no pain, but rather the greatest flow of love I have ever felt in my life. I stood motionless and silent as tears poured from my eyes.

Mom never stopped for a second as I silently turned and walked slowly back to my bedroom. I have had love in my life and received some elaborate gifts through the years, but how can I ever hope to receive more costly gifts or more sacrificial love? I shall never forget my mother or the Christmas of 1925.

John Doll

Kevin and the Saint

"Santa for special kids on tomorrow's broadcast. See you then."

The tag line caught my attention. I raised my head from my book and saw a picture of a waving Santa on the television screen as the Channel 6 news credits rolled by. My heart began to pound. *Could this be the Santa I've been looking for?*

I picked up the phone and called the station, "That Santa tomorrow, can he communicate with deaf children?" I asked.

Over the rumble of the newsroom, I heard, "Yes, he's a retired schoolteacher who signs. He won't release his name but he's scheduled to be at the Memphis city mall tomorrow. We'll be picking up the story through our affiliate news station."

"Memphis? You mean Tennessee, not in Florida?"

"Yes, can I help you with anything else?" He was pressuring me to end the conversation.

"No, thank you." I hung up, disappointed.

Just then Jessica came into the office. Her face changed after seeing my saddened expression. "What's wrong?"

"You know I love your son like a nephew, right?"

She smiled. "Of course. You're his favorite baby-sitter."

"Well, I'd like to take him to Tennessee tomorrow to the Memphis mall. There's a Santa who knows sign language scheduled to appear."

A twinkle sparkled in her eyes. "Kevin's six. He doesn't need to visit Santa Claus any more. That's really sweet of you to think of him. But I'd rather instill in him the true meaning of Christmas—Jesus' birth—not just exchanging presents."

My heart broke. I wanted her to know how much it would mean to Kevin. He'd never met a Santa who could understand him. Last year when we took him to our local mall, he signed his name to the Santa there.

"Yes, I'll bring you that," the Santa had replied.

Kevin had cried for hours. He decided Santa didn't give gifts to children who couldn't speak. That wasn't good enough, not for Kevin, I thought. He deserved a Santa who could relate.

"You really want to drive all that way just so he can tell him he wants a Pokeman?"

"Santa isn't just a man in a red suit," I explained. "He's the spirit of giving. He's Jesus' helper, spreading cheer to all the little girls and boys, even the deaf ones. For the first time Kevin will be able to think Santa knows who he is."

She nodded. "Well, all right, we'll go tonight. Bring a map and your camera?"

"Of course." I happily laughed. "We have to make a memento!"

Later in the evening Kevin piled into the minivan clutching his pillow.

His mother signed, "Don't you want to see Saint Nick?"

Kevin moved his fingers. "He doesn't like me unless I write."

"That's not true," his mother mouthed slowly.

Soon, Kevin snuggled in his backseat bed as mile after mile drifted by. Palm trees and scrub brush gave way to reddened clay. We drove until the air chilled and the land grew hilly.

I wasn't sure if I was overstepping my bounds, but I hoped this would be a wonderful experience for Kevin. He deserved to communicate with Santa.

When we arrived early the next afternoon at the mall, his mother signed to Kevin, who was staring back at her, "We're here."

Wiggling in anticipation, he signed, "Do you think Santa cares that I came?"

I looked around at all the cars and knew enough to nod my head yes.

Kevin jumped out of the minivan and took his mother's hand and mine. Together we walked through the crowded walkways to the open courtyard. There, on top of a platform, was an older man with real gray hair. His stomach looked pillow-plumped, but there was no mistaking his outfit of red and white. He sat enthroned next to a sparkling, bedecked Christmas tree.

His mother gestured, "That's him, straight from the North Pole."

Kevin's eyes suddenly lit up at the whole Yule scene. He vaulted up the steps and stood in front of Santa. His mother and I scampered to catch up. By the time we got to Santa's chair, Kevin was signing, "I'm Kevin Johnson from Orlando, Florida."

"Hello, Kevin. You live near Disney World," Santa signed back. "You've been very good this year. What would you like for Christmas. Let me guess . . . a Pokeman?"

I knew that was probably what all the little boys had asked Santa for, but Kevin's eyes lit up as if Santa knew him personally.

"You're the real Santa," Kevin signed.

"Anything else?" the smiling, rosy-cheeked Santa asked.

Kevin quickly moved his hands to cross his chest.

Knowing what Kevin wanted, Santa stretched his arms to give a giant hug.

Tears came to my eyes as I raised my camera to capture the moment. All children are special, I know that, but seeing Kevin hug Santa reminded me of how important every individual is. Whenever I look at my framed picture of Santa hugging Kevin, I want to thank him for a memory that will never fade for Kevin, his family or me.

Michele Wallace Campanelli

Heaven-Sent

I went through a time in which I felt everyone was taking advantage of me, and I wasn't the least bit happy about it. It seemed that all the people I had decided to show kindness to were overstepping their boundaries. I wrestled with the idea that if I was doing good just because God said we should, but if my heart wasn't cheerful about doing it, was I really doing God a favor? Wasn't my bad attitude canceling out the good?

I had spent many hours and dollars on some disadvantaged kids in our neighborhood, and it was getting to the point where things were being expected of me by their grandma, with whom they lived. I was feeling resentful of her and the fact that the kids didn't seem to be a priority in her life. I got a call from her one day as Christmas was approaching and she started telling me about some girl she knew who wasn't going to have much of a Christmas, and could I maybe buy her something.

I stewed on that request. I couldn't get over the nerve of her calling and asking me to do something for someone I didn't even know. *Wasn't I doing enough already for her kids? Now I have to take on someone else's?* It's not as if we had a lot of money.

As I was shopping a few days later, I saw a box with two dolls in it, one dark-haired and one light-haired. I thought about that little girl. Because it seemed like a bargain at fifteen dollars, I bought it, but I wasn't happy about it. I tossed it in my cart with some begrudging mutter and took it home and wrapped it up. Right before Christmas, I gave it to the grandma, and I never heard a word about it after that. For all I knew, the girl never got it, or the grandma said it was from her.

When I was growing up, l wasn't allowed to see my paternal grandma, who never failed to buy us Christmas gifts and leave them with my maternal grandma. My maternal grandma would change the name tags to say they were from her. As an adult I found out my favorite childhood doll had really come from my other grandma. I was sure this was a similar situation. *Oh, well,* I thought, *just let it go.* And so I did.

About a year and a half later, I was out walking my dog and I saw a little girl about seven years old playing in a yard.

When I passed by her she yelled out, "I've seen that dog before!" I told her we live around the corner, and sometimes I walk him by here. She came over and bent down to pet the dog. It struck me that she might know the neighborhood kids I knew. They always told me they had a friend named Joan (not her real name) who lived on our block. I asked the girl if her name was Joan. "No, that's my grandma's name," she answered.

Then the light bulb went on.

I asked her if she knew Aaron and Nick and Melanie, and she did. Then I got curious and wondered if she might have been the unknown little girl l bought the dolls for. I asked her, "Not last Christmas, but the one before that, did you get a couple of dolls for Christmas?"

"Oh yes, Lucy is the light-haired one, and Debbie is the

dark-haired one. They are inside sleeping right now," she replied.

"Was that all you got that year?" I asked.

"I think I got some other stuff, but I don't remember," she said.

"Who gave you the dolls?" I asked.

"Aaron's grandma," she answered.

Ah ha! That was it . . . the grandma was going to take all the credit. To prove myself right I asked, "Who did she say they were from?" And God, in his mysterious ways, had to show me I can never give too much—even if I do it with a rotten heart.

I got a lump in my throat when the response came from her: "She said they were from an angel."

Mickey Bambrick

Secret Santa

Generosity is giving more than you can and pride is taking less than you need.

Kahlil Gibran

Manuel and I work in the same building. I'm a music talent agent with a firm on the eighteenth floor. Manuel has his own space near the escalator from the garage to the lobby. He sells newspapers, magazines, gum and candy. I pass Manuel each day as I make my way from the underground parking to the lobby.

Hundreds of people working in the building pass by Manuel each day, and he seems to know everyone's name.

Each morning I stop to buy a newspaper, and Manuel greets me. "Good morning, Miss Tanja. How are you today?"

Last year I convinced him to stop calling me "Miss Crouch," but he refuses to drop the "Miss" in front of my first name. Some mornings I stop to chat a moment and marvel at the fact he supports a wife, three boys and a daughter on his salary.

Prior to Christmas, my assistant learned that Manuel not only supported his own family but had recently taken in his widowed sister and her two children. Manuel's wife, Rosa, stays home to care for the six children while Manuel and his sister work to support the family. When my assistant heard about this, she decided we needed to become secret Santas to Manuel's family.

Throughout the month of December, several of us made it our mission to learn all we could about Manuel and his family. We rejoiced as something new was discovered, such as Manuel's oldest son, Jose, was ten years old. He loved baseball and hoped to one day play professionally. He would get a baseball, bat, glove and cap. Manuel's only daughter Maria was just learning to read and she loved bears. A special teddy bear and books were selected.

We charted facts, listed gift ideas, then cross-referenced them with what had been purchased. One of the partners in the firm got into the spirit and bought a VCR, then charged a new television set to another partner! Everyone was caught up telling stories of how Manuel had touched our lives with his warm spirit and the details we were learning about his life.

We arranged for UPS to deliver our gifts the day before Christmas. The return address was simply North Pole. We speculated at how surprised Manuel would be and could hardly wait to return from the holidays to hear if he would mention it. We never in our wildest dreams anticipated what we would learn.

Manuel had packed up all the gifts and sent them away! The television and VCR went to a nursing home where Manuel's sister worked as a maid. Clothes were shipped to relatives in Mexico. Food was shared with the neighbors. On and on it went. Manuel considered his family so blessed that they had shared all the wonderful gifts they received with others less fortunate.

"We had the best Christmas ever, Miss Tanja!" Manuel beamed.

"Me, too," I smiled.

Tanja Crouch

An Angel in Chains

It was only a few weeks before Christmas when Becky, our four-and-one-half-year-old daughter, cheeks flushed with excitement, climbed over the fence of the corral where I was bottle-feeding an orphan calf, and squealed, "Mama! Mama! You have to come see! Angels wear chains!"

I was about to ask, "Becky, what on earth do you mean?" when my heart plunged to the pit of my stomach.

Outside the wooden gate amid the cactus and mesquite towered a stranger, his skin gleaming like oiled mahogany in the blistering Arizona sun. Nearly eight feet tall in giant-sized motorcycle boots, he wore a red sweatband that failed to control the black braids leaping wildly from his head, and in the early morning December breeze he seemed to sway like a genie uncorked from desert sand.

Heavily muscled arms stained with purple tattoos burst from a leather vest. A deep scar crimped his left cheek and a small silver dagger swung from one ear. But it was the chains on his boots, chains on his belt and chains cascading down his massive chest that made me wonder, *Why does Becky think he's an angel?*

Then I spied the Harley-Davidson beside the water pump at the end of our long dirt road. On the far side of the barbed-wire fence a gang of wind-whipped, grease-streaked, smoke-shrouded motorcyclists milled around, "HELL'S ANGELS" glinting across the shoulders of more than one black jacket.

This was 1974. I'd read about the Hell's Angels—terror-riddled tales of large groups of men who adhered to no boundaries of human decency, infamous for murder, rape, theft, guns and drugs. My husband was at a bull sale in Casa Grande. The children and I were alone. Why was this group here on our ranch a hundred miles from Tucson?

"His name's Rip because his muscles ripple," Becky piped as she ducked beneath the fence and took the stranger by the hand. "His motorcycle broke." She tugged him toward me, and although he seemed bigger with each step, I noticed he looked down at my little girl as though seeking reassurance.

Finally, he bowed his head and his uneasy, hooded eyes met mine. "Rip Balou, missus. I know it's gettin' late, but two of my buddies took off for the city to get me a new clutch. They won't get back till morning and I wondered if we could camp near the gate for the night? We won't bother you none . . . and . . . all we need is water."

Dared I say no? It was a chance I had to take, yet something beyond Rip Balou's frightening appearance—and The Hell's Angel's reputation—made it seem safe to say, "Sure." I glanced at the group by the gate. "But please," I said, "don't smoke. Fire danger is at a peak right now."

"Don't you worry yourself none about no fire," Rip said. The thought seemed to have humbled him a bit. "Those warning signs are posted all the way from New Mexico." He thanked me before walking back toward his friends.

"But Mama, what about supper?" Becky asked. "They don't have any food."

"How many are there?"

"Eleven . . . no, nine. Zack and Ty went to Tucson . . . and

Rip makes ten." She answered so quickly.

Zack? . . . Ty? . . . Rip? I wondered how long she'd been down by the gate. Long enough to count—to know their names—and to make a friend! Such a natural thing for a child to do, especially one without playmates. I vowed to keep a closer eye on her, but at that moment, my thoughts were on food. I fed everyone else who stopped by—ranchers, cowboys and Mexican *mehados* hoping for work. What harm could possibly come from feeding a band of . . . Angels?

Later, back at the house, ten men sat at the picnic table under the cottonwood tree drinking iced tea from Styrofoam cups while Becky held them spellbound with a Barbie-doll fashion show. As they wolfed down tacos and beans, I asked questions. "Where are you going?" "Los Angeles," they chorused. They had been on the road for two years, ever since they had met at the Harley-Davidson rally in Sturgis, South Dakota. Before that time, some had come from major cities across the country. Chicago. New Orleans. Boston. New York. "What about home and family?" I asked. Few responded, but Rip, the obvious leader, muttered "Baltimore, 2,647 miles away."

The following morning, Rip's huge frame darkened the kitchen doorway. He didn't look happy. "Zack's back. They had to order the clutch from Phoenix," he said. "It'll take a couple a days. Could we stay? We could rake . . . clean stalls . . . do somethin' to help out?"

"Okay. I guess you can't get very far without a clutch." I thought I was being funny. He didn't.

"And missus. There's twelve of us now." I knew he was referring to meals.

Soon, more hands than I would ever need, or find again, unloaded a double semi-trailer load of hay, repaired fences, and rode back and forth to Tucson to buy food that I hadn't even asked for. I noticed they laughed and talked

a lot among themselves. *Why not?* I thought. *No responsibil-
ities. No family ties.*

Strangely, it was big Rip Balou who not only worked
the hardest but continued to be drawn to Becky—and she
to him. She let him help bottle-feed the orphan calf and
collect eggs in a basket from the chicken coop where the
ceiling was so low he couldn't stand up straight. Then,
when she placed a day-old chick in his enormous hands,
his mouth opened like a child who had just touched Santa.

Three meals a day at the picnic table left time to share
more than her Barbie doll. Although not yet in school, Becky
could read, and I watched a remarkable friendship tighten
between her and the giant man as they hovered over a book
together. *Was it possible that a little girl could make a difference in
his life?* Rip's tough, big-shot countenance seemed to soften,
and the face of a boy emerged; I saw a whole life flash by in
his eyes as Becky ran a tiny finger beneath magic words that
introduced an Angel to *Beauty and the Beast.* Rip watched. He
listened. I wondered . . . *could he read?*

What did it matter? It was Becky's crayons and coloring
books that caused those haunted eyes to brighten. "Red
and blue are my favorite colors," she told him, "but we can
share. Can't we?"

It wasn't long before the crayons in his pie-sized hands
created magic of their own. Rip banished another Angel to
Tucson to "buy more." During the two days that followed,
he taught Becky how to coax pastels from primary colors
and fill empty skies with sunrises, sunsets and rainbows.
Gradually, every page in the coloring books became a Rip
Balou masterpiece.

"I don't like ugly, dark colors," Rip told Becky. "Anyone
can color like that." Then over and over again, he covered
her small white hand with his huge dark one, and said,
"Honey, the most important thing to remember is that
you gotta stay inside the lines."

It was on the third day that Becky popped the question. "Do you have a mommy and a daddy?" Rip didn't answer. Instead, he flexed his muscles so the ship on one arm seemed to roll in a storm and the dragon on the other coiled to strike. But he'd shown her these wonders before. And now there was something else on her mind. She asked again.

Reluctantly, Rip unhooked a leather pouch from the chain around his waist and pulled out a photograph of a gray-haired woman with glasses. Her hand rested gently on the shoulder of a little girl. "That's my mama," he said, " . . . and that's Jasmine . . . my baby. She'd be just about your age now."

"I wish she could come play with me," Becky said.

Rip stared at the picture for a long time. "Mama's raisin' her," he said, "but she's got the glaucoma. She can't see so good no more."

Becky fixed her eyes on Rip and, in the infinite wisdom of a child, she asked, "If your mama can't see so good, who's going to teach Jasmine to stay inside the lines?"

Rip shook his head. "I . . . don't know." He answered softly, but I could hear the pain in his voice, his heart and his soul.

Late Thursday evening, the gang members who had gone in quest of the new clutch finally returned. Rip must have worked throughout the night to get his bike running for they were all ready to leave at daybreak. Although the barnyard and corrals had been raked and the men were filling their canteens with cool water I sensed unrest among them. "No breakfast, Ma'am," one Angel said. "We gotta hit the road." He glared at Rip. Had there been an argument? A disagreement?

Careful not to scare the horses and chickens, motors purred softly as one by one the Hell's Angels cruised over to say "good-bye" and "thanks." Rip Balou was last.

"Thank you, missus," he murmured, ". . . for a lot of things."

"And thank you for being such a wonderful playmate and teacher." I wanted to say more, ask him why he had chosen such a life, but suddenly his eyes were brimming with tears over which he had little control.

"I don't see Becky," he said, glancing over at the picnic table. "I . . . I need to tell her somethin' . . . remind her of somethin' real important . . ."

"She's down by the gate." I hugged him quickly, straightened the chains around his neck and found myself wishing I could do the same to the chains that had stolen his life. I pointed to a very little girl sitting alone on top of the fence. By now Becky was waving and shouting good-bye above the roar of impatient engines as one by one the Angels turned west on Frontier Road—west to Los Angeles—leaving the peaceful desert of moments ago drowned in swirling dust. "You better hurry, Rip," I urged. "They're going to leave you behind."

He smiled at me then—for the first time a big smile—before coasting down to Becky on the high ground between ruts worn by tires. I watched him set the kickstand before he dismounted and walked over to the little girl he'd grown to love. He lifted her off the fence and set her down on the leather seat. Then, crouching beside her so they could speak face-to-face, Beauty and the Beast talked . . . about sunrises? . . . sunsets? . . . rainbows? Who knows?

What I do know is that the good-bye hug he gave Becky brought tears to my eyes. Then the last angel swung a long leg over his gleaming Harley, revved up the engine and turned east on Frontier Road—east, to Baltimore— "2,647 miles away—in time for Christmas," where a little girl waited for a lesson on the importance of "staying inside the lines," and a Daddy to show her how.

Penny Porter

Timber!

Never worry about the size of your Christmas tree. In the eyes of children, they are all thirty feet tall.

Larry Wilde

We went Christmas tree hunting at the local U-cut farm this weekend.

"How about this one?" my wife shouted.

I trudged through the icy mud to where she was standing. Kneeling down, I looked at the massive base of the tree. "Honey, I think we're in the old growth section. Where are the trees you don't need Paul Bunyan to cut?"

"But this one looks good," she argued. "See how the branches are soft and supple, the angles are proportionate, and there isn't a bald spot?"

"Sweetie, you are looking for a tree, not a date. That's too big to cut."

"But it's perfect," she insisted.

I looked incredulously at her. "Oh, I see. The tree can't have any defects, but it's okay that I'm in bed all week with a dislocated shoulder?"

I was about to win when she brought out the holiday guilt. "Don't you want the best tree for your kids?"

I looked at my children. Pine needles were stuck to the candy cane sheen they had all over their faces.

"Fine," I conceded. "But grab my medical insurance card now in case the medevac guys need it right away."

An hour later, the mighty tree fell to the earth. And for my two pulled muscles and splitting headache, I paid forty dollars.

Dragging the tree to the car, I starred blankly at my wife.

"What are you waiting for?" she asked.

"A crane to lift the tree onto the car roof."

After several attempts to hoist the tree up myself, I heard my daughter's voice: "Where's Daddy?"

"On the ground," my wife answered. "Ken, what are you doing down there?"

"I'm just resting," I replied. "When you guys finish your hot chocolate, I'll probably be ready to roll the tree off my chest."

I finally managed to tie the tree down to my roof, and we drove home. The next challenge was fitting the huge stump into the little tree stand.

"How's it going?" my wife asked, stepping out into the garage where I was trimming the stump with a Skill saw.

"How do you feel about an ornamental tree for the dining room table?" I asked. "I could cut off the top third of this thing and throw away the rest."

"So on Christmas morning we can sit around the table and open gifts?" she asked sarcastically. "That will be fun. If you put it on your nightstand, we don't even have to get out of bed."

When the tree was finally in the stand, I brought General Sherman into the living room. Kneeling by the stand, I asked my family to help me line it straight.

"How's that look?" I asked, immersed in tree limbs.

"A little to the left," they sang.

"Is that good?"

"To the right."

"There?"

"Left."

"Okay?"

"There—don't move!" my wife shouted. "That's perfect. It's standing straighter than ever before—how'd you do that?"

"By accidentally wedging my hand in the tree stand," I answered. "This is probably going to be awkward during our holiday party next week."

Later that night, after the lights were strung, and my wounds were bandaged, my wife and kids decorated the tree.

"Look, Daddy's pretending to be a step stool," my daughter said, standing on me to place an ornament up high on a branch.

"Actually," my wife said. "I think Daddy passed out."

Ow Tannenbaum!

Ken Swarner

Christmas in the Country of Miracles

It was the day after my Aunt Mim's funeral, and I was in the third-floor storeroom of her house, sorting through her things. I wanted to spare Uncle Ken any difficult moments, but he was with me when we found the Christmas ornaments.

There were boxes and boxes of them. "Oh, my," Uncle Ken said quietly, "you take any of these you want, Jane. I don't believe I'll be putting up a Christmas tree around here anymore." He left me alone in the big, cedar-scented room.

As I sorted through the ornaments, many of which I had sent Mim over the years from my various travels, I thought of the aunt I had lost. Mim was my mother's identical twin. I loved my gentle, self-effacing mother, but I adored Mim and wanted to be just like her. She was the fiercest Welsh nationalist of all our large clan of Thomases and Lloyds. "I'm Welsh, black Welsh," she told me over and over. "And you're half Welsh. The best half of you."

During Mim's last illness, my husband, Michael, and I drove frequently from our home in New York City to New Hope, Pennsylvania, to visit her and Uncle Ken. The last time I saw her, she looked slim and young, even with her white hair.

We had a few minutes alone, and we were candid with each other, as we always had been. "What am I going to do without you?" I asked her.

"Just remember me," she said.

I promised her I always would. Mim died the next day.

Now I picked up a larger, carefully wrapped ornament. The tissue came away and there was the angel who had always stood at the top of the tree all the Christmases of my childhood.

My mother's family, the Lloyds and Thomases, had emigrated from Wales to the United States in the 1840s. They had been coal miners in Wales, so they became coal miners in Pennsylvania, settling in the town of Shamokin.

My grandmother told us that her own parents had brought the angel with them from Wales. She was an old-fashioned Victorian figure with a sweet, childish face, blonde hair and a sky-blue robe. Though she had lost most of her nose and her blue robe was faded, I remembered her vividly.

I recognized Mim's handwriting on a note in the bottom of the box of ornaments. She was constantly making lists or jotting notes to herself.

"New Year's Eve, 1985," I read. "We took the tree down early this year. A good Christmas, but next Christmas, as God is my witness, I am going to Wales. To see if there are any of our Lloyd and Thomas family still there."

She hadn't made it to Wales. Then, as I wrapped the angel back in tissue paper, I knew that I would make the journey for her.

As Michael and I made plans to spend the following Christmas in Wales, the biggest question was: Where should we hunt for these long-lost cousins? The trail had grown cold. The only Welsh uncle left said he remembered vaguely that the family came from Carmarthenshire, now part of the county of Dyfed, in the southwest.

In our research, we found some Lloyds who lived in a medieval mill in the town of St. David's. They had remodeled it and took visitors on a bed-and-breakfast basis.

I telephoned the Lloyds and found David Lloyd at home. He was skeptical and a bit gruff. Yes, he said, he had Thomases in his family, and some of his forebears had emigrated to America. But, he hastened to add, Lloyd and Thomas were among the most common names in all of Wales. He seemed puzzled by my call and obviously did not share my enthusiasm for this quest.

Nevertheless, Michael and I arranged to stay at the mill our last two nights in Wales. Before our departure from America, I made another call to confirm dates. This time I spoke with David's wife, Gail, who said she had invited her sister, a student of family trees, to dinner with us. David got on the phone to ask when my family had left Wales for the United States. "In the 1840s," I told him.

"That's when my family left, too," he acknowledged. "But that's not a coincidence. Everybody left then because of the economy. Where did your family settle?"

"In Pennsylvania. Shamokin, Pennsylvania."

"Well, God knows where mine went," David said. "Don't get your hopes up. It's a needle in a haystack."

Our departure day came at last. We were just about to leave for the airport when I called to Michael, "Wait!" Then I darted back into the bedroom.

"What in God's name is that?" Michael asked as I emerged with my tissue-paper-wrapped bundle.

"A Christmas-tree ornament."

"Just what we needed. Now are you ready to go?"

I said I had been ready to go to Wales all my life.

We spent five wonderful days sightseeing, meeting some of the Welsh people, and finding them warm and welcoming. On Christmas Day, I called the Lloyd family from our hotel.

David answered. He sounded brusque. I said we were simply calling to wish them a happy holiday and were looking forward to seeing them on Monday. "Is this a bad moment to call you?"

"Well, not the best moment, I would say. You know how it is on Christmas Day. We are concentrating on our family."

There was a pause. I think he knew he had hurt my feelings without being quite sure why.

"Happy Christmas," David said. And just before he hung up, added, "We are looking forward to seeing you, too."

I woke up on Monday with a feeling of expectation. Today we would meet the Lloyds. But could they possibly be the family I wanted to find?

At breakfast, Michael watched me quietly over his coffee cup. "If it's as important to you as I think it is, we can get a professional to do a real search."

"It is important," I told him, "but for now, in the lap of the gods."

We set off towards the old mill.

Gail Lloyd must have been watching for our car. She came out into the courtyard to greet us. She was a tall attractive woman in her forties with chestnut hair. "Welcome to Felin Isaf."

Felin Isaf means the lowest mill she told us as she helped us carry our luggage inside, and we walked through the two-story central hall, where the great wooden wheel of the mill was on display behind a glass panel.

In our bedroom, on the bureau beside a vase of fresh flowers, was a Christmas card from the Lloyd family. "*Croeso i Gymru!*" it read. Welcome to Wales!

We settled ourselves and went downstairs quickly, curious to learn more about our host and hostess. We found Gail in the kitchen. A big round table filled the center of the room, easy chairs stood about and books were stacked everywhere. A huge stove took up one entire wall. "That stove is never allowed to go out," Gail said, following my glance.

As she chopped vegetables for the stockpot, Gail told us a little about her husband, carefully, as if she were preparing us. "David is a good man, a good husband and father. He's a bit brusque sometimes. And he's not one for showing affection. But once he decides you're his kind of people, he will be loyal for life."

The prologue was over. Gail put the lid on the stockpot and led the way into the parlor to the master of Felin Isaf.

David Lloyd had twin barricades in case he needed them—his newspaper and television set, tuned to sporting news. He shook hands with us gravely, then surveyed me. "So this is the American who wants to be our cousin." He would not be easily won over.

He poured four glasses of sherry and retreated behind his newspaper.

Gail and I discussed my family genealogy, from the Thomas/Lloyd beginnings somewhere here in Dyfed to the coal regions of Pennsylvania.

David Lloyd had been paying attention after all. He peered over his newspaper and commented again, "Needle in a haystack."

That night at dinner, Gail's sister Carole, who had been married to David's brother, showed us a scrapbook of family trees she had researched.

There was one tree she thought would be interesting to us. It showed where the Lloyd side of David's family had married the Thomas side. And two of the Thomases went to America!

I could feel my eyes widen. Was I going to get my wish? "They went to Pennsylvania?"

"No," Carole said. "These two went to Oregon."

I'm sure my disappointment showed on my face.

The next day we set out for a last round of sightseeing. In the car I was quiet.

"Last-day blues?" Michael asked.

"I was really hoping the Lloyds might turn out to be my cousins," I said. "It's crazy, but exactly the kind of craziness Mim loved."

He shook his head. "It wasn't very probable."

"But as Mim always said, 'This is a country that believes in miracles,'" I retorted.

When we arrived back at the mill that evening, David Lloyd ran out towards us before we stopped the car.

"Hurry," he called, waving us inside. "Come see what Gail's found!"

Gail was holding a black book. "I went through some boxes nobody's opened for years. And I found this old Bible from David's family. He didn't even remember having it." It was opened to the pages for recording births, deaths and marriages.

She squinted at the page. "Does the name Cham-o-king, Pennsylvania, mean anything to you?"

"Cham-o-king?" I breathed. "Could that possibly be Shamokin?"

Gail handed the Bible to me, and I squinted at the spidery, faded script. There it was. Born in 1885, in the town of Cham-o-king, Pennsylvania, to David Thomas and Mary Lloyd, a son named Garfield. My great-uncle Garf.

Oh, Mim, I said silently. *We are home. We are home.*

Everybody hugged everyone else, and David poured sherry for a toast to the family. "Welcome home," he said simply, echoing my own thoughts. Dinner passed in a blur as we all exchanged backgrounds and filled in gaps.

We sat around drinking wine and reading poetry after dinner. David read Dylan Thomas's *A Child's Christmas in Wales*. He made the funny parts funnier than I remembered.

We laughed, then grew quiet as David read the last

lines—the bedtime scene, the end of Christmas Day:

"'Looking through my bedroom window, out into the moonlight and the unending smoke-colored snow, I could see the lights in the windows of all the other houses on our hill and hear the music ringing from them up the long, steadily falling night. I turned the gas down, I got into bed. I said some words to the close and holy darkness, and then I slept.'"

Then we all said good night. Our Christmas in Wales was over.

In our bedroom, Michael was asleep in a moment, but I wasn't quite ready to let this day end. I fussed with the packing and heard the rustle of tissue paper. Suddenly I remembered something I had to do.

Downstairs, the living room was dark except for the tiny lights on the Christmas tree. I took the angel out of the tissue, reached up as high as I could and placed her on the tree. "You're home, too," I told her.

Back upstairs, I got into bed, I said some words to the close and holy darkness, and then I slept.

Jane and Michael Maas

/

The Heavenly Salesman

It was going to be a lean Christmas, Barbara and Ray Thill realized as they surveyed their budget in December 1973. Unexpected medical bills, major repairs on their house and the ongoing needs of a family of nine young children left nothing extra for holiday presents. All of the kids needed pajamas, so Barbara and Ray decided they could afford those and maybe some candy. The children would just have to understand.

"This Christmas we're going to give instead of receive," Barbara explained to the children the next day. Her brother, a father of four, had been out of work for many weeks, and it would be a rough holiday for his family, too. "Why don't each of you choose one of your toys and wrap it up for Uncle Dick's family?" Barbara suggested. "Otherwise, they won't have any celebration at all."

Everyone agreed. The oldest child, Ray Jr., hid his disappointment at not receiving a longed-for sled and decided to buy some small gifts for his cousins out of his paper-route earnings. Barbara was proud of her children, but her heart still ached at the thought of disappointing them.

After the children went to bed on December 24, Barbara and Ray laid out nine pajama-filled packages, stuffed nine stockings with candy and smiled at each other. Their family was together, safe and well, and there was even a collection of gifts for Uncle Dick's kids.

Tomorrow would still be a good day.

An hour later a neighbor called. Her husband was on his way home from a business trip and had just telephoned from a highway oasis. He'd stopped for coffee and struck up a conversation with the man sitting next to him—a toy salesman and bachelor with a station wagon full of beat-up samples and no place to donate them at this late hour. "My husband thought of you," the neighbor told Barbara, "so if you can use the toys, we'll drop them off when he gets home."

If she could use them! "Yes, thank you!" Barbara heard herself saying. Soon the doorbell rang. Ray went out to help the neighbors unload, and as the pile of "beat-up samples" grew on the porch, Barbara's eyes filled with tears.

The toys were beautiful, much nicer than anything they'd have been able to afford even in a good year. But even more amazing, there was one perfectly suited toy for each of her children. There were dolls for the girls, a fire engine almost as large as Larry, even a red sled for Ray Jr. There were nine toys for her brood and—incredibly—four extras, ideal for her brother's four kids. It was as if God had gone shopping just for them.

Nearly twenty years later, the Thill family still wonders about the toy salesman. How strange that he should have been on the road so late, waiting until the last moment to dispose of his samples. Perhaps, they think, he was not a salesman at all, but a Christmas angel, sent from heaven to reassure a faithful family that God keeps his promises.

"Give and it shall be given unto you," the Scriptures tell us. The Thills gave from loving hearts and were blessed in abundance.

Joan Wester Anderson

A Christmas Gift I'll Never Forget

A child's life is like a piece of paper on which every passerby leaves a mark.

Chinese Proverb

He entered my life twenty years ago, leaning against the doorjamb of Room 202, where I taught fifth grade. He wore sneakers three sizes too large and checkered pants ripped at the knees.

Daniel made this undistinguished entrance in the school of a quaint lakeside village known for its old money, white colonial homes and brass mailboxes. He told us his last school had been in a neighboring county. "We were pickin' fruit," he said matter-of-factly.

I suspected this friendly, scruffy, smiling boy from an immigrant family had no idea he had been thrown into a den of fifth-grade lions who had never before seen torn pants. If he noticed snickering, he didn't let on. There was no chip on his shoulder.

Twenty-five children eyed Daniel suspiciously until the kick-ball game that afternoon. Then he led off the first inning with a home run. With it came a bit of respect from the wardrobe critics of Room 202.

Next was Charles's turn. Charles was the least athletic, most overweight child in the history of fifth grade. After his second strike, amid the rolled eyes and groans of the class, Daniel edged up and spoke quietly to Charles's dejected back. "Forget them, kid. You can do it."

Charles warmed, smiled, stood taller and promptly struck out anyway. But at that precise moment, defying the social order of this jungle he had entered, Daniel gently began to change things—and us.

By autumn's end, we had all gravitated toward him. He taught us all kinds of lessons. How to call a wild turkey. How to tell whether fruit is ripe before that first bite. How to treat others, even Charles. Especially Charles. He never did use our names, calling me "Miss" and the students "kid."

The day before Christmas vacation, the students always brought gifts for the teacher. It was a ritual—opening each department-store box, surveying the expensive perfume or scarf or leather wallet, and thanking the child.

That afternoon, Daniel walked to my desk and bent close to my ear. "Our packing boxes came out last night," he said without emotion. "We're leavin' tomorrow."

As I grasped the news, my eyes filled with tears. He countered the awkward silence by telling me about the move. Then, as I regained my composure, he pulled a gray rock from his pocket. Deliberately and with great style, he pushed it gently across my desk.

I sensed that this was something remarkable, but all my practice with perfume and silk had left me pitifully unprepared to respond. "It's for you," he said, fixing his eyes on mine. "I polished it up special."

I've never forgotten that moment.

Years have passed since then. Each Christmas my daughter asks me to tell this story. It always begins after she picks up the small polished rock that sits on my desk. Then she nestles herself in my lap and I begin. The first words of the story never vary. "The last time I ever saw Daniel, he gave me this rock as a gift and told me about his boxes. That was a long time ago, even before you were born.

"He's a grown-up now," I finish. Together we wonder where he is and what he has become.

"Someone good I bet," my daughter says. Then she adds, "Do the end of the story."

I know what she wants to hear—the lesson of love and caring learned by a teacher from a boy with nothing and everything—to give. A boy who lived out of boxes. I touch the rock, remembering.

"Hi, kid," I say softly. "This is Miss. I hope you no longer need the packing boxes. And Merry Christmas, wherever you are."

Linda DeMers Hummel

The Other Reindeer

Taking the children to visit Santa has always ben a highlight of the season but no visit was so memorable as the year the big guy presented each child with a pair of cardboard antlers.

Delighted with their new headgear, my daughter, Courtney then age four and son, Colton, age one, raced frantically about the house pretending to be reindeer. While I was busy with Christmas preparations, the two snuck into the kitchen and acquired some much-needed supplies.

After an uncomfortable length of silence had passed, I put down what I was working on and turned to go check on my little hoofed ones. As I turned, I was greeted by two beaming sets of big brown eyes and smiles as proud as you please. My daughter had donned her treasured antlers and with the aid of a red, felt pen, had coloured the entire center of her face.

"I'm Rudolph!" she announced with admiration for herself, little chest thrust forward. Holding very tightly to her hand was my young son, also wearing his antlers but with a large crumpled-up piece of tin foil adhered to the center of his face.

"That's nice." I said. "And who is your little friend?"

Courtney's regimental stance drooped as in with disgust by the mere mention of any confusion. "Mommy!" she clarified, "He's Olive. You know, Olive. . . . The other reindeer!"

Carrie Powell-Davidson

You Better Watch Out!

The holidays were fast approaching. Many of the homes in our neighborhood were decorated with lights, snowmen and reindeer. It was a real treat to drive around with my two-year-old daughter and hear the oohs and ahhs as she took it all in.

Kendall was a very precocious child, talking early and with great expression and drama. As she was very apt to repeat excerpts from every adult conversation she overheard, it became obvious that we needed to watch what was said around her.

It was a shock to me one day as Kendall dropped her toy and said "Jesus Christ." My first instinct was to reprimand her, then I realized she was just repeating words she had heard me say in frustration.

"You can't say that, Kendall. It's not nice."

"You say it, Mom. What do I get to say?"

"Mommy shouldn't say it either, so let's say 'darn it' instead," I suggested.

That seemed to pacify her and the holidays were now rid of any unexpected and embarrassing outbursts of swearing in front of family or friends.

A few days later, my mother called and asked if I would

bring Kendall over for lunch so she could show off her granddaughter to her friends. On the way to my mom's house, we passed a beautiful manger scene on the center divider of the road. Never having seen anything like it, Kendall asked what it was. She was fascinated and seemed to enjoy the story when I explained it to her.

When we reached Grandma's, she couldn't wait to get in the house and tell everyone what she had just seen. The door opened and she ran in. Out of breath and excited, she told everyone how she had just seen Joseph, Mary and the Baby "Darn it" in the manger.

Kristine Byron

Oh What a Day!

Last year, exasperated with epicurean excess overshadowing the blessed event and fearful of maxing out my credit cards once again, I began planning a simpler Christmas, unaware that I was about to create an unforgettable moment and a pretty terrific day.

I decided that, although I would buy gifts for our twelve grandchildren, I absolutely would not buy presents for our seven adult kids. Absolutely not. Well then, I thought, I'll just make up a nice basket of goodies for each couple.

In August, I traveled to the outlet mall and purchased seven big baskets. I went to yard sales and bought cookie tins and cute little containers. Really saved some money, too. Next, I chose a few crystal and porcelain dishes just to dress things up a bit (I'm into elegant). I also bought red, green, silver and gold spray paint.

I wanted to personalize the baskets somewhat (I detest "cookie-cutter" gifts). So I decided to decoupage tall cans to match the decor of each family's home. Good grief! I had no concept of how much cutting or how many pictures and scraps it takes to arrange one simple design. I cut from our albums, encyclopedias, history texts, magazines and flyers. My husband's toes curled when he saw the job I did on his *National Geographics*. Of course, then I had to buy all the glue, brushes and decoupage stuff. One entire bedroom was set aside, and locked, for this project.

Meanwhile, I pored over new recipes seeking something special for each person. The decisions took me weeks. Next, I was off to the farmer's market to purchase bushels of apples for chutney, pies and applesauce. I foraged for days to find special salt to make beef sticks for the guys.

I chopped, sliced and diced until my hands resembled crazy explorer's maps. Oh, the pain. Homemade candied fruit, madeleines, mustards, relish, special sauces, rolled candies, decorated petite fours, dried fruit slices, potpourri. I was driven, a madwoman on a quest for perfection. I was on a complete Martha Stewart binge.

Did I mention the fifteen-cubic-foot freezer I bought just for this endeavor? Oh, yeah. Real savings there.

Time was running out. The pace quickened: shopping, wrapping, tagging, decorating, cleaning, baking. Spare moments were spent creating tiny marzipan flowers and fruits. My husband (and the dog) had the audacity to expect dinner every night in the midst of this frenzy. An additional little chore nagged at the back of my mind: Christmas dinner for thirty-five people. Just another incidental.

Finally, after scouring boutiques for cute little gold cards, I meticulously arranged the baskets. Now, the final touch: bows. I bought yards and yards of gold and silver ribbon; gorgeous stuff. I won't bore you with the details. Suffice to say, I failed Ribbon Making 101. Checkbook in hand, I stormed out of the house and dashed to the craft store. People dispersed in every direction as I entered; they saw the crazed look of a woman "on a mission." No one in my path was safe. I exuded danger. Quickly, I placed my order for seven huge bows with streamers. They were lovely and only cost eighty-eight dollars. Plus tax.

Earlier in the year, I'd made cookbooks for each daughter and daughter-in-law. These contained recipes of family favorites and little cut-outs of my favorite hymns, quotes and prayers.

The crowning touch was a personal poem for each, emphasizing individual traits, with endearments to match. Oh, they were such fun to do!

The great day arrived, and I was anxious. Just to be sure the fellas wouldn't be too disappointed by the excess of feminine accoutrements, I'd gone out Christmas Eve and found seven Star Trek mugs. They were only twenty dollars each. Well, my dears, the baskets were a raging success. "Oohs" and "aahs," and "Oh, Mom, this must have taken you days." (Excuse me—days?)

Suddenly, like a gentle ocean wave, a hush overcame the room (Ever notice when we women stop talking, no matter how many fellas are around, there is a hush?). Pages turned as silent tears fell—then audible sniffles—then, as the poems were shared, uproarious laughter filled the moment. Surrounded by hugs and wet faces, I glanced across the room at my husband. He grinned back with happy eyes. Love personified the moment. What a day.

Lynne Zielinski

A Blessed Bounty

Early on Christmas morning in 1986, members of the Gospel Lighthouse Church in Blytheville, Arkansas, were preparing to serve dinner to the needy. "Fifteen or twenty families had brought their own turkey and trimmings to the church and had made extra to share," explains Jeanne Templeton, a church member and mother of two. Word of the free dinner had spread, and the volunteers expected a crowd. Would there be enough to go around?

At about eleven that morning, church members took their places at the serving tables, the doors opened and guests streamed in, each taking a plate and passing it along, cafeteria-style. So many to be fed! Jeanne sliced turkey, scooped mashed potatoes and prayed that the food would last.

Time passed, but the needy kept arriving. *Odd,* Jeanne mused. They weren't running out of anything. Even the pans of dressing, which had been few in number when dinner began, still seemed full. She caught the eye of a perplexed friend spooning vegetables from a seemingly bottomless bowl. What was going on?

Finally, as the last guest was served a brimming plate of all the church group had to offer, Jeanne looked at her

watch. Four o'clock! Could it be? There was still food
remaining. Baffled, the volunteers packed the leftovers.
"The men carried everything to the church buses and drove
away," Jeanne recalls. "They would go door-to-door, to
make sure no one in the area had missed the dinner." The
women went back to the empty kitchen and, still somewhat dazed, they scoured, tidied and compared notes.

"Was it my imagination . . . ?"

"No, I saw it, too. The turkeys seemed to . . . to multiply!"

"But we had only six or seven. How . . . ?"

"Two thousand," Jeanne murmured. "I think we fed
almost two thousand people."

Just then a knock sounded on the kitchen door. A volunteer opened it to a man, a woman and eight young children, all of them shabbily dressed. "We're a little late," the
man acknowledged shyly. "Would you have anything left
over from dinner?"

Oh no! The women glanced around the spotless kitchen.
All the food was gone, they had put it on the buses themselves. But how could they turn this hungry group away?

"Come and sit down," said one helper, leading the
family to a table, while the others quickly conferred.
Perhaps there was a store open, or a restaurant in town
where they could buy something. Suddenly someone
pointed: "Look!" The others turned to stare. Sitting on a
counter in plain view was a freshly baked loaf of bread. It
had not been there moments before, Jeanne knew. But no
one had come to the kitchen except the family, and they
had been empty-handed.

"How did we miss this?" Jeanne's friend cried in aston-
ishment. She had found an institutional-sized can of green
beans and corn in a cupboard. Another woman peeked
under a cabinet.

There on a shelf she had previously inspected now sat a
large tray of dressing with big chunks of cut-up turkey in it.

"We packed up the containers and sent the family home to enjoy their holiday," Jeanne says. Then, tears spilling down their cheeks, the women praised the Lord for his wonderful care. They had offered him an early birthday present by caring for the least of his children. But he had multiplied their gift a hundredfold and given them a Christmas they would never forget.

Joan Wester Anderson

Homestead Holiday

I had so wanted to celebrate Christmas at the two-hundred-year-old farmhouse, surrounded by the love of the dear relatives who had labored to preserve it. A delightful throwback to an era of simplicity—no phones to jangle nerves, no electric lights to glare in eyes—the place veritably shouted, "*Christmas!*" But first things first; we had to settle in.

"Let's make it easier for our folks to get up," I said to my cousins on our first morning at the old homestead.

We drew well water in tall buckets and carried split logs chin high. Soon a kettle whistled on the cast-iron stove. In each bedroom, we poured warm water into the pitchers of porcelain wash sets.

Our efforts paid off. Our sleepy-eyed parents climbed out of Victorian beds to chat over cinnamon rolls and coffee.

We girls cranked the Victrola in the parlor and pedaled the empty spinning wheel in the hall. Everything about this place was a novelty. We read century-old magazines in the barn and memorized epitaphs in the family cemetery.

We bathed in the fresh waters of Connor Pond and shared teen secrets on the two-holers at "the end of the line." We purchased a block of ice for the antique box in the shed and even scrubbed down the "Grouch House" for would-be guests.

But we wanted so much more.

We wanted Christmas!

"It might be a little odd," one cousin said.

"Sure would," echoed the other.

"Let's ignore that," I said.

Cross-legged on the antique bed in our upstairs hideaway, we plotted how we could pull it off.

"We'll handcraft decorations for the tree," said one cousin.

"We'll pick up gifts in the village . . . even a holiday meal," chimed the other.

"And we'll send out invitations," I said.

The wide plank flooring quivered under our combined energy.

On stationery found in the parlor desk, we composed rhymed couplets penned in our best script. Convinced Keats would be proud, we lost no time in posting them.

We begged our moms to pick up a few items at the grocery store—okay, maybe not a turkey, but how about a holiday brunch with eggs Benedict and a fresh fruit cup? "And don't forget maple syrup for waffles!"

We popped corn in a pan and strung garland, yet so much was missing. There were no ornaments to be found anywhere. We poked through brush along a New England stone wall and fell upon a treasure trove of cones, seedpods and nuts. We tied loops around red-berry sprigs and green crabapple stems. Scissors soon fashioned white paper into snowflakes and tinfoil into a star.

Thoughts of the tree encouraged us—but the mailbox didn't. Every afternoon, we rode down the mountain to check it. Still no reply to our invitations—even though the event was upon us.

On the morning of the anticipated day, our folks

distracted us with an excursion to the mountains. We arrived home late and tired.

Dad went in first to light the kerosene lamps. When the windows were aglow, we girls ambled upstairs. We stopped at the sound of bells.

"What is it?" I craned over the stairwell.

"Ho, ho, ho," resounded in the distance.

"It's *got* to be Chesley!" Dad said, lamp in hand, as he peered out the front door into the darkness.

Chesley and Barbara, I thought. *The guests are arriving!*

I jumped down the stairs in time to see a fully regaled Santa leap into the lamplight. A prim Mrs. Claus joined him by the house.

"You didn't think it was a dumb idea, after all!" we girls shouted.

"Oh, we thought it was wonderful," they said.

Such gameness of spirit spurred us cousins to action. We chopped down a forest fir, placed it in the sitting room and smothered it with our handmade treasures.

Before the crackling fire in the hearth, Mrs. Claus rocked while Santa distributed our carefully selected gifts. Chocolate mints, knickknacks and a dainty handkerchief . . . even Roy Tan cigars for Dad.

The impossible had actually happened: a farmhouse Christmas . . . *in August!*

True, this was a most uncommon New Hampshire Christmas. Instead of frost nipping at our toes, perspiration beaded our foreheads. Rather than windows iced shut, fragrant breezes blew past. In place of quietly falling snow, a chorus of crickets performed. Where snowsuits would have hung, swimsuits dried on pegs.

Yet the love of celebrating, which knew no season, abounded. And therein lay the joy.

Margaret Lang

With Gladness and Glue

While Christmas shopping in a jewelry store, I discovered a clearance table of gilded ornaments. Detailed and delicate in design, each had a personality all its own. I sorted among the hundreds of filigreed masterpieces, picked out a few and took them home.

Deciding they were much too pretty to disappear among the clutter of a Christmas tree, I used them instead to decorate small eight-inch wreaths. When I stood back to admire my handiwork, a thought crossed my mind: *Wouldn't some of our family and friends like these, too?*

I raced back to the jewelry store to discover that the stack of ornaments had been reduced even further. This time I bought dozens as I thought of the many people who might enjoy one for the holidays.

Armed with a glue gun and bright ribbons of every color, I eagerly began my creative project. The wreaths multiplied like measles and dotted every flat surface in our house. For days, my family tiptoed around, elbowed their way through and slept among the miniature masterpieces.

While I tied dainty bows and glued golden ornaments, my mind wandered to Christmases past, and I pondered how special each had been. I thought about others perhaps not so fortunate. Some people in our community didn't have a family to share the joy of Christmas. Some didn't bother with holiday decorations. Some never left their homes to celebrate the season.

I nodded my head in determined satisfaction. They would be at the top of my list to receive a little wreath. My husband joined me in the plan, and we set out together to put it into action.

We visited the aged. We visited the widowed. We visited the lonely. Each one was thrilled with our cheery stops and immediately hung our small gifts—often the only signs of celebration in their homes.

After several days, I realized we had made and given almost two hundred wreaths. Decorated with love and delivered with delight, they filled many homes and hearts with the joy of Christmas.

And I came to the simple realization that *we* were actually the ones who received the greatest blessing that year. We had found *our* Christmas spirit in the doing.

Nancy B. Gibbs

Decking the Halls with Balls of Jolly

A number of years ago, NBA All-Star Cedric Ceballos hosted a free basketball clinic for a couple hundred youngsters. At the end of the event, Ceballos—then playing for the Los Angeles Lakers—handed out half a dozen autographed basketballs.

One lucky recipient, a boy about eleven years old, hugged Ceballos and then hugged the ball. But what really touched me was this: As I left the gym, I saw the boy outside shooting baskets on one of the blacktop courts ... using his autographed ball.

While the other handful of lucky kids surely went home and put theirs in places of honor, this boy had already dribbled, shot and worn off Ceballos's valuable signature.

Curious, I asked the boy why he hadn't taken the ball straight home.

"I've never had my own ball to shoot with before," he explained happily.

It made me wonder about similar kids—kids who don't have their own basketballs to shoot, their own soccer balls to kick, their own footballs to throw or their own baseballs to play catch. And so it was that I began using my regular sports column to ask readers to step up to the plate. I started an annual ball drive for underprivileged children.

Great gifts, with no batteries required and no breakable parts.

The first year, about one hundred were donated. That just got the ball rolling, so to speak. The next year's total was 363, then 764 and 877.

Which brings us to this past Christmas. And Briana.

After reading my Thanksgiving Day column announcing "Woody's Holiday Ball Drive," Briana responded like an All-Star point guard. The nine-year-old dished out assists like a mini–Magic Johnson. In notes attached to her generous gifts for other kids, she wrote, in neat printing that would make her teacher proud, a message that should make her parents even prouder:

> *I saw your wish list in the paper and I wanted to help. I know how important it is to help others. So this year I saved money by collecting recyclables (sic). So here I give to you: 5 basketballs, 2 footballs, 2 soccer balls, 1 volleyball, 1 bag of baseballs, 1 bag of softballs. I hope this helps.*
>
> *Happy holidays,*
> *Briana Aoki*

Her generosity kicked off a heartwarming campaign of kids helping kids in need.

As a result, ten-year-old Sarah and eight-year-old Mitch emptied "The Jar." Kept on the family's fireplace hearth, it collected pocket change, some chore money and even coins found in the laundry. Sarah chose a soccer ball and Mitch selected a football to buy and share.

Professional tennis players Mike and Bob Bryan, identical twins, served up a donation of twenty-five footballs and one hundred top-of-the-line basketballs. Others stepped forward, too.

The life lesson here is this: A lot of great kids find joy in giving and joy in sharing—loose change in a jar, wages for chores, allowance money, coins from recycling—just to make a difference. A big difference. A difference of . . .

397 basketballs
218 footballs
178 playground balls
161 soccer balls
104 baseballs
 29 softballs
 26 cans of tennis balls
 14 volleyballs

GRAND TOTAL: 1,127 balls—and smiles
—for kids in need this
Christmas morning.

Woody Woodburn

The Debut

"Mom, where's the roll of butcher paper?" JoAnn asked as she rummaged in the kitchen drawer for scissors and tape. Off she trotted down the hall, clasping the items.

Gathered for our family Christmas party, all three generations had finished eating. Now, the little cousins eagerly left parents and grandparents behind to begin preparations for the annual nativity pageant. Sequestered in the far recesses of the house, the youngsters plotted behind closed doors.

Grateful for peace and quiet, we adults basked in the festive glow of the fire, nibbled remnants of our delicious dinner and continued chatting. We felt no need to hurry our budding geniuses, tickled that they found delight in planning this project together.

An occasional burst of dialogue erupted through the open door as first one then another child was dispatched on a crucial errand. A jar of craft paint, then a wide paintbrush disappeared into their inner sanctum. Intense forays commenced throughout the house as armloads of towels, bathrobes, scarves, bed sheets, belts and jewelry joined their stash. Giggles and whispers intensified as their conspiracy continued.

We knew the project must be coming together when they mounted an intense search for bobby pins, large safety pins, paper clips, even clothespins—anything to hold costumes and props in place. Everyone's anticipation heightened as the cast and crew finished their preparations.

When the designated spokesperson called for our attention, a hush fell over the room.

Two stagehands wrestled a long, butcher-paper poster and, with copious lengths of tape, secured it to the wall. Emblazoned in bright paint it read:

Bethlehem Memorial Hospital

The makeshift stage became a busy reception area of the hospital. One bossy cousin greeted newcomers, summoned aides and kept employees scurrying. Instead of halos, "nurse-angels" wore folded-paper caps with red painted crosses. They assessed each case, wielding their make-believe stethoscopes and thermometers before sending patients off to imaginary treatments.

Mary, endowed with a plump throw pillow, entered, leaning on Joseph's sturdy arm for support. Rejected by the insensitive innkeeper, they found a warm welcome at Bethlehem Memorial where one escort whisked Mary off to delivery and another led Joseph to the waiting room.

Joseph paced; he wrung his hands; he nodded off while shuffling through old magazines. He begged for the latest news on Mary's condition. At proper intervals, a nurse appeared with an encouraging, "It won't be long now."

After our young thespians had milked the scene dry, unseen hands shoved the last performer onto the stage.

There stood Connie Beth, the youngest nurse-angel in the troupe. Her scrap of angel robe in disarray, her nurse cap askew, she inched toward Joseph. Having outgrown her role as babe-in-the-manger, this year—oh, joy—she had a speaking part.

Suddenly aware of her audience, Connie Beth froze. She ducked her head, lowered her eyes and studied the floor. Her tongue probed the inside of her cheek and lower lip. A tiny finger crept toward her mouth. The toe of her little tennis shoe bore into the carpet fibers.

Would stage fright be her undoing?

Offstage, a loud whisper shattered the silence. "Tell Joseph about the baby!"

Connie's head lifted. Her countenance brightened. Resolve replaced fear.

She hesitated, searching for the right words. Taking a deep breath, she stood before Joseph and quietly delivered her joyous message:

"It's a girl!"

Mary Kerr Danielson

Music to My Ears

I sat silently in the backseat as we drove home from an evening church program where I'd heard once again the wondrous story of Jesus' birth. And my heart flooded with happiness as the three of us hummed to familiar Christmas carols drifting from the car radio.

With my nose pressed against the side glass, I gawked at the department-store displays. As we passed houses with lighted Christmas trees in the windows, I imagined the gifts piled under them. Holiday cheer was everywhere.

My happiness lasted only until we came to the gravel road leading to our home. My father turned onto the dark country lane where the house sat two hundred yards back. No welcoming lights greeted us; no Christmas tree glowed in the window. Gloom seeped into my nine-year-old heart.

I couldn't help but wish for trees and presents like other children. But the year was 1939, and I was taught to be grateful for the clothes on my back and the shoes on my feet, to be thankful for a home—no matter how humble— and for simple food to fill my growling belly.

More than once, I'd heard my folks say, "Christmas trees are a waste of money."

I guessed gifts must be, too.

Although my parents had climbed out of the car and gone into the house, I lingered outside and sank down on the porch steps—dreading to lose the holiday joy I'd felt in town, wishing for Christmas at *my* house. When the late-night chill finally cut through my thin dress and sweater, I shuddered and wrapped my arms around myself in a hug. Even the hot tears streaking down my cheeks couldn't warm me.

And then I heard it. Music. And singing.

I listened and looked up at the stars crowding the sky, shining more brightly than I'd ever seen them. The singing surrounded me, uplifting me. After a time, I headed inside to listen to the radio where it was warm.

But the living room was dark and still. How odd.

I walked back out and listened again to the singing. Where was it coming from? Maybe the neighbor's radio? I padded down the long road, glorious music accompanying me all the way. But the neighbor's car was gone, and their house was quiet. Even their Christmas tree stood dark.

The glorious music, however, was as loud as ever, following me and echoing around me. Could it be coming from the other neighbor's house? Even at this distance, I could plainly see no one was there. Still, I covered the three hundred yards separating their house and ours.

But there was nothing and no one.

Yet to my ears the singing rang clear and pure. To my eyes the night stars shone with such radiance that I wasn't afraid to walk home alone. Once I reached my house, I sat again on the porch steps and pondered this miracle. And it *was* a miracle. For I knew in my young heart and soul I was being serenaded by the angels.

I was no longer cold and sad. Now I felt warm and happy, inside and out. As I gazed upward into eternity, surrounded by the praise of heavenly hosts, I knew I had received a joyous Christmas gift after all—a gift straight from God.

The gift of love.

The shining star.

And an everlasting Christmas.

Margaret Middleton

I Wonder

I wonder if that precious babe
were born somewhere today,
Would he recline on Bubble-Pak®
instead of straw or hay?

Would the message of the angel
be broadcast on TV—
Just one more televangelist
ignored by you and me?

Would the anthems of that heavenly choir
hit Nashville from the start?
With concerts, tapes and CDs,
no doubt they'd climb the charts.

Would we confuse that glowing star
with satellites in space,
Or think it just a UFO
from a distant, cosmic place?

The "Jesus news" would travel fast
in this Information Age—
By phone, by fax, by e-mail,
perhaps his own Web page.

Would we gladly leave our tasks behind
and travel far and wide,
Not hesitating in our quest
to worship at his side?

The answer lies within each soul.
Each year we get to choose
How we will celebrate his birth
and greet the wondrous news.

He comes! He comes! (though not a babe)
so softly none can hear,
And creeps into your life and mine
this joyous time of year.

And listen. Oh, just listen,
his sounds are all around—
The choir's song, the call of friends,
snow crunching on the ground.

The laughter of the children,
the ringing of each bell,
The stories and the carols
we've learned to love so well.

So pause amid the craziness,
embrace each mem'ry dear.
Let tastes and smells and sights and sounds
delight nose, eyes and ears.

And welcome him this holiday
with laughter and with joy,
His gift of hope, his gift of life,
That blessed, holy boy.

Mary Kerr Danielson

Tending the Home Fires

Our hardworking parents always did their best to provide memorable holidays for their family of seven.

Weeks before Christmas, my father pulled double and even triple shifts at the cement mill to make sure there would be presents under the tree. Coated in ashes and soot, he'd drag into the house each night, bone-weary from cleaning out smokestacks. Besides one full-time job as city clerk and another one mothering us, Mom did all the things necessary back in the 1960s to make our budget stretch: sewing clothing into the wee hours of the morning, mending hand-me-downs, packing school lunches and laundering cloth diapers.

Even so, my parents emphasized the memory-making moments: designing elaborate macaroni ornaments to decorate the tree, hanging dozens of cheery greeting cards from loved ones around our bedroom doorframes, and singing carols as we hauled aging boxes of decorations from the basement to the living room. In mid-December, Mom gathered her baking sheets, her huge wooden rolling pin and her kids to spend an entire day in the cramped kitchen baking and decorating sugar cookies.

And she always delegated one duty to me.

Because our scant living room had no fireplace to hang stockings, we used a cardboard-kit substitute. It was my job to assemble it each year, that special place where Santa would soon leave his few presents for us.

Against one wall, I unfolded the fireplace front. Then I placed and balanced the black cardboard mantle that bore wounds from dozens of punctures where we'd thumb-tacked our stockings during holidays past. After I inserted a red lightbulb into the hole near the metal spinner, I plugged in the cord so the logs would "burn."

Satisfied at last, I settled to the floor in my favorite nook across from the fireplace—directly in front of a furnace vent. I knew the warm air blew from the basement, but in my mind, the heat spread from the cardboard logs to ignite my imagination. It was there that I spun my boyish dreams and lived my foolish fantasies.

The years drifted on, and so did I.

When all of us kids were grown and on our own, our parents hit the jackpot. I mean, *really* hit the jackpot. In a big way. They won over two million dollars in the Illinois State Lottery!

As instant millionaires, the first thing they did was look for a new place to live. My father insisted on only two musts: an attached garage and . . . a working fireplace. My mom wanted more space. And they found it: a beautiful two-story house with four bedrooms, a spacious kitchen, a dining area, a two-car garage, a roomy basement—and a living room with a working fireplace.

In December after their move, we all came home for our first holiday together in years. While everyone lazed and chatted by the fireside on Christmas Eve, I rose to my feet to stroll through the house on a private tour.

Mom had decorated with recently purchased crystal ornaments and a hand-carved Santa from Germany. Embroidered holiday doilies graced new end tables, and expensive wrapping paper enveloped dozens of presents under the beautifully lit tree. From top to bottom, the place murmured, *"New. Gorgeous. Tasteful."* It certainly wasn't home as I remembered it.

Near the stairwell, I glanced up . . . and did a double take. Perched at the top, like a forgotten old friend I might bump into on the corner, stood the raggedy cardboard fireplace. With a smile as wide as Mom's rolling pin, I climbed the stairs and sank to the top step as a wave of boyhood memories washed over me.

Before long, Mom found me upstairs and stood silently at my side. I looked up, waiting for her eyes to meet mine.

"You kept it, this old fireplace in your new home. Why?"

After a long moment, she placed her hand on my shoulder and bent toward me. "Because I don't ever want any of us to forget the simple joys of Christmas," she whispered.

And I nodded in understanding, pleased that I could still feel the warmth radiating from the old, cardboard fireplace.

Jim West

Whittle-ed Away

"Connie Ann!" Mom caught the piece of tinfoil in midair. "We might need this next time we bake potatoes. You know better than that."

Ashamed, Connie Ann gave a gusty, seven-year-old sigh and retreated from the kitchen. Yes, she knew better. The Whittle family creed demanded that everything, even a piece of foil, be used again . . . and again. Especially now, with the divorce and all.

And she knew about other things, too. Like salvaging buttons and zippers from old clothes to use on the new ones her mom sewed. Like gagging on dust clouds each time someone emptied the vacuum bag instead of throwing it away. Like walking everywhere when most of her friends rode in cars. Of course, the Whittles didn't own a car; Dad had left them the Pumpkin.

The bronzey colored, short-bed pickup couldn't hold all ten children at once, so the Whittle children walked. To school. To church. To get a gallon of milk. Mom said it was simpler than buying a car. Besides, they got exercise and saved on gas at the same time.

Mom said she liked doing things the simple way. In fact, that's how she got rid of the Christmas tree, too.

Without Dad there to haul it out that year, she puzzled over the problem. "How will we get rid of this monstrosity?"

She circled the tree.

"It seems like a waste to just throw it away. It should be good for something, shouldn't it?"

Connie Ann nodded in agreement, knowing Whittles never wasted *anything.*

"It still smells good." Mom poked both arms through the brittle needles to heft its weight. *"Hmmm."* Her brow furrowed a bit, and she glanced over her shoulder where coals still glowed in the fireplace.

"Our gas bill has been sky high." She scooted the tree from its nook in front of the window. "If I just push it in . . . a bit at a time . . . as it burns. . . ." She wrestled the tree to the floor.

"Connie Ann, you grab that end while I drag the bottom."

Wincing from the pain and prickles of the browning evergreen, they struggled to get their handholds.

"What could be simpler?" Mom half-shoved it across the floor with a grunt. "A fragrant room freshener," she tugged at the trunk, *"and* free heat," she gave one final push, *"and* we get rid of this thing."

With a precise aim, she poked the tippy-top of the tree right into the middle of the glowing embers.

KA-VOOOOM!

In a roar as loud as a sonic boom, the entire tree—from its bushy head to its board-shod feet—burst into one giant flame. Screaming, Mom dropped the trunk, and they both jumped across the room.

WHOOOOOSH!

All the branches disappeared. In one big breath. Just like magic. Nothing was left of the Christmas tree except a charred trunk, some scraggly Charlie Brown twigs—and a trailing, tree-shaped shadow of white ashes.

For one long, bug-eyed moment, Mom caught her

breath. Then she pulled Connie Ann close to search for burns and swept a glance over herself for singes. And she examined the carpet for damage. Finding none, she slowly shook her head in wonder.

After a stunned silence, Mom brushed her hands together efficiently. "Well! I guess that takes care of that."

Then she picked from among the newly formed crowd of wide-eyed, jabbering children.

"You and you and you," Mom pointed at the oldest, "help me haul this tree outside. At least *now* it's manageable."

Connie Ann nodded in agreement. She knew how much Mom liked things kept simple. It was, after all, the Whittle way.

Carol McAdoo Rehme

Secret Ingredients

I press "play" on the VCR and sit back to watch the ten-year-old video. On it was my kids' attempt to record my father's secret ingredients as he prepared our annual Christmas meat pies.

"Hi, Mom." I see myself looking out of the screen, gesturing for Lisa to aim the camera at her grandfather instead.

"Hi, Grandpa," she says next as the camera sweeps his direction.

My dad nods in acknowledgement while he pries open the lid of a spice can.

"Mom, what are you doing now?" The camera swings back to me.

"The hard part, as usual." I make a production of stirring the meat in a large pot. "Dad, don't strain yourself shaking that spice can," I tease over my shoulder.

We're making meat pies—my family's holiday tradition.

As an adolescent, I was not particularly close to my father. After driving a delivery truck and unloading heavy packages all day to support our large family, he barely had energy left to talk to me, except to ask me to get him another beer from the fridge or go buy him a carton of cigarettes.

But one Christmas, he expressed a desire to make meat pies like his mother had. Although he could figure out the filling, he didn't have a clue about the crust. Then my junior high home ec teacher gave me a recipe for no-fail pastry.

Mustering my courage, I approached Dad and suggested we team up and experiment with the pies. Much to my delight, he agreed to give it a shot.

I began the pastry crust in the morning. Following the instructions precisely, I blended the dough while Dad sautéed the meat in a large pot—equal amounts of ground chuck and ground pork. He added onions and then debated on the spices.

They were the tricky part. Allspice, savory, sage, thyme, cloves, salt and pepper. He added them all on instinct, guessing at the amounts. The meat simmered and teased our noses.

Meanwhile, I successfully rolled out the crust and placed it in a greased and floured pie plate. I held the empty pie shell close to the pot while my father ladled in bubbling meat. When we judged it full enough, I positioned the top crust, crimped the edges with the tines of a fork, brushed it all with milk, and popped it into the oven. We put together several for dinner.

The aroma of baking pies was encouraging. By the time they were done, the whole family was salivating. But, would the meat pies taste as good as they smelled?

Dad placed a slice on each of our plates. The pastry flaked when our forks cut through it. Then the first taste: eyes closed, nostrils flared, smiles appeared and a unanimous "mmm ... mm" resounded around the kitchen table.

"This is really good," Dad winked at me, "but I think the meat is the best part."

"Oh, really? I don't think so," I teased back. "The crust is delicious; the meat is a close second."

The bantering continued until we finally agreed that neither would be any good without the other. I glowed with pride. We had worked—side-by-side—to replicate the old family recipe, my dad and I.

That was the start of our Christmas tradition.

As he aged, it became more difficult for my dad to do his part. Some years we made as many as fifteen pies and stirring such a large pot of meat was not an easy task. Finally, I recruited my children, Brian and Lisa, as our kitchen assistants.

One year, Dad got pneumonia and never fully recovered. The Christmas after he died, I couldn't bear the thought of making meat pies. Besides, they wouldn't be the same without his secret seasonings. But Brian and Lisa insisted we continue the thirty-five-year-old holiday ritual.

Forcing my mind to the present, I focus again on the video, curious to see what he adds to the pot.

But Dad smiles now from the television screen while he scrapes the last of his savory meat into a pie shell. As I struggle to position the top crust on this final, skimpy pie, someone off-camera suggests it should be for Uncle Bruce, who's always first in line to get his.

"Here, let me spit on it." I wink. "I hope he's not watching this video." Everyone laughs and the screen goes white.

Silence.

It occurs to me that I hadn't noticed a single label on the spices Dad used in the video. Yet a huge grin sweeps across my face when I realize we'd captured the secret ingredients after all.

The secret wasn't in the seasonings. It was in the people. The teasing and joking. The laughing and loving. And I know it was the working together—side-by-side— that made our Christmas meat pies so special.

Jane Zaffino

Fair Game

The real intent of our holiday trips to my wife's family in Oregon is for her to visit with her sisters and niece, along with shopping and cooking, of course. So I'm left twiddling my thumbs a lot, nobody to play with. Except my nephews Adam, Jimmy and Tyler.

A few years ago, I initiated an "Uncle and Nephews' Day" when we go out in force and spend time together doing something, somewhere. Bowling, skiing on Mt. Hood, whatever. Unbridled fun and freedom from parents with rules that only uncles and nephews share. Secrets and promises kept, love secured.

This time, I suggest a drive to the Coast Range west of Portland to an elk refuge called Jewell Meadows where hundreds of magnificent Roosevelt elk congregate.

"It's awesome," I assure my nephews. "Warm steam shoots from their black nostrils as they sound an eerie paean," I wax poetic. "We'll hear big bulls bugle their mating calls and see them proudly standing at attention as they oversee their harems."

The nephews say they're game.

On a cold, damp December morning, nephews and uncle—puffed in parkas—pile into an old sedan and head west in anticipation. The guys are loose again!

Now, Uncle hasn't been to Jewell Meadows in a couple of years maybe, but feels certain he knows the way.

Wrong.

Taking the well-remembered turnoff to the north and the I'm-sure-we-go-left-here crossroad, the beige Volvo wanders onto snowy mountain roads that become more and more unfamiliar.

The three nephews, ages twelve to fifteen, hurl taunts that are immediately challenged, which escalates into an exchange of witticisms and good-natured personal insults.

It's a guy thing.

It's how guys show love: taking potshots at each other, poking at each other's weaknesses and sensitivities. It's primitive preparation for the competitiveness they'll face as men in this still occasionally Neanderthal world of aggressive mentalities. Whether blue- or white-collar combat, it's all the same. This banter toughens them and keeps them tough, with an underlying, supportive subtext of love.

An uncle is a special being, both buddy and adult authority figure. More slack than dad, more unguarded camaraderie. An equal for a nephew—but an equal with acknowledged wisdom amid his playfulness.

An uncle is like a god, but pleasantly flawed and bemused by earthly existence. An uncle lets you in on the secret: Nobody really knows what life is all about, but don't worry about it. Be a good person and enjoy life to its fullest.

Heck, everyone's lost in the winter woods looking for elk and laughing their tails off over Uncle's ramblings. Ain't it great?

After two hours of wandering—with the required detours: roadside pit stops to pee, snowball fights in drifts with dog piles of nephews on top of Uncle, then pushing the car back onto the road from icy shoulders—Uncle stumbles onto the road to Jewell Meadows.

But today, the long-sought meadow—historically popu-
lated with 400 to 500 regal animals against verdant green
grass and bucolic woods beyond—is abo-so-lutely . . . *empty*.

Not an elk in sight.

"So, Uncle, where's the elk? We don't see any elk."
Nephews are on Uncle's case.

Uncle's heart sinks; his male ego falters; his child leadership merit badge is at risk. Uncle's macho dissolves into
nacho.

"I don't know," Uncle stammers. "They're *always* here,
hundreds of them. This is weird. Maybe they're off in the
tree line browsing. They do that sometimes. Let's get out
of the car and walk up to the fence. Take the binoculars,
too. They've got to be here somewhere."

All four guys zip up parkas, snug down wool caps, grab
the binocs and creep to the fence.

Eyeing the tree line some three hundred yards across
the meadow, they stare and stare. They begin to halluci-
nate. First, individually, then en masse.

"I see one."

"Look over there, just past that big, funny-looking bush."

"THERE. See it? See, it's moving."

But no amount of conviction unearths an elk. It's cold;
snow is on the ground; they've crossed the continent for
the Promised Land and there's no gold. No milk. No honey.
Nothin'.

Uncle rallies. "Oh, I get it."

Eyes hopeful, the three defeated nephews swivel their
heads as one in his direction.

Uncle nods knowingly. "It's Christmas time, that's why."

"Huh? What's that got to do with it?" all three demand.

"Remember . . ." and, on the spot, Uncle begins a sere-
nade. His voice floats over the entire meadow, a new twist
on an old carol.

"No-o-elk, No-elk . . ."

The nephews are stunned. They actually lean away from Uncle, mouths agape, struck dumb, incredulous.

"No-o-elk, No-elk . . ."

They can't believe what they're hearing. Adam, the eldest, recovers first. "You brought us all the way out here to do THAT?"

In turn, the others arrive at the same conclusion: They've been had. Shagged. Deceived. Misled. Tricked.

"Aw, man."

"I can't believe it."

"Du-ude . . ."

They turn from the fence and toward Uncle. He's about to be a dead man. He knows it—and he can't wait.

The nephews attack full force, wrestle him down, pound on him, sit on him, jump on him and pelt him with snow. He resists not at all.

It's great. He earned it; he loves it. He loves *them.*

And they love him.

James Daigh

Nothin' Says Lovin' Like . . .

Christmas was coming, and I didn't have one ounce of spirit or energy. I couldn't even muster a half-hearted "ho-ho." I was a gray heap of sorrow, enmeshed in my own pity party.

I had taken a last walk with my closest friend that year and still grieved her passing. Neither of my away-from-home daughters would be able to get back for the holidays. My recently retired husband, grappling with his own identity, didn't or couldn't see that I was a mess. My joints ached; I felt old, looked old and was losing my grip on things that had always been so sure and steady in my life. I slogged through my days, unable to even recognize myself.

I mourned for the past when everything ran smoothly: The girls were growing; I was busy and involved in their lives; my husband was working. My grief had reached crisis proportions after our move across town a few months earlier. Even my neighbors had been replaced with strangers.

I tried walking the new neighborhood. I tried holiday shopping. I even saw a movie or two. But I felt like I had lost my way. Then the phone rang one afternoon.

"Isabel," a voice chirped. "It's Julie. Nicholas is wondering if you're planning your annual cookie-baking day. Are you?"

Ever since Nicholas was able to toddle across my kitchen in the old neighborhood, we'd had tea together and baked cookies. This year, his younger brother Zachary was old enough to join the activities.

"Oh Julie, I don't think . . ." I paused and mustered some false enthusiasm. "Of course I'm going to bake with Nicholas. And send Zachary along, too. It'll be great!"

I set the date and hung up the phone with a weight sitting in the bottom of my stomach like a wad of raw cookie dough. This was the last thing in the world I wanted—two little boys racing all over my house, my kitchen and my life. Still, it *would* be nice to carry on an old tradition.

Down the block lived another child, a quiet little thing, sometimes peeking out at me from behind a large ash tree in her front yard. One day I saw her sitting idly on the curb and, recognizing a kindred spirit, joined her.

"Hi. I'm Isabel. I moved in over there," I pointed, "and I'm lonesome because I don't know anybody. What's your name?"

"Kelsey," she answered. "I don't have anything to do."

"Hmm. Well, I've got just the thing," I heard myself saying. "Tomorrow my friends Nicholas and Zachary are coming to bake cookies. Would you like to come?"

Kelsey's mother eagerly brought her over the next morning. Standing on my doorstep were three grinning kids and two parents. I told the grown-ups that it would take about three hours, but I'd call when everybody was ready to go home.

And the four of us got started.

We measured.

We mixed.

We laughed when flour powdered our faces and hair.

The dough was over-rolled and over-handled, but it didn't seem to matter. Nor did anyone care when the cookie-cutter shapes were crooked or lopsided. And there were no tears shed over the burned sheet of Christmas trees that set off the smoke alarm. Instead, we discovered they made splendid Frisbees to bulls-eye the frozen bird-bath out back.

Amid singing and conversations both long and short, I hauled out the frosting: red and green pastry tubes that oozed both top and bottom. After a minilesson in rosette making, the three little ones practiced squeezing the sugar concoction onto the countertop. Did you know that red and green icing turns mouth, teeth and tongue an awful purple? Even my own!

Tiny fingers pressed raisin eyes and red cinnamon buttons onto gingerbread fronts. The kids ate two for every one they used. Colored sugar sprinkled the table, the Santa cookies and the floor.

Secrets were whispered, little hurts mended and problems solved while we downed three refills of beyond-sugary sugarplum tea in real china cups.

And—miracle of miracles—frosted holiday cookies, divided by lacy paper doilies, were all neatly packed in white boxes decorated with "Merry-Christmas-I-love-you" tags when the doorbell rang. *Six* hours later.

"I thought you came here to decorate cookies, not your-selves," Kelsey's mother teased. All three kids grinned back with purple teeth. I kept my own mouth closed.

"I miss you, Isabel." Nicholas grabbed me around the waist before he left. "The lady in your old house doesn't make us cookies or tea."

"Yeah," chimed in Zachary.

"One day," I smiled, holding Nick's rosy cheeks in both my hands, "you're going to grow up, and you won't want to bake Christmas cookies anymore. And I'll understand."

"Oh no, Isabel! I will never, never be too old for you. I love you."

"I love you, too," said Zachary.

"Me, too," whispered Kelsey.

And suddenly they were stuck to me like Velcro.

Christmas came. I invited all the old neighbors and a few of the new ones. My daughters phoned, bereft and homesick, and, of course, we all cried. I still missed my friend. And my husband didn't change at all. But the most important thing I learned that year was:

When life seems sorrowful—reach out.

Find children.

Bake cookies.

Isabel Bearman Bucher

Flashing Back

It wouldn't be Christmas without the memory of my dad taking the annual holiday photo. I carry a mental image of his hairline with the camera blocking his face and the unsnapped case dangling beneath it like the protective gear of a catcher's mask.

But nothing protected Dad from the hubbub of five kids on Christmas Day. The Christmas commotion clashed with his German temperament, driving him to create order out of the chaos.

So he created the ritual. None of us could eat dinner, or even touch our forks, before he took the holiday picture. His payoff was some peace, if only for a precious few minutes.

"I need quiet," he commanded, "or else it will take me even longer to set up."

We rolled our eyes—the only things we could move without disturbing the pose. The focus of his attention was a Zeiss Ikon Contaflex One, purchased when we were stationed in Europe. A manual 35 millimeter camera, it required endless calculations and adjustments before he dared click the shutter. I'm sure it was a dad just like him who inspired some kid to invent the Kodak Instamatic®!

For what seemed like hours leading up to the photo, he

made us sit still in our assigned places around the table. He looked through the viewfinder every few seconds. He read—and reread—the instruction booklet. He peered through reading glasses to carefully manipulate the camera's settings.

And Mom offered us no sympathy.

"Be patient with your father," she advised. "Someday, when you're grown up, you'll thank him for doing this."

It turns out Mom was right.

Years after leaving home, I pawed through a box in her basement and discovered the Christmas pictures. I looked closely at each one and realized that, instinctively, Dad had almost replicated the poses each year. The changes were so minor that the photos resembled animation cells. I placed them in chronological order, earliest at the bottom, and began to flip through the years.

I notice how the images changed at the sides of the table where a highchair moved in and out of the frame like a ping-pong ball as each toddler grew out of it. Finally, Gretchen, Carolyn, Jan and I were all seated at the table. Seven frames later the high chair moved into place again with the family caboose, Bart. Our heights increased with the years and so did our hairstyles: from pixie, to beehive, to pageboy. We were always in Sunday dress, and Mom's clothes mirrored the decades.

But little changed at the head of the table.

With no evidence of him dashing to his own spot in front of the camera, Dad sported an every-hair-in-place military crew cut. He always wore a white shirt and a necktie that exactly matched his trousers. His left hand gripped an oversized fork impaling the turkey breast. His right hand held a knife poised to carve. It is a sign of the times when I see a white cord that stretched from a wall socket to Dad's new electric knife.

It's all there, captured year after year, as we held our

places and our smiles, waiting for the Dad's diligently pre-set timer to click our pose.

My life story is told in those photographs, in all that is seen and unseen. And I smile, recalling the adage about what a picture is worth. Thank goodness Dad loved us enough to ignore our groans and snap them.

Kathryn Beisner

Presence and Accounted For

Every gift had been wrapped, each recipe prepared, and all the ornaments hung. I had seen to every detail; I knew I hadn't overlooked a thing. And now, with my three anxious children tucked in bed at last, I leaned back in my favorite recliner—satisfied—to survey our perfect, shimmering tree.

I admired the gay packages arranged meticulously underneath. Thanks to my early planning and a little extra money this year, Christmas was going to be wonderful. I couldn't wait to see my children's faces when they tore into their presents the next morning, discovering all of the new clothes and great toys I had bought for them.

I began a mental accounting of the treasures tucked inside each package: the Dallas Cowboys jacket for Brandon, the Fisher Price castle for Jared, the Victorian dollhouse for Brittany . . .

Basking in the glow of twinkling lights and my own thoughts, I barely noticed Jared sneak into the room. My normal reaction would be to jump up and rush him back to bed. Languidly curious this time, I chose to sit still and watch, hoping he wouldn't notice my presence.

I needn't have worried.

Jared was a five-year-old with a mission. The glimmering tree illuminated his small figure as he made his way straight to the nativity beneath it. Sinking to his knees, he held out a paper and whispered, "See, Jesus, I drew this picture for you."

Not wanting to miss a word, I held my breath and leaned forward.

"On the left side, that's me." Jared's finger traced a path across the page. "On the right side, that's you." He pointed. "In the middle is my heart." He smiled sweetly. "I'm giving it to you."

With tenderness, Jared placed the picture beneath the tree.

"Merry Christmas, Jesus," he said and scurried back to bed.

My throat tightened, and my eyes filled. All the sparkling decorations and all the shiny wrappings in the room suddenly dulled in comparison to Jared's innocent crayon drawing. It took my small child's gift of love to remind me that only Jesus can make Christmas wonderful this year. And he always does.

Vickie Ryan Koehler

Let's Get Real

For years and years, our family celebrated Christmas with an artificial tree. The tradition caught on during the seventies when we were living in Australia and it was *hotter'n all get-out* during the month of December. While the Aussies smothered themselves with zinc cream as they sunbaked on the beach, our family held tenaciously to its American customs, insisting on a traditional sit-down Christmas dinner and, of course, a real-looking tree.

Unfortunately, the heat was too extreme to trust an evergreen, and those who did were soon sorry. Fearing a not-so-festive display of bare branches or, worse yet, a house fire, we opted for the artificial. White plastic, to be exact.

"It looks gross," my kids whined.

And try as we might to cover it with handmade or imported ornaments, it somehow never made the grade. Meanwhile, year after year, we piled our gifts underneath the fake tree—never even noticing that, with age, it had slowly turned yellow.

Our first yuletide back in America was electric. Dallas, Texas, was never billed as Christmas-in-Vermont, but the possibilities were everywhere. Nurseries from Plano to

Waco showcased a winter wonderland of snow-flocked, bushy Scotch pines. Roadside stands, advertised solely by a single strand of swinging lightbulbs, beckoned at dusk for highway travelers to stop and shop in a forest of firs. And supermarkets all around the city did their bit by offering a variety of spruce and cedars to their customers.

Once again, we considered the possibility of buying a *real* tree. Having discarded our white plastic tradition on a friend's doorstep when we left Australia, our kids had high hopes that America could make all their dreams come true. But eventually, dreams gave way to budget, and we hauled home yet another inexpensive imitation.

"At least this one is green," I told them, "and besides, we won't have the repeated cost of buying a freshly cut tree every Christmas."

So, for the next fifteen years, we piled our gifts beneath the branches of a manufactured pine—never even noticing that, with age, it had slowly lost its beauty.

This year, however, something magical took place. It happened one night as I approached the electronic doors of our neighborhood grocery store. Out of the corner of my eye, I spied a breathtakingly beautiful, real-live Christmas tree, leaning near the entrance. It was there with all the others, yet standing apart. I made a detour to take a second look.

The grand fir that caught my attention stood ten feet high. It was indeed a lofty tree, and I ran my fingers over the needles, surprised by their softness.

Hmmm, maybe this is why children love real trees at Christmas, I thought, smelling the woodsy fragrance in the air.

A store clerk was working at the far end, slowly watering the trees and making his way in my direction. But I was in no hurry, so I waited. When he saw me admiring the fir, he called out, "Hey, great tree for hanging ornaments!"

I acknowledged him by waving and stepping back to

make my final decision. At that very moment, a pre-recorded Christmas carol cascaded through the sound system, out into the night. Customers rushed past—some going in, some going out—more or less oblivious to the majestic music filling the air. And the words spilled across the busy parking lot, "No-el, No-el, No-el, No-el. Born is the king of Is-rael," to the accompaniment of a Salvation Army bell ringer just outside the door.

As I stood in the shadow of that noble fir, I knew this was the year I needed to buy a *real* tree. For no other reason than this is a *real* story being told, a *real* message being sung, and a *real* occasion to celebrate.

So this year, for the very first time ever, our family will pile all our Christmas gifts underneath a towering noble fir—never even noticing that, with age, we're slowly becoming believers all over again.

Charlotte A. Lanham

The Right Touch

It was four days before Christmas and the town sat still, as if Old Man Winter had forgotten the snow everyone was wishing for.

Grandpa and I worked at the department store where he asked kids what they wanted for Christmas while I distributed candy canes and small presents. Grandpa's beard was real, bushy and full. Some of the kids who tugged it were quite surprised. And when he ho ho-ed, his stomach shook. Grandpa *was* Santa Claus, no question.

Most of the lap-sitters were under ten. They were pretty much alike, asking for bikes, dolls, radios and games. But one little girl was different. Her mother led her up, and Grandpa hoisted her onto his lap. Her name was Tina. She was blind.

"What do you want for Christmas, Tina?" Grandpa asked.

"Snow," she answered shyly.

Grandpa smiled. His eyes twinkled. "Well, I'll see what I can do about that. But how about something just for you? Something special?"

Tina hesitated and whispered in Grandpa's ear. I saw a smile creep over his face.

"Sure, Tina," was all he said.

He took her hands in his and placed them on his cheeks. His eyes drifted shut, and he sat there smiling as the girl began to sculpt his face with her fingers. She paused here and there to linger, paying close attention to every wrinkle and whisker. Her fingers seemed to be memorizing the laugh lines under Grandpa's eyes and at the corners of his mouth. She stroked his beard and rolled its wiry ringlets between her thumbs and forefingers. When she finished, she paused to rest her palms on Grandpa's shoulders.

He opened his eyes. They were twinkling.

Suddenly her arms flew out, encircling Grandpa's neck in a crushing hug. "Oh, Santa," she cried. "You look just like I knew you did. You're perfect, just perfect."

As Tina's mother lifted her down from his lap, Grandpa smiled, then blinked, and a tear rolled down his cheek.

That night when my grandmother came to pick us up, I watched her help Grandpa transfer into his wheelchair and position his limp legs on the footrests. "So, Santa," she winked, "how was your day?"

He looked up at me and pressed his lips together. Then he looked at Grandma, cleared his throat, and said with a tiny smile, "Sweetheart, it was perfect, just perfect."

Outside it began to snow.

Steve Burt

'Twas the Night

When I was a child, our family traditionally caroled on Christmas Eve. It was a joint venture, with the neighborhood churches all participating. Not only did we brave the cold winds to sing door-to-door, but our caroling benefited the Fannie Battle Day Home, a local organization for unwed mothers.

The procedure was routine. We met at the local Methodist church, divided into teams and conducted a quick rehearsal. A child was commissioned as spokesperson for the evening and given a modest, wooden box with a slit in the top to collect donations.

Assuming a seven-year-old could easily pull the heartstrings of any Scrooge that lived in the district, someone handed *me* the collection box that year. My assignment was elementary: Wait patiently until someone opened the door, and then cheerfully announce, "Merry Christmas! We're collecting money for the Fannie Battle Day Home. Would you like to make a donation?"

I memorized my lines before leaving the church and walked proudly ahead of the others, protecting the box with my tiny, gloved hands.

A dusty snow fell around us, and halos around the

streetlamps provided our only light—except for the flash-lights used to read music. Some houses felt inviting, others intimidating, but—sensing the choir was never far behind—I boldly approached each home and knocked loudly.

A towering old man, dressed in his pajamas, came to a window and peered through the curtains before opening his door. My knees trembled, but I waited until he acknowledged me and courageously blurted out my rehearsed appeal.

"Merry Christmas! We're from the Dannie Hattle Fay Bome. Would you like to make a monation?"

The man chuckled and motioned his wife to bring his wallet. Together they dropped in a few dollars. Ah, success! On to the next house.

"Merry Christmas! We're from the Hannie Dattle Bay Fome. Would you care to make a dolation?"

And at another door, "Merry Christmas! We're from the Bannie Fattle Hay Dome. Would you need to make some domations?"

No doubt about it, I was *cute*. And in spite of the fact that I couldn't get the words right, people were generous and good-hearted. But I was young and cold and growing weary.

Too tired to carry on, I surrendered my position at the front line of duty to a more experienced caroler. Huddling close to the others, I stomped my feet and blew my breath into my palms like I watched others do. It wasn't long before we arrived at the end of Cephas Avenue, complet-ing the circle back to the Methodist Church.

Hot chocolate, doughnuts and my mother waited for us in the warm hall. Once my toes were thawed and my tummy full, Mama took me home and nestled me all snug in my wee little bed.

But there were no sugarplums dancing in my head that

night. No visions of candy canes or lollipops. Instead, I fell asleep remembering the faces of those who gladly put money into my little wooden box . . . remembering the house where we sang around the bedside of a wrinkled, old lady in a hospital gown . . . remembering how she cried when we left . . . remembering the carolers softly singing "Away in a Manger" under a light snow.

The night's music and magic stayed with me. And I remember it still—each Christmas Eve—when I'm nestled all snug in my wee little bed.

Charlotte A. Lanham

Taffy Twist

The most wasted day of all is that during which we have not laughed.

Sebastian R. N. Chamfort

"How's it look?" my mother asked me. I stared into the boiling pink goo bubbling up in the pan. My mom had decided that we should have an "old-fashioned" Christmas this year, and we were experimenting with making taffy for the first time in our lives.

"I think it's ready," I said. The candy thermometer read 265 degrees. My mother checked it.

"It's definitely ready," she said. "Let's pour it out."

My little sister, Janet, had a large cookie sheet buttered and ready to go. My brother Mike and his best friend, Jimmy, looked on as my mother took the hot pan off the stove and poured the pink taffy slowly onto the cookie sheet. It looked shiny and delicious.

"While we wait for that to cool, let's pull this one," my mom said, pointing to the white taffy we'd made earlier.

"Yeah!" we shouted. It was the moment we'd been waiting for. My mom cut the white taffy into two halves and gave one hunk to Mike and Jimmy, and the other hunk to Janet and me. As teams, we began pulling on opposite sides of our taffy, making long stringy lengths, folding it in half and pulling it out again. We did this over and over until our sticky taffy turned smooth and satiny. It was hot work, but no one minded on such a cold December night in Alaska. It made us feel cozy even though huge snowflakes spun past the streetlights outside.

Now that the taffy was pulled, we rolled it into one big ball. From there, we took small pieces and formed them into little taffy "snakes." When the pink taffy was cool enough, we repeated the process.

"Now," my mother said, "watch this." She picked up a length of white taffy and a length of pink taffy and twisted them together. She pinched the ends and formed a crook at the top. "It's a candy cane!" she said.

"How cool!" we said, excited to be making our own candy canes from scratch. We got busy twisting the taffy and soon had a large batch of candy canes ready. We took them out to the living room and hung them one by one on our Christmas tree. Our tree was decorated with home-made ornaments in the spirit of an old-fashioned Christmas and the freshly made candy canes added just the right touch. We took a moment to admire our handi-work and then headed back into the kitchen to clean up our mess.

After the last pan had been washed and dried and the kitchen was tidied up, we returned to the living room to enjoy our creations and relax in front of the fire. But when we entered the living room, the sight of our tree made us stop and stare in amazement.

The homemade taffy candy canes were now two and three feet long! They oozed from branch to branch like thick pink and white spider webs.

"Oh no!" my mother shrieked. "The heat from the fire-place is melting the taffy!"

Mike stifled a laugh. That did it. In an instant, we were all hysterical with laughter as we watched the blobs of taffy slowly plop onto the carpet.

The next year at Christmas, we bought candy canes from the store.

Sandra J. Payne

The Drummer Boy

Give what you have. To some it may be better than you dare think.

Henry Wadsworth Longfellow

I couldn't have been more excited. The pastor and his wife were coming for dinner! I had a few favorite people in the world—and one of them was Pastor Shick. No matter where I saw him, he would always open up his big arms and give me a bear hug.

When my parents told me that he was coming for dinner, I jumped up and down with as much excitement as a seven-year-old could show. Then I realized I didn't have a present for him, and it was a week before Christmas.

Kneeling down near the wrapped gifts under the tree, I burrowed around the mountain of presents, hoping my mom or dad had left him one. Nothing was labeled Pastor Shick. Just as I was getting up, an ornament caught my eye; it was a hand-painted wooden drummer boy, about three inches tall. I thought to myself, *Pastor Shick's son, James, had played his drum during church last night while a teenager sang, "The Little Drummer Boy." The pastor must like that song to have his son play it at Christmastime.*

Hurrying, I yanked the wooden figure off the tree, grabbed some wrapping paper and ran to my mom's bedroom. Quickly, I covered the ornament with the colorful paper and began encircling the small package with Mom's entire roll of cellophane tape.

Soon the pastor and his wife arrived. We sat down at the dining-room table, and I began eating meatballs and spaghetti while the adults talked. The meal was so delicious and the conversation so interesting that I almost forgot about my gift until dessert.

Reaching under my chair, I grabbed my secret surprise. "Here," I tossed the mummy-taped gift over the table with no introduction. "Merry Christmas!"

My parents' faces went pale. They had no idea what I had given him.

The pastor reached for the gift with a smile. "How sweet of you, Michele." For several minutes he tried to unfurl the tape, then he turned to my father, saying, "I think I might need a pair of scissors. Would you have some handy?"

My father rose and grabbed a pair from a drawer.

With a few cuts and a hard pull, the minister discovered what I had bundled: the wooden drummer boy. It was very small and looked a bit worse from the tape.

"My goodness!" the minister gasped. "This is really something, young lady."

"It reminded me of last night when James played the drum," I smiled. "I love 'The Little Drummer Boy' song!"

After we finished our ice cream, the pastor gave me another warm hug, and he and his wife left. I wasn't too sure if he had really liked my gift, but I was still glad that I had remembered him in a special way.

The moment Pastor Shick was out the door, my father

turned to me and questioned, "Why did you give him that old ornament?"

"I thought he'd like it," I sputtered.

"Next time, ask before you take something off the tree," my father warned. "If you wanted to give him an ornament, you should have given him one of these big, fancy glass or crystal ones."

"Oh." Now I felt my gift wasn't good enough and my eyes fell to the floor. "Sorry."

The next Sunday, I was almost too embarrassed to go to church. I thought that my dad was probably right. I should have given him a larger ornament, one with fancy colors that glistened or twinkled with lights. After all, Pastor Shick was a very important person.

We sat in the first pew as usual, but I couldn't even look up. When it came time for the sermon, I began fidgeting in my seat, kicking my feet.

"I want to tell you all of a wonderful Christmas gift that was given to me this past week," the pastor said, holding up the familiar drummer-boy ornament. "It's one that shows that even a seven-year-old knows the true reason why we give to one another at Christmastime. Out of all of the presents I received this year, this one means the most to me. And let me tell you why. . . . For those who didn't attend the Christmas concert service, my son played his snare drum for 'The Little Drummer Boy' song. Yesterday, my son left to go back to college. Now I will keep this on my desk, reminding me that wherever he is, he is my drummer boy."

The congregation clapped.

He continued, "Over the years, I prayed to God that my family would impact your lives and that we'd make beautiful memories together. And now I know that my son's music meant something to a special little girl, as much as it meant to my family. I would like to thank her from the bottom of my heart." His eyes got teary. "She reminded me that it isn't the gift that is most important, but the love that prompted it."

After the service I went up to the pastor and received my big Sunday hug. He thanked me again for the precious ornament. Those surrounding us realized I was the girl who'd given the drummer boy gift and smiled at me knowingly.

"After I gave it to you, I was worried if you'd like it because it was so small," I finally stammered.

"Well, you're small, and I love you," the pastor said.

"But it's not fancy; it doesn't have lots of sparkles."

"Well, Jesus didn't have fancy things when he walked on Earth, but I love Him very much, too."

To this day, each Christmas when I hear "The Little Drummer Boy," I remember Pastor Shick's family fondly. That ornament was so tiny, but the meaning became larger than life to me. I learned at seven years old that it's not the gifts themselves that are important; it's making someone happy, and being willing to show love by sharing, that represent the true spirit of giving.

Michele Wallace Campanelli

Snowball's Miracle

Where there is great love, there are always miracles.

Willa Cather

When I looked into her big brown eyes, my heart melted. She won me over instantly with her big sloppy kisses. That Christmas Eve morning, I received my most-wanted Christmas gift and a wonderful, new friend. Since the weather was freezing cold and the puppy was nothing but a little ball of white fur, the name Snowball seemed to be very fitting.

Snowball snuggled closely to me and went to sleep. Later that afternoon, I noticed that her eyes were turning red. She started coughing and sneezing. Her nose was running. I called the pet store where we adopted Snowball. The manager offered to refund our money or give us another puppy. The choice was ours.

"No way!" I shouted. "I already love her!" Instead, I called the veterinarian's office and explained the circumstances. The receptionist told us to come right over since they were leaving early that day for the holidays. After checking her over thoroughly, the doctor had a sorrowful expression on his face.

"It will be a miracle if this puppy lives through the night," he sadly whispered. "My recommendation would be to put her under. You should be able to obtain a full refund from the pet store."

"I won't let her die without a fight," I cried. "I'm taking Snowball home with me."

When the doctor realized how determined I was, he gave Snowball a shot and handed me a bottle of medication to take home.

All night long, I held and nursed Snowball. Together, we sat beside the brightly lit Christmas tree and watched it twinkle. I fed her chicken broth and water with an eyedropper. When I finally dozed off, even though her breathing was labored, Snowball rested contently in my lap.

I was surprised when I awoke to a fabulous Christmas miracle. Even though she was still very sick, Snowball was alive. She had made it through the night. We became best friends that day. As the days passed, Snowball became stronger and stronger. Before long, she was the picture of health.

I'm so glad that I expected a miracle to occur that Christmas Eve. She was the best Christmas gift I've ever received. Today, sixteen years later, Snowball is still alive and continues to demonstrate a zest for living. Even though Snowball can no longer see very well, her big brown eyes are still captivating. They continue to warm my heart each time I gaze into them.

Nancy B. Gibbs

The Cat and the Christmas Star

As white snowflakes fall quietly and thickly on a winter day, answers to prayer will settle down upon you at every step you take. . . .

O. Hallesby

Tears fell from my eyes onto the posterboard below and mixed with the ink from the felt marker I was using to write "Missing: Gray tabby cat with white paws and green eyes."

Linda, my missing cat, had shared a close relationship with me ever since I had adopted him about two years before. Despite the fact that I had given him a female name (after an exam, our vet mistakenly told us he was female and we didn't find out the truth until much later), he didn't seem to mind. And even now, when we had taken him out of his familiar South Carolina neighborhood and moved him to Virginia, he seemed to bear it well. Linda continued to faithfully greet me every day when I returned home from school. But my younger sister had recently adopted a kitten, and Linda hadn't taken this change well. The image of the hurt look he had given me after meeting the kitten was still etched vividly in my memory.

One night soon afterward, he didn't come home for his evening meal, and none of my repeated calls throughout the neighborhood brought him running. The cheerfulness of the Christmas decorations on the houses failed to excite me the way they usually did. I went to bed reluctantly, certain he would turn up first thing the next morning. But I was wrong. And after two days, I started to panic.

Frantically, I dialed the local animal shelter, but no cats fitting his description had come in. So, with my family's help, I'd made and distributed the posters and even found a local radio station willing to announce Linda's disappearance and plead for his return. Every day after school, I spent hours either on foot or bike scanning the neighborhood for him and calling his name until my voice was hoarse. Every night in bed I asked God to bring him home.

By the time Christmas Eve had arrived, Linda still had not. He had been missing for eight days. After spending the church service and our Christmas Eve dinner distracted by my sadness and anxiety, I glumly went to bed where I dutifully prayed once more that God would bring Linda home. Then exhausted, I fell into a deep sleep.

Several hours later, my clock radio blinked 11:59 P.M. I suddenly awoke. It was rare for me to wake in the middle of the night; I'd always been a sound sleeper. But as I lay in the darkness, I was fully awake and consumed with a desire to get up and look at the stars outside.

For several years, I'd had a personal Christmas Eve tradition of scanning the sky for the brightest star, which I liked to imagine was the "Christmas star." Whether it was actually the North Star that led the ancient wise men to baby Jesus in the manger, I didn't know. But I enjoyed viewing it anyway, and usually looked for it before I went to bed on Christmas Eve. As I lay there wondering why I was awake all of a sudden, I realized that I hadn't even bothered to look for it this year.

Eagerly, I leapt from my bed and peeked through the blinds on my bedroom window, but I couldn't discern any stars. Then a thought came to me with surprising strength. *Try the front door. Now.*

The thought of opening the door to the icy wind outside didn't excite me, but somehow, I felt, I *had* to find the Christmas star. So I unfastened both locks and swung the door open. Shivering in my nightgown, I scanned the sky until a silvery white dot came into view. The Christmas star! At that moment, I knew that no matter where Linda was, or if he ever returned, God still cared for me.

I stared at the star for a moment, then reached for the door to pull it shut, looking down to the front stoop as I did so. And then I saw him—Linda—thin, shivering and reeking of gasoline. He sat quietly before me. His green eyes searched mine, as if to say, "I'm sorry. Will you take me back?"

Immediately, I scooped him up. But before I closed the door, I stood with Linda in my arms to gaze once more at the Christmas star. Then I said a prayer of thanks to the God who watches over all his creation—from the most distant star to the purring cat I held closely.

Whitney Von Lake Hopler

4

HOLIDAY
TRADITIONS

Christmas is time to sing "happy birthday" to someone in the form of Christmas carols.

Carmen Rutlen

The Christmas Phantom

*Christmas waves a magic wand over this world,
and behold, everything is softer and more
beautiful.*

Norman Vincent Peale

My parents had a ritual of reading in bed before turning in for the night. If they would find something particularly interesting, they would share it with each other. One night, my mother found a wonderful story about a family that was blessed with the "Christmas Phantom." I'd like to recall this story to you and how she became the Christmas Phantom.

It was a little after 9 P.M., and all was quiet at the Markley's house. All the children were tucked in their beds and Mary was finishing up the dishes and cleaning the kitchen. Dan sat at his desk going over the bills. It was almost Christmas again, and as usual, the pile of bills was growing and growing. Dan didn't really like what Christmas did to the family budget and had nearly become a scrooge during this time of year.

When he was a little boy things were so much easier and cost so much less. Christmas was a joyous time for everyone and most of the gifts were handmade. Things had changed so much since that time.

A light snow had begun to fall as Dan gazed out the window. It was December 14, only twelve days till Christmas. A light knock at the door brought Dan's thoughts back to the present, and he went to answer the door. No one was there, but on the steps in the new fallen snow lay a small package wrapped in gold paper. Mary joined him at the door wondering who could be calling at this hour. Together they stared at the small gift in wonderment. They found a small card attached, but it only read, "On the first day of Christmas." After a brief discussion they decided to open it and see if there was a card inside. Inside the box they found an adorable little drummer boy ornament, and nothing else. The little drummer boy found a prominent place on their Christmas tree and the incident was all but forgotten.

The next evening about dinner time, Brad, age six, answered a light knock on the door. Again no one was there, but on the step was another small package with a card that read, "On the second day of Christmas." Inside were two candy canes. Three angels arrived "on the third day of Christmas" in a similar fashion; these all took their place on the Christmas tree.

By the fourth day, curiosity getting the better of them, Dan and Mary were peeking out the window every few minutes in hope of catching a glimpse of the stealthy delivery person. Mary was sure it was her friend Tracy. Dan thought it must be Sam and Kate from next door, and that's how they disappeared so fast. But nine and then ten o'clock passed and so finally Dan and Mary gave up and went to bed. At eleven o'clock the light knock was loud in the sleeping house. Dan was quick and ran to the door as

Mary peeked out the window, neither seeing hide nor hair of anyone. When Dan returned to the room, he held a large package in his hands. "On the fourth day of Christmas" were four hot chocolate mugs.

"On the fifth day of Christmas," with a heavy knock, a stranger appeared at the door with a package in his hands. He said he was sworn to secrecy and wouldn't tell anyone the names of the givers. This time five gold balls joined the other gifts on the tree.

"On the sixth day . . . ," six packets of hot chocolate arrived.

"On the seventh day . . . ," seven white candles wrapped in gold twine.

"On the eighth day . . . ," eight gold sparkling pine cones came nestled in a basket.

By the ninth day of Christmas, all the children had become involved and were trying to set watch to find out who was doing this. Every night someone sat up watching for the mystery person, and everyone tried to guess who was behind this. Dan finally decided that they might never find out who it was. Perhaps the person didn't want to be thanked and just wanted to share a little of the Christmas spirit. Everyone agreed that this was getting to be really fun with the anticipation of when and what the next gift would be. Mary was sure the cards would be signed by the twelfth night.

"On the ninth day of Christmas," nine kisses arrived.

"On the tenth day of Christmas," a different stranger delivered ten sheets of wrapping paper. "On the eleventh day . . . ," eleven red bows.

"On the twelfth day of Christmas" it was nearly midnight when the knock came to the quiet Markley house. In a small canister on the step were twelve pieces of fudge, the card unsigned. The Christmas Phantom would remain anonymous after all. Mary was a little disappointed, but

Dan was happy. He had found someone who truly shared the spirit of Christmas without expecting a return gift or even a thank-you. Isn't that the true meaning of Christmas after all? Maybe next year the Christmas Phantom would come again . . . or maybe Dan and Mary would share their love in this special way by being the Christmas Phantom to their friends.

My mother read this and decided to become the Christmas Phantom in 1985 to her friends. Her sons and daughter joined in and eventually became Christmas Phantoms to their friends. For well over a decade we continued this tradition of being the "Christmas Phantom" to many friends and strangers. Last year my mother lost her ongoing battle with ovarian cancer. One of her last wishes was for us to carry on this tradition. I hope that you adopt this tradition with me in becoming the "Christmas Phantom" to the many who have lost the Christmas spirit.

Shawn and Melissa Pittman

The Holly Trees

Growing up in the sixties wasn't easy when your parents were divorced and your dad seemed to have disappeared off the face of the planet—especially when everyone else seemed to be living like Ozzie and Harriet. And although my mom worked hard to keep us clothed and fed, when Christmastime rolled around, life suddenly seemed rather bleak and barren. About the time of the school Christmas party, all I could think about was making that three-hour drive to my grandparents' house where Christmas was really Christmas. Where food and relatives abounded, and artificial trees, like the cheesy tinfoil job in our tiny living room, were not allowed. You see, every year, my grandpa cut down a tree tall enough to touch the high ceiling in their old Victorian house. We often got to help; but some years, especially if we arrived just before Christmas, the tree would already be up, but we'd still help decorate it.

One year, just two days before Christmas, we arrived and the tree wasn't up. I asked Grandpa if we were going out to the woods to get one. He just smiled his little half smile, blue eyes twinkling mischievously, and said we weren't going out to the woods this year. I worried and watched my grandpa all afternoon, wondering what we were going to do about the tree, but he just went about his business as if nothing whatsoever was unusual. Finally just after dinner, Grandpa went and got his ax. At last, I thought, we are going to cut down a tree. But in the dark?

Grandpa grinned and told me to come outside. I followed him, wondering where he could cut a tree down at night. My grandparents' large home was situated on a small lot in the middle of town, with no U-cut trees anywhere nearby. But Grandpa went out to the parking strip next to their house and began whacking away at the trunk of one of his own mature holly trees—the tallest one, a beautiful tree loaded with bright red berries. I stared at him, in silent shock. What in the world was he doing? And what would Grandma say?

"The city says I gotta cut these trees down," he explained between whacks. "They're too close to the street. I figure if I take one out each Christmas, it will keep us in trees for three years." He grinned down at me, and the tree fell. Then my sister and I helped him carry it into the house, getting poked and pricked with every step of the way. I still wasn't sure what I thought about having a holly tree for a Christmas tree. I'd never heard of such a thing.

But when we had the tree in the stand and situated in its place of honor in one of the big bay windows, I knew that it was not a mistake. It was absolutely gorgeous. We all just stood and stared at its dark green glossy leaves and abundant bright red berries. "It's so beautiful," said Grandma. "It doesn't even need decorations." But my sister and I loved the process of decorating, and we insisted it did. We began to hang lights and ornaments—carefully. It isn't easy decorating a holly tree. But with each new poke we laughed and complained good-naturedly.

For three years, we had holly trees for Christmas. And now, whenever I get pricked by holly, I think of Grandpa.

Later on in life, after my grandpa passed away, I learned about the symbolism of holly and why we use it at Christmas—and how the red berries represent droplets of Christ's blood. I don't know if my grandpa knew about all that, but he did know how to be a father to the fatherless. And he knew how to salvage good from evil. My grandpa didn't like to waste anything.

Melody Carlson

A True Christmas

I plopped the last of the ready-made cookie dough onto the cookie sheet and shoved it into the oven. These standard-issue chocolate chip cookies would be a far cry from the bejeweled affairs I'd baked for twenty-six years, but the only reason I'd even summoned the effort was because my youngest son, Ross, had opened and re-opened the cookie jar four times the previous night, saying with fourteen-year-old tact, "What? No Christmas cookies this year?"

Since today was the twenty-third, and his older siblings, Patrick and Molly, would be arriving Christmas Eve, Ross informed me that they would be "big-time disappointed" if there wasn't "cool stuff" to eat. This from the same kid who had never watched a Christmas TV special in his life and who had to be dragged into the family photo for the annual Christmas card.

I never considered a family picture this year. A big piece of the family was now missing—or hadn't anybody noticed?

All my friends had been telling me the same thing since the day of the funeral:

"Pam, the first year after you lose your husband is the hardest. You have to go through the first Valentine's Day without him, the first birthday, the first anniversary . . ."

They hadn't been kidding. What they hadn't told me was that Christmas was going to top them all in hard-to-take. It wasn't that Tom had loved Christmas that much. He'd always complained that the whole thing was too commercial and that when you really thought about it, Easter seemed to be a much more important Christ-centered celebration in the church.

The phone rang. Molly was calling collect from the road. She and two dorm buddies were driving home after finals.

"Do you know what I'm looking forward to?" she said.

"Sleeping for seventy-two straight hours?" I asked.

"No." She sounded a little deflated. "Coming home from Christmas Eve services and seeing all those presents piled up under the tree. It's been years since I've cared what was in them or how many were for me—I just like seeing them there. How weird is that?"

Not weird at all, my love, I thought. I sighed, took a piece of paper and penciled in a few gift ideas for Ross, Molly, Patrick, his wife Amy and my grandson, Shane.

And then I snapped the pencil down on the counter. A part of me understood that the kids were in denial. Tom's sudden death eleven months earlier had left them bewildered and scared. And now at Christmas, their shock was translated into exaggerated enthusiasm. The Cobb family Christmas traditions provided a sense of normalcy for them. Patrick had even asked me last week if I still had the old John Denver Christmas album.

But as far as I was concerned, there just wasn't that much to deck the halls about. Tom was gone. I was empty and unmotivated. At worst, I wished they'd all just open the presents and carve the turkey without me.

When the oven dinged, I piled two dozen brown circles on a plate and left a note for Ross: "I don't want to hear any more complaining! Gone shopping. I love you, Mom."

The complaining, however, went on in my head as I elbowed my way through the mob at the mall.

Tom was right, I thought. *This is all a joke.*

It really was everything he hated: canned music droning its false merriment, garish signs luring me to buy, tired-looking families dragging themselves around, worrying about their credit card limits as they snapped at their children.

Funny, I thought while gazing at a display of earrings I knew Molly wouldn't wear. *All the time Tom was here pointing this out to me, it never bothered me. Now it's all I can see.*

I abandoned the earring idea and took to wandering the mall, hoping for inspiration so Molly would have something to look at under the tree. It wasn't going to be like years past—I should have told her that. She wasn't going to see a knee-deep collection of exquisitely wrapped treasures that Tom always shook his head over.

"You've gone hog-wild again," he would always tell me—before adding one more contribution. Instead of buying me a gift, he'd write a check in my name to Compassion International or a local food pantry, place it in a red envelope, and tuck it onto a branch of our Christmas tree.

"This is a true Christmas gift," he'd tell me. "It's a small demonstration that Christ is real in our lives."

I stopped mid-mall, letting the crowds swirl past me.

Tom wasn't there, a fact that the rest of the family didn't want to face or discuss. But he could still be with us, maybe just a little.

I left the mall and quickly found a Christmas tree lot. The man looked happy to unload one very dry tree for half price. He even tied it to my roof rack.

Then it was off to Safeway, where I bought a twenty-four-pound Butterball turkey and all the trimmings. Back home, the decoration boxes weren't buried too deeply in the garage. I'd barely gotten them put away last year when Tom had his heart attack.

I was still sorting boxes when Ross emerged from the kitchen, munching the last of the two dozen cookies.

"Oh, I thought we weren't going to have a tree this year," he said between mouthfuls.

"Well, we are. Can you give me a hand getting it up?"

Two hours later, Ross and I stood back and admired our Christmas tree. The lights winked softly as I straightened a misshapen glittery angel Molly had made in second grade and Ross's first birthday Christmas ball.

I wanted to cry.

The house sprang to life when everyone arrived Christmas Eve. In the middle of our church service, however, my spirits sagged. There was no lonelier feeling than standing in the midst of one's family singing "Silent Night"—surrounded by a vivacious college daughter; a sweet, gentle daughter-in-law; a handsome, successful twenty-five-year-old son; a wide-eyed, mile-a-minute three-year-old grandson; and an awkward teenager whose hugs were like wet shoelaces—and being keenly aware that someone was missing.

Back at home everyone continued to avoid the subject.

"The tree is gorgeous, Mom," Molly said. She knelt down and began hauling gifts out of a shopping bag to add to my pile.

"I love what you did with the wrappings, Pam," Amy said. "You're always so creative."

"I forgot to buy wrapping paper," I told her. "I had to use newspaper."

It was Christmas as usual—easier to pretend everything was normal than to deal with harsh reality. Ross and Patrick sparred over whose stocking was whose, and Shane parked himself in front of a bowl of M&Ms. They all got to open the customary one present on Christmas Eve, and after doing so, they schlepped off to bed.

But there was one more thing that had to be done. I went over to Tom's desk, found a red envelope in the top drawer, and stuck into it a check made out to the American Heart Association. It seemed appropriate.

"I know the kids—and even I—have to go on with our lives, Tom," I whispered. "But I wish you were here."

It occurred to me as I tucked the red envelope midway up the tree that one of the kids would say, "Oh, yeah—I remember, he always did that," and then there would be an awkward silence and perhaps sheepish looks.

I hoped so.

Morning, or at least dawn—came way too soon. Shane was up before the paper carrier. I dragged myself into the kitchen and found it already smelling like a Seattle coffee-house.

"This is what we drink at school," Molly told me and handed me a cup.

"Is anyone else awake?" I asked.

She nodded her head, and for the first time I noticed a twinkle in her eye that was unprecedented for this hour of the morning. "What are you up to?" I asked.

"Mom!" Patrick yelled from the living room. "You've got to see this!"

"At this hour of the . . ."

What I saw was my family perched on the couch like a row of deliciously guilty canaries. What I saw next was our Christmas tree, dotted with bright red envelopes.

"Man, it got crowded in here last night," Ross said. "I came down here about one o'clock and freaked Amy out."

"I almost called 911 when I came down," Patrick said, until I saw it was Molly and not some burglar."

I had never heard a thing. I walked over to the tree and touched each one of the five envelopes I hadn't put there.

"Open them, Mom," Molly said. "This was always the best part of Christmas."

From Patrick, there was a check to Youth for Christ, to help kids go on mission trips like the one Dad supported him on to Haiti five years earlier. From Amy, a check to our church for sheet music, because some of her best memories of her father-in-law were of him helping the children's choir. From Molly, several twenty-dollar bills for the local crisis pregnancy center, "because many of the women who go there have probably never experienced the love of a husband like Daddy," she said. From Ross, a twenty-dollar bill for a local drug program for kids, "since Dad was all freaked out about me staying clean."

The last envelope was lumpy. When I opened it, a handful of change spilled out.

"Mine, Gamma," Shane said, his little bow-mouth pursed importantly. Amy finished his thought. "He wants this to go to the animal shelter—you know, for lost dogs. Like the one he visited with Dad just before he died."

I pulled all the envelopes against my chest and hugged them.

"You know what's weird?" Molly said. "I feel like Daddy's right here with us."

"Yeah, that's pretty weird," Ross said.

"But true," Patrick said. "I feel like he's been here this whole time. I thought I'd be all bummed out this Christmas—but I don't need to be."

"No, you don't, my love," I said. To myself, I added, *Neither do I. I have my family, and I have my faith.*

Nancy Rue

Deck the Halls . . . and Save Some Tinsel for the Goat!

"It followed me home, Mom, can I keep it?"

If you live in the city, this usually means your child has brought home a stray kitten or a puppy. If you live in the country, it could mean your child has brought home anything from a chicken to a pig. Today it was a goat.

"Isn't she beautiful, Mom?" Peter hugged the smelly, black nanny goat who looked at me with blank eyes that showed no sign of intelligence.

"She looks very valuable, I'm sure some farmer has lost her and wants her back." I hoped that was true.

"I'll put an ad in the lost and found, and if nobody claims her in a week, can I keep her?" he begged.

"Okay," I agreed, not realizing I had just destroyed my entire life.

No one claimed the goat even though I ran the ad an extra week. Some very smart farmer had dumped her on our doorstep and wasn't about to admit it and get stuck with the goat again.

Nanny goat ate every living thing in the yard except the cat. She mowed the flowers to the ground, ate the weeping willow tree my husband had given me on our anniversary and she tap-danced on the hood of my car. No fence was high enough or tight enough to keep her in the pasture.

Nanny grew and grew and it became obvious she was pregnant. On Thanksgiving Day, she produced triplets. That night an ice storm came sweeping through the Ozarks and the goats had to be moved into the house to keep them from freezing to death.

That was also the night our new minister came to visit. He said he'd never known anyone who kept goats in their living room before. He only stayed a few minutes. He said he wanted to get home before the roads got too slick. Nanny chewing on his shoelaces probably didn't help.

We discovered a goat only four hours old can jump on a chair, bounce on a sofa and slide across the coffee table forty-two times an hour. Triplets can do 126 jumps, bounces and slides per hour. Nanny sat in the recliner, chewed her cud and showed no signs of intelligence.

The Christmas parade was just around the corner and what animal reminds us all of Christmas more than a goat and three baby goats? My husband promised to take the goats to the parade in his truck, but he was working at the auction and running late. I had to get four children and four goats to town or they would miss the parade.

I'd have to be crazy to load my children and the goats into my station wagon and drive six miles to town just so they could be in a Christmas parade.

Nanny loved riding in the car, but she insisted on a window seat. She sat upright with a seat belt holding her securely in place. Three of the children each held a baby goat in their lap. As other cars passed us, people stared and pointed and I hoped they knew I had four goats in my car and not four very ugly children.

When we arrived in town, Peter dressed the four goats in tinsel, bobbles and bells, and walked down the street behind the band and the float with Santa Claus riding on it.

The band struck up "Hark, the Herald Angels" and the goats bolted through the middle of the trumpet players and made short work of the elves. Santa jumped off the float and helped us corner the goats in the doorway of the donut shop.

The goats were dragged back out onto the street and placed at the front of the parade to keep them as far away from the band as possible.

Peter and his goats won the first place trophy for the most unusual entry. Nanny's picture was in the newspaper, and she looked brilliant.

If you look closely at the newspaper picture, you can see me in the background, showing no sign of intelligence.

Time has passed, and Peter's goat herd has grown to over thirty. These smelly, wonderful animals have changed our lives and Christmas just doesn't seem like Christmas until someone asks, "Who's going to hang up the stockings on the mantle, and who's going to decorate the goats?"

April Knight

Sweets for the Sweet

Every year, between Thanksgiving and December 26, something mystical happens to me. The festive foods of Thanksgiving dinner start the process. Then Christmas music, piped from radio and DIRECTTV for an entire month, trips my alarm to *shrill*. Recipe ideas, over a half-century of them, cork to the surface like soda fizz.

Each chorus of "Rockin' Around the Christmas Tree" and "I'll Be Home for Christmas" transports me deeper and deeper into a rhapsodic trance that has my husband, Lee, shaking his head, mumbling and slanting me knowing looks.

"What?" I snap, stirring candy.

"You're doing it again." He saunters past, sniffing the chocolate mixture.

"Why do you want to spoil Christmas for me?" I glare at his back. He just doesn't *get* it.

"I hate to see you work yourself to death," he says, munching spoils from my fudge heap.

"Hey, I *love* working myself to death."

At the same time, something deep inside concedes that I *do* actually go a little mad. I can't rest until I whip up thirty pounds of walnut fudge, fifteen pounds of Mounds candy, five gallons of Rice Krispies/Snickers balls (so the grandkids can, once a year, eat to their hearts' content), ten dozen peanut-butter balls, twenty pounds of butter-scotch fudge, and—although I *swear* each year I'll not do them again—I cannot resist making several batches of yummy chocolate-toffee bars.

"But why so *much*?" Lee snatches a couple of toffee bars and crams his mouth full. I roll my eyes at his duplicity.

"Tradition," I say.

And, dear Lord, on one level, it *is*. But, I ask myself, does tradition alone justify my annual cooking frenzy? I've done it since I was a teen practicing home ec class recipes. During ensuing years, I involved the children in the fun, building happy memories, packaging gifts of food for friends and family.

Now, with the kids raised, the activity has become, at times, tiresome. Yet the urge persists. Mystified, I wonder, *What is the core of this crazy compulsion?*

Later, I browse through some old family photos.

"Look, here's my Two-Mama," I tell Lee. "Remember how, after we married, we used to visit during Christmas? As far back as I can remember, she always had goodies of every description to feed us. I loved the way she would always . . ."

Tears spring to my eyes. I *miss* her. She and PaPa have been gone for many years. I remind Lee how my grand-parents' fragrant house welcomed and cheered me during childhood holidays, how their table sprouted delectable treats and how she always had plenty. Two-Mama made sure her loved ones never left her home hungry, even loading us down with carry-home bags.

That's it!

My Yuletide frenzy evokes memories of Two-Mama's gift to me. *That's* what motivates me! I never felt more loved than there, in her home, knowing in my child's mind that she'd prepared all this in honor of me. She celebrated me with all those goodies. That was her way of loving.

I smile at Lee. "I guess now it's my turn to celebrate my loved ones. It's my way of loving them." He squeezes my hand in understanding.

So, five weeks later, here I am: ten pounds heavier, crash-landed back to sanity. I'm also exhausted.

"Y'know," I admit to Lee, propping my swollen feet on the coffee table, "I'm getting older. I believe next year I'll skip the candy-making thing."

"That's a good idea, hon." He winks at me.

This time, I vow I'll remain staunch. Immovable. At least until Thanksgiving rolls around, and I hear those first strains, "I'll be ho-o-me for Christ-maaaas . . ."

Emily Sue Harvey

Everybody Loves Santa

One Christmas season I helped Santa Claus by filling in for him at a small shopping mall. Instead of the usual assembly line of children, I enjoyed spontaneous visits with little tots bearing lists of toys, as well as the occasional surprise visits with teenagers and adults.

A bright, happy and chatty three-and-a-half-year-old sat on my lap, asking questions and answering mine. Finally, looking me in the eye, she said, "I thought you were fake. You're real!" Her doubts removed, I'm sure she had a magical Christmas.

A pair of fifteen-year-old boys ran up, hugged me lovingly and, grinning, asked, "Will you bring us each a motorcycle?" After a brief chat, they walked away chuckling.

A young father paid the elf photographer for a single picture. "I don't have custody of my children," he explained, "and I want to show them a picture of you and me shaking hands." He received the finished photo, mouthed "thank you" and left.

Three teenage girls skipped and twirled over. Giggling, one teased, "I want a sports car."

The second one topped her. "I want a mansion."

The last girl whispered in my ear, "I'd like a job for my dad."

As they walked away, her friends probed, "What did you ask for?"

"That's between me and Santa," she sighed.

Substitute Santa swallowed hard and wiped his eyes with his handkerchief. I truly believe the girl's father found a job becuse, you see, that night Santa prayed he would.

Robert H. Bickmeyer

Away from the Manger

"Okay, that's the last of it." Michael stacked the final box in my entry hall.

I surveyed the tattered, dusty containers with anticipation. To me, these Christmas decorations from Michael's childhood, in storage since his mother's death, signified our future together as a couple. We were sharing all sorts of holiday activities—parties, shopping and, now, decorating. In a few months we'd be married, and I was eager to create some traditions of our own. I yearned for meaningful practices, significant and unique to the two of us.

Opening the crates was a start.

"Hey, here's our old nativity set." Michael pulled out a well-packed box. "Mom always put it under the Christmas tree."

I carefully unwrapped Mary and Joseph and the manger. Stuffed deep in the newspapers was a stable. I placed it on the floor beneath the tree and arranged three wise men, a shepherd boy, a lamb and a cow. All accounted for, except . . .

I double-checked the loose packing and looked under the wadded newspapers, hoping to find the missing figure. Nothing.

"Honey," I called to Michael, who was busily arranging Santa's toyshop in the dining room. "I can't find Jesus."

Walking to my side, he playfully squeezed my shoulder. "Excuse me?"

"The baby Jesus for the nativity. He's not here!" I rummaged through more wrappings.

Michael's expression tensed. "He's here. He has to be. He was here the last Christmas Mom was alive."

Hours later, all the boxes were unpacked, but Jesus never appeared. Michael regretfully suggested we pack the nativity scene back in the crate.

"No," I said. "I'll find a baby that matches the set tomorrow."

We kissed good night, and Michael went home.

The next day, I stuffed the manger into my purse and headed to the hobby store during my lunch hour. No Jesus there. After work, I searched for him at several other stores only to discover that baby Jesus *wasn't sold separately*. I considered buying another nativity just to replace the Jesus in Michael's, but none of the infants fit the manger.

Michael arrived for dinner a few days later, and I broke the news to him. After we ate, I began to repack the figurines in their box. Michael stilled my hands with his.

"I think we should leave it up."

"Honey, we can't. There's no baby," I replied. "We can't have a nativity without Jesus."

"Wait a minute." Michael pulled me away from the tree. "Now look from back here."

He pointed. "At first glance, you don't notice anything missing. It's not until you look closely that you see the Christ Child is gone."

I cocked my head and looked at the scene. He was right. "But I don't get your point."

"Amid the decorations, shopping lists and parties, sometimes we lose sight of Jesus," he explained.

"Somehow, he gets lost in the midst of Christmas."

And then I understood.

So began our first Christmas tradition—significant and unique to our family. Each year, we position the treasured figures in their customary places. The manger remains empty. It's our gentle reminder to look for Christ at Christmas.

Stephanie Welcher Thompson

Let It Snow!

"Wasn't tonight's church service wonderful, Beth?"

"Hmm? I'm sorry. What did you say, dear?"

Roe glanced at his wife. "I asked what you thought of the Christmas Eve program."

"Nice. It was . . . nice." Beth looked over her shoulder. All three kids slumped against each other in the backseat, sound asleep.

"But?"

Beth didn't answer. She turned to stare out the windshield. A steady stream of traffic slinked like a glowworm, inching its way along the interstate at the foothills of Colorado's Front Range.

"Beth? What's wrong?"

"Wrong? Oh, I'm not sure that anything in particular is wrong, but it's not exactly right, either." She sighed. "Or maybe it's just that everything is so . . . different."

"Well, this isn't Minnesota," Roe chuckled.

"No, it's not, and that's the problem. I guess I'm homesick. Christmas in Minnesota was . . ." Beth's voice trailed off, and her mind followed.

Christmas—in Minnesota.

Where stars glittered over a frozen wonderland. How

well she knew those winter scenes with steepled churches, fence posts, fields and barns. All covered with icy snow, wonderful for sledding and old-fashioned sleigh rides and building igloos and forts and massive snow sculptures and . . .

Christmas—at church.

Where friends whispered seasonal greetings. Where aunts, uncles and giggling young cousins crowded into pews. Where grandparents still sang the old carols in Norwegian.

Christmas—at home.

Where getting a tree meant a trip to the woods on the family farm and a lively debate over the merits of each person's chosen favorite. Where Grandpa's axe always made the first cut and the kids dragged the tree to the car by its trunk. Where sticky sap glued their mittens to the bark.

To her, Christmas was Minnesota. Her childhood was gift-wrapped in those warm memories of tradition, and she had planned on more of the same for her own kids. Until this move changed everything.

Instead, here they were, heading back to a new house in a new neighborhood after participating in a—different— Christmas Eve service with new people in a new church.

"I'm sorry, Roe. Tonight's program really went well. I guess I just missed our traditional sing-a-long, bell choir and candlelight vespers."

"Different places do different things, Beth. You'll get used to it." Roe signaled to change lanes.

"I suppose."

"Truthfully, I think your homesickness is nothing that a good snowfall couldn't cure," Roe teased as he eased the car toward the exit ramp.

"Well, I must admit, when we moved here this autumn and I got my first glimpse of those towering Rocky Mountains, I just assumed snowy winters were a given."

Beth looked at the dark peaks silhouetted against the clear night sky and shivered. "But all this cold weather and not a flake in sight!"

"Only in the upper elevations." Roe pointed to Long's Peak, favored hiking destination of the locals. "There's the nearest snow and plenty of it."

"A lot of good that does!"

"It's probably only a hour's drive to the trailhead. What do you say we head up there tomorrow with the kids and spend Christmas afternoon in the mountains?"

Beth grimaced. Spending part of Christmas Day driving to find snow didn't fit her mood, and it certainly didn't fill the mold of traditional holiday activities.

"It's not the same as shoveling sidewalks or building a snowman in the yard or making an arsenal." She paused. "Remember the snowball fights we used to have?"

Roe and Beth grinned at each other.

"Yeah," Roe said. "In fact, just today I was telling that nice Ben Johnston across the alley how much we'll miss the neighborhood snowball challenges we hosted in Minnesota each Christmas. He got a good chuckle when I told him it was kids against adults—and the adults usually lost."

"That's what I want for Christmas, Roe."

"What?"

"I want to look out the window Christmas morning and see something more than winter-brown grass. I want snow and an old-fashioned snowball fight with friends. Home *means* tradition. Is tradition too much to ask for?"

Slowing, Roe turned down Logan Drive.

"Oh, Beth, I'm sorry this move has been so rough on . . . Well, I'll be!" Roe braked in the middle of the street. "Look!"

Beth gasped. Their lawn—bare and brown only hours before—was covered with several inches of snow. The grass, the walks, the porch and the bushes all sparkled under the streetlight's glow.

"Snow, kids, snow! Wake up and look at our yard!"

Rubbing sleep from their eyes, all three kids tumbled from the car and raced to the glittery powder. Beth and Roe sat spellbound.

"I can't believe my eyes," said Beth. "Snow! SNOW! But . . . it's only in OUR yard. How? And . . . why?"

"Who knows, Hon? But you certainly got your Christmas wish, or part of it, anyway."

Roe pointed down the street. "Well, would you look at that!" Ben Johnston's muddied pickup—loaded with snowblowers and shovels, headlights dimmed—slipped around the corner, leaving a fine trail of white.

"And tomorrow you get the rest." He smiled at his wife. "What do you say we revive an old snowball tradition—with a brand-new neighborhood of friends!"

Carol McAdoo Rehme

The Easter Egg Christmas

Christmas is not a time nor a season, but a state of mind. To cherish peace and goodwill, to be plenteous in mercy, is to have the real spirit of Christmas.

Calvin Coolidge

Easter was just a week away when the radio announcements began. Each day, as the holiday approached, my five-year-old daughter, Ashley, and I would hear updates about the Easter egg hunts coming up at local parks in our area.

With the first mention of the events, Ashley began pleading with me to take her to one of the big egg hunts the coming weekend. I knew in my heart that sometimes events like these could set kids up for disappointment. With so many kids scrambling for only so many eggs, the odds of her not finding any at all were very real. Still, I did not want to be the reason why she might feel let down, so I smiled at her and agreed to take her, all the while hoping that she would be able to find at least one egg.

Saturday came and we drove to the hunt that Ashley had decided would be best. The parking lot was jammed with cars loaded with children. Frustrated by all the chaos, I considered leaving and just going home again when Ashley jumped out of the car with basket in hand, eager to begin hunting. She was not discouraged in the least by the crowds.

After I parked the car, I joined Ashley and as we began walking toward the event area we heard an announcement on the loud speaker. The Easter Bunny had hidden hundreds of eggs early that morning, and each and every one contained a surprise inside. Ashley's eyes lit up as she imagined what treasure she might find inside the special eggs.

I glanced across the field that was roped off for the hunt and was easily able to see several eggs lying out in the open area. To make sure that the hunt was fair for kids of all ages, the field was roped off in sections and each section had an age limit. Ashley signed in and was directed to the proper line for her age group. When the whistle blew and the rope was dropped, the children ran into the field searching quickly for all the eggs they could find. After the hunt was officially over, each child began his journey back across the field.

Disappointment showed on the faces of the children who didn't find any eggs. Huge smiles were on those who did. I searched the crowd for Ashley, growing concerned that she might be in the group of children who didn't find anything. I hoped that her heart had not been broken.

Just then, I spotted her in the distance running toward me with her basket. To my relief, she was smiling. Once she reached me, I counted three eggs lying in her basket. She plopped down on the grass and reached for one, which she quickly twisted open.

The egg contained a certificate for a Happy Meal™

compliments of McDonald's. That made her day right there, regardless of what else might be in the other two eggs. We decided we'd go there for lunch.

The second egg rattled when she shook it. The mystery was quickly solved when several golden tokens to Chuck E. Cheese Pizza Palace fell from the plastic egg. Ashley looked up at me with pleading eyes and asked if we could go there and play for a while after we ate at McDonald's. I agreed as she reached for the last egg.

I didn't think that anything would top what she had found in the first two eggs until we saw it with our own eyes. There, inside egg number three, was a gift certificate to Toys "R" Us for fifty dollars!

Ashley had won the grand prize!

She jumped up and down, thrilled, as I expected she would be. But I had no idea that her happiness wasn't simply because she had won a toy-shopping spree until we got in the car.

"Mommy, can we stop by the mall on the way home?" Ashley asked.

I assumed that she wanted to spend her gift certificate, and I agreed. As I buckled her into her seat, I quizzed her on what toy she had in mind.

"I don't want any toys for me, Mom. I want to buy some toys for an angel," she replied.

"An angel?" I questioned. I couldn't understand what she was talking about. And then I remembered what had happened during the previous holiday season.

Last Christmas, Ashley and I had been doing our Christmas shopping in the mall. We came upon a gigantic tree in the middle of the mall with paper angels hanging from the tree branches. Each angel had the name of a child written on it. Ashley asked me what they were for. I explained that sometimes Santa can't visit every child's house on Christmas Eve, so he sends a list of kids to the Salvation Army. They put the names on angels and hang them on this special tree in the mall. That way, people can help Santa out by giving presents to one of the children whose name is on an angel. The tree is called an Angel Tree.

Ashley just stood there, looking at the tree and all the names hanging there. Distracted with thoughts of completing my Christmas shopping and thinking that I had satisfied her curiosity, I rushed her off so I could finish looking for the items I had on my Christmas list.

Later that night, as Ashley was getting ready for bed, she wanted to know what happens to the angels who no one buys presents for. "Will they get any toys?" she asked.

I explained that the Salvation Army would try and see to it that every child would have a visit from Santa on Christmas. Her concern touched me so much that I suggested we say a special prayer for every kid whose name was on the Angel Tree. So we offered a prayer that all of the Angel Tree children would get presents for Christmas. She closed her eyes and drifted off to sleep.

I had thought that was the end of it, but now, months later, I realized that she had never forgotten about the Angel Tree children. I pulled over to the side of the road and looked into the eyes of this little girl sitting beside me. Though small in size, her compassion for others was huge. I explained to her that the Angel Tree is only in the mall at Christmas and it was now Easter. There would be no Angels to adopt at this time of year.

Ashley sat there in silence for a minute and then she looked at me.

"Mommy, can we save this money until Christmas?" she asked.

"Yes, we can," I answered. "And we will make some girl or boy very happy!"

I looked at the excitement on Ashley's face and realized

that all along I had acted like Christmas was all about buying the right gifts for my family and friends, decorating our home and creating a wonderful Christmas dinner. It had taken my five-year-old daughter to make me realize that it is up to all of us to help the less fortunate, especially at Christmas. Her compassion woke me up to what the true spirit of Christmas is all about. As I pulled back onto the highway, I knew in my heart that I had developed a respect for my daughter that I would carry with me forever.

That next Christmas, Ashley and I went to the mall on the very first day that the Salvation Army put up the big, beautiful Angel Tree. We quickly picked out *two* Angels, one for Ashley and one for me, and with smiles on our faces we set off for an extra-special shopping trip.

That early December day, we began a Christmas tradition that all started because of an extraordinary Easter egg hunt and a little girl with a very big heart.

Denise Peebles

[EDITORS' NOTE: *Ashley is now seventeen years old and has been actively involved in the Salvation Army Angel Tree Project each year, wrapping and distributing gifts to children. In many cases, the Angel gifts are the only Christmas presents these children receive. To become involved in the Angel Tree Project in your area, call your local branch of the Salvation Army or go to* www.salvationarmyusa.org.]

The Twelve (Silly) Days of Christmas

On the first day of Christmas
My mother gave to me
A toothbrush I didn't really need.

On the second day of Christmas
My mother gave to me
Two pairs of new socks
And a toothbrush I didn't really need.

On the third day of Christmas
My mother gave to me
Three hairbrushes
(I guess my hair was messy)
Two pairs of new socks
And a toothbrush I didn't really need.

On the fourth day of Christmas
My mother gave to me
Four Canadian coins
(Which, as it turns out, are pretty useless 'cause
   I don't live in Canada)
Three hairbrushes
Two pairs of new socks

And a toothbrush I didn't really need.
On the fifth day of Christmas
My mother gave to me
Five Barbie rings
(They're really tiny, and I'm way too old for Barbie)
Four Canadian coins
Three hairbrushes
Two pairs of new socks
And a toothbrush I didn't really need.

On the sixth day of Christmas
My mother gave to me
Six comic books
Five Barbie rings
Four Canadian coins
Three hairbrushes
Two pairs of new socks
And a toothbrush I didn't really need.

On the seventh day of Christmas
My mother gave to me
Seven "days of the week" undies
(I hope no one from school ever sees these)
Six comic books
Five Barbie rings
Four Canadian coins
Two pairs of new socks
And a toothbrush I didn't really need.

On the eighth day of Christmas
My mother gave to me
Eight electronic games
(Enough to drive her crazy)
Seven "days of the week" undies
Six comic books
Five Barbie rings

Four Canadian coins
Three hairbrushes
Two pairs of new socks
And a toothbrush I didn't really need.

On the ninth day of Christmas
My mother gave to me
Nine candy kisses
(I really like this gift, I think I'll give
    her one of my Barbie rings)
Eight electronic games
Seven "days of the week" undies
Six comic books
Five Barbie rings
Four Canadian coins
Three hairbrushes
Two pairs of new socks
And a toothbrush I didn't really need.

On the tenth day of Christmas
My mother gave to me
Ten blue flyswatters
(My mom's losing it; what happened to the
    candy kisses?)
Nine candy kisses
Eight electronic games
Seven "days of the week" undies
Six comic books
Five Barbie rings
Four Canadian coins
Three hairbrushes
Two pairs of new socks
And a toothbrush I didn't really need.

On the eleventh day of Christmas
My mother gave to me

Eleven novelty ice-cube trays
(Now I know she's really lost it)
Ten blue flyswatters
Nine candy kisses
Eight electronic games
Seven "days of the week" undies
Six comic books
Five Barbie rings
Four Canadian coins
Three hairbrushes
Two pairs of new socks
And a toothbrush I didn't really need.

On the twelfth day of Christmas
My mother gave to me
Twelve Snoopy Band-Aids
(I scratched myself trying to get
    the ice out of the novelty ice trays—
    how did she know I would need these?)
Eleven novelty ice trays
Ten blue flyswatters
Nine candy kisses
Eight electronic games
Seven "days of the week" undies
Six comic books
Five Barbie rings
Four Canadian coins
Three hairbrushes
Two pairs of new socks
And a toothbrush I didn't really need.

Kristina Richardson

5

BOUGHS, HOLLY AND MISTLE . . . ANEOUS

When the song of the angels is stilled,
when the star in the sky is gone.
When the kings and princess are home,
when the shepherds are back with their
flock. The work of Christmas begins:
to find the lost, to heal the broken,
to feed the hungry, to release the prisoner,
to rebuild the nations, to bring peace
among brothers, to make music in the heart.

Howard Thurman

Chocolate-Covered Cherries

[EDITORS' NOTE: *This Christmas letter was sent to friends and family along with a box of chocolate-covered cherries.*]

What a terrible way to spend Christmas! My oldest son, Cameron, had been diagnosed with acute myleoblastic leukemia on June 30, 1997. After a harrowing ride in a military helicopter to Walter Reed Hospital, three rounds of horrendous chemotherapy, an excruciating lung resection and a disappointing bone marrow search, now here we were . . . at Duke University Hospital. Cameron had a cord blood transplant, a last-ditch effort to save his life, on December 4. Now, here it was . . . Christmas Eve.

A very small room on ward 9200 was a different place to spend Christmas. We had always spent weeks baking cookies. Now the cookies were sent from family and friends because I wanted to spend my time with Cameron, trying to ease the long, tedious hours. He had been in isolation for weeks because he had no immune system, the result of even more chemotherapy and drugs that would hopefully make his new bone marrow engraft. As some presents had arrived in the mail, we had opened them immediately . . . anything to make a bright moment . . . here or there.

Christmas Eve, 6:00 P.M., was always the magic hour. The time when my family, in Iowa . . . Wisconsin . . . California . . . or Washington, D.C. . . . all opened our presents at the same time, somehow bringing the family together, even though apart. Cameron's father, stepmother, sister and brother would also be opening presents at their house in Fayetteville, North Carolina. This Christmas, it would just be Cameron and me in the small room with few decorations, since they weren't allowed in the sterile environment.

With the drone of the HEPA filter and the beeping of his six infusion pumps hooked to a catheter in his heart, Cameron waited until 6:00 P.M. exactly. He insisted we follow this small tradition, some semblance of normalcy abandoned six months earlier. I gave him a few presents I had saved, his favorite being a Hug Me Elmo that said "I love you" when you squeezed him. It was over too quickly. Christmas was over. Or so I thought.

Cameron carefully reached over the side of his hospital bed and handed me a small green box. It was wrapped beautifully, obviously by a gift store—perfect edges, a folded piece of ribbon held down with a gold embossed sticker. Surprised, I said, "For me?"

"Of course. It wouldn't be Christmas unless you had something to unwrap from me," he replied.

I was almost speechless. "But how did you get this? Did you ask a nurse to run down to the gift store?"

Cameron leaned back in his bed, and gave me this most devilish smile. "Nope. Yesterday, when you went home for a few hours to take a shower, I sneaked downstairs."

"Cameron! You aren't supposed to leave the floor. You know you are neutropenic. They let you leave the ward?"

"Nope!" His smile was even bigger now. "They weren't looking. I just walked out."

This was no small feat, because Cameron had grown weaker after the cord blood transplant. He could barely walk, and certainly not unassisted. It took every ounce of strength just to cruise the small ward halls, pushing the heavy medication and pain pump IV pole. How could he possibly have made it nine floors to the gift store? "Don't worry, Mom. I wore my mask, and I used the cane. Man, they gave me hell when I got back. I didn't get to sneak back in; they had been looking for me."

I held the box even tighter now. I couldn't look up. I had already started to cry. "Open it! It's not much, but it wouldn't be Christmas if you didn't have something from me to open."

I opened the box of gift-store-wrapped chocolate-covered cherries. "They are your favorite, right?" he asked hopefully.

I finally looked at my poor eighteen-year-old baby, who had begun all this suffering so soon after high school graduation and who taught me so much about what being a family really meant. "Oh . . . absolutely my favorite!"

Cameron chuckled a little bit. "See, we still have our traditions, even in here."

"Cameron, this is the best present I've ever received, *ever*," I told him, and I meant every word. "Let's start a new tradition. Every Christmas, let's only give each other a box of chocolate-covered cherries, and we'll reminisce about how we spent Christmas 1997 at Duke University Hospital, battling leukemia, and we'll remember how horrible all of it was and how glad we are that it is finally over." And we made that pact right then and there, sharing the box of chocolate-covered cherries. What a wonderful way to spend Christmas!

Cameron died on March 4, 1998, after two unsuccessful cord blood transplants. He was so brave—never giving in, never giving up. This will be my first Christmas without him. The first Christmas without something from him to unwrap.

This is my gift to you. A box of chocolate-covered cherries, and when you open it I hope it will remind you what the holidays are really about: being with your friends and family, recreating traditions, maybe starting some new ones, but most of all, love.

What a beautiful way to spend Christmas.

Dawn Holt

Gold, Common Sense and Fur

My husband and I had been happily (most of the time) married for five years but hadn't been blessed with a baby. I decided to do some serious praying and promised God that if he would give us a child, I would be a perfect mother, love it with all my heart and raise it with his word as my guide.

God answered my prayers and blessed us with a son. The next year God blessed us with another son. The following year, he blessed us with yet another son. The year after that we were blessed with a daughter.

My husband thought we'd been blessed right into poverty. We now had four children, and the oldest was only four years old.

I learned never to ask God for anything unless I meant it. As a minister once told me, "If you pray for rain, make sure you carry an umbrella."

I began reading a few verses of the Bible to the children each day as they lay in their cribs. I was off to a good start. God had entrusted me with four children and I didn't want to disappoint him.

I tried to be patient the day the children smashed two dozen eggs on the kitchen floor searching for baby chicks.

I tried to be understanding when they started a hotel for homeless frogs in the spare bedroom, although it took me nearly two hours to catch all twenty-three frogs.

When my daughter poured ketchup all over herself and rolled up in a blanket to see how it felt to be a hot dog, I tried to see the humor rather than the mess.

In spite of changing over twenty-five thousand diapers, never eating a hot meal and never sleeping for more than thirty minutes at a time, I still thank God daily for my children.

While I couldn't keep my promise to be a perfect mother—I didn't even come close—I did keep my promise to raise them in the Word of God.

I knew I was missing the mark just a little when I told my daughter we were going to church to worship God, and she wanted to bring a bar of soap along to "wash up" Jesus, too.

Something was lost in the translation when I explained that God gave us everlasting life, and my son thought it was generous of God to give us his "last wife."

My proudest moment came during the children's Christmas pageant. My daughter was playing Mary, two of my sons were shepherds and my youngest son was a wise man. This was their moment to shine.

My five-year-old shepherd had practiced his line, "We found the babe wrapped in swaddling clothes." But he was nervous and said, "The baby was wrapped in wrinkled clothes."

My four-year-old "Mary" said, "That's not 'wrinkled clothes,' silly. That's dirty, rotten clothes."

A wrestling match broke out between Mary and the shepherd and was stopped by an angel, who bent her halo and lost her left wing.

I slouched a little lower in my seat when Mary dropped the doll representing Baby Jesus, and it bounced down the aisle crying, "Mama-mama." Mary grabbed the doll, wrapped it back up and held it tightly as the wise men arrived.

My other son stepped forward wearing a bathrobe and a paper crown, knelt at the manger and announced, "We are the three wise men, and we are bringing gifts of gold, common sense and fur."

The congregation dissolved into laughter, and the pageant got a standing ovation.

"I've never enjoyed a Christmas program as much as this one," Father Brian laughed, wiping tears from his eyes. "For the rest of my life, I'll never hear the Christmas story without thinking of gold, common sense and fur."

"My children are my pride and my joy and my greatest blessing," I said as I dug through my purse for an aspirin.

Linda Stafford

A Letter to Santa

My five-year-old scribbled out his Christmas list. It's there by the fireplace. The Coke and chocolates are from him, in case you're hungry. You know five-year-olds these days. The Cheez-Its are from me.

Santa, if you don't mind, I thought I'd go ahead and leave my list, too. It's long, but do what you can.

It's all I want for Christmas.

- Santa, let my little boy grow up still believing that he has the funniest dad in the neighborhood.
- Give him many close friends, both boys and girls. May they fill his days with adventure, security and dirty fingernails.
- Leave his mom and me some magic dust that will keep him just the size he is now. We'd just as soon he stayed five years old and three feet, four inches tall.
- If he must grow up, Santa, make sure he still wants to sit on my lap at bedtime and read *Frog & Toad* together.
- If you can help it, Santa, never let him be sent into war. His mother and I love our country, but we love our five-year-old boy more.

- While you're at it, give our world leaders a copy of *The Killer Angels,* Michael Shara's retelling of the Battle of Gettysburg. May it remind them that too many moms and dads have wept at Christmas for soldiers who died in battles that needn't have been fought.
- Let our house always be filled with slamming doors and toilet seats, which are the official sounds of little boys.
- Break it to him gently, Santa, that his dad won't always be able to carry him to bed at night or brush his teeth for him. Teach him courage in the face of such change.
- Let him understand that no matter how nice you are to everyone, the world will sometimes break your heart. As you know, Santa, child's feelings are as fragile as moth wings.
- Let him become a piano player, a soccer star or a clergyman. Or all three. Anything but a politician.
- Give him a hunger for books, music and geography. May he be the first kid in kindergarten to be able to find Madagascar on a map.
- The kid's a born artist, Santa, so send more crayons. May our kitchen window and refrigerator doors be ever plastered with his sketches of surreal rainbows and horses with big ears.
- Steer him oh-so-carefully to that little girl destined to be his bride. Let his mother and me still be around when he walks her down the aisle. If there is a just God, let her daddy be obscenely rich.
- Grant him a heart that will cherish what his parents did right, and forgive us for the mistakes we surely will have made over a lifetime of raising him.
- Let him not hold it against us that he was born with my chin and his mother's ears. Time will teach him that these are God's ways of girding him for life's adversities.

• Hold him steady on the day that he learns the truth about you and the Easter Bunny. May he take the news better than I did.
• While you're flying around the heavens, Santa, make sure God has heard our prayer for this child: Lead our little boy not into temptation; deliver him from evil.

Be careful out there, Santa. And close the flue on your way up.

David V. Chartrand

I'm Dreaming of a
Normal Christmas

It's not often that us urbanites get the opportunity to journey back to those glorious days when nature reigned supreme and every moment was a test of one's mettle.

That's why December is such a time of rejuvenation. It's the one month of the year when we must once again draw upon our innermost strengths and venture forth into the wilds of . . . the Christmas tree farm.

Yes, armed only with a pair of Armani gloves and a checkbook, we stand at the edge of that carefully coifed forest, scanning the unfamiliar terrain with but one goal—to find the perfect conifer.

And no easy task is that. For strategically interwoven amongst nature's flawless creations are a number of trees that look just like the others—until you get them home. That's when the urbanite family, who doesn't understand the complexities of Mother Nature, sometimes questions the final choice.

Family: It leans.

Me: I know.

Family: And it's missing branches.

Me: I know.

Family: The Norvilles' tree doesn't lean. They always have a perfect tree.

Me: I know!

This year was different. For just as the village leaders learned to refine their techniques in order to become better hunters, I, too, had grown wiser and more cunning. . . .

Norvilles: Ernie? Is that you?

Me: What a coincidence. Here to get a tree?

I waved nonchalantly as they wandered off, pretending my intentions lay elsewhere. Then I doubled back and stealthily began my mission, crawling from tree to tree, practically invisible to all but the trained eye.

Tree Farm Manager: Ah, can I help you?

I knew my clandestine operation was beyond the scope of his young, urbanite mind, so I grabbed a stick and drew my plan in the dirt. I sketched the entire Norville family pointing at a tree, and then added myself swinging in on a rope claiming the prize for myself. He nodded several times, then spoke.

Tree Farm Manager: Please don't use any of the sharp saws yourself. Ask one of the workers for help.

Then he left. Quickly, I erased my plan and dashed ahead to catch up with my quarry. I circled left, then right, then left again, but the Norvilles were nowhere to be found. I panicked and began crashing through the evergreens, squeezing by parents, leaping over pets, sending startled workers scurrying. At one point, I almost tipped over a hay wagon full of gleeful, urbanite children. But still no Norvilles.

I stopped to reassess. That's when I felt a hand on my shoulder.

Tree Farm Manager: Look, I've never dealt with Prozac overdose before. Is there someone I can call? Your psychiatrist, maybe?

Me: You don't understand. I need a tree.

Tree Farm Manager: Yes. Well, maybe they have a tree at the home. Maybe they'll be so glad to have you back they'll let you help decorate it. Although I doubt it.

I caught a glint of sunlight on metal. There they were. The Norvilles. Loading a tree into their van. I wiggled out of the grasp of the manager and ran toward them.

Me: Wait. That's my tree.

Norvilles: This tree?

Me: Yes. I left to get a saw. And when I returned it was gone.

Norvilles: Are you sure it was this tree?

Me: Yes. I must have it. Here's fifty dollars.

Norvilles: But we only paid twenty.

I felt impending danger, as I noticed the manager talking on a cell phone.

Me: Please.

Reluctantly, the Norvilles took the tree from their van and tied it on my roof. I gave them the fifty bucks and sped away.

Hours later, back in the safety of my urban surroundings, I elevated my prize, awaiting the accolades of approval.

Family: It leans.

Me: What?

Family: And it's missing branches.

Me: That can't be.

Quickly, I grabbed the phone and called the Norvilles.

Norvilles: It was for Tommy's school play—"Charlie Brown's Christmas Tree." In the play, they learn to love it. Hope you can.

I thought briefly of Christmases past and future, then I picked up the box of extra large ornaments and slowly began filling the holes.

Ernie Witham

Martha's Christmas Wonderland

The Christmas season is one of my favorite times of year. I always thought I did a pretty good job of celebrating it by putting up lots of holiday decorations throughout the house—but that was before I met my friend Martha. I was amazed at how she magically transformed their entire home into a Christmas extravaganza. I had no idea you could put so many garlands and ornaments and lights on a tree and still have it look good, let alone stand up. Everyone marvelled at the wonderland she created.

One day Martha told our friend Maureen the reason she went to such lengths to celebrate Christmas. She said it was because she had never really had much of one when she was growing up. In fact, she said her family had never even had a Christmas tree.

Maureen was deeply moved by Martha's missing out on this childhood experience. She reached over, touched her lightly on the arm and said, "Oh, Martha, were you poor?"

Martha looked at her in a puzzled sort of way, then said, "No! . . . We were Jewish!"

Nancy Mueller

Sugarplums

'Twas the night before Christmas and all through the street
Not a creature was sleeping, my body was beat;
The stockings were taped to the chimney quite snug,
In hopes that my kids wouldn't give them a tug;

My daughter was jumping on top of my bed,
While visions of broken things danced in my head;
And Mamma getting ready, and I with a comb,
Were almost prepared to drive to my folks' home,

When somewhere downstairs there arose such a clatter,
I sprang from my room to see what was the matter.
Away to the stairs I flew like an ace,
Tripped over the Legos and fell on my face.

The bruise on my head and my pain-swelling side,
Gave a luster of midnight to objects inside,
When, what to my crestfallen eyes should appear,
But my rambunctious son, with a face full of tears,

With a little hors d'oeuvre plate, so empty and bare,
I knew in a moment he dropped it downstairs.
More rapid than squirrels my anger it came,
and I whistled, and shouted and called them by name;

"You dropped fruit! Rocky road! The truffles! And sweets!
The tea cakes! The crackers! What will Uncle Dutch eat?!
To the top of the stairs! To the rooms down the hall!
Now sweep it up! Sweep it up! Sweep it up, all!"

As mad dogs that before the wild tornado fly,
When they meet with their parent-folk, fit to be tied,
So out to the auto my family we flew,
With an armful of gifts and the damaged treats, too.

And then, in a flurry, we arrived at my folks'
Their puppy was barking, my kids gave it pokes
As I fell in a chair and was spinning around,
Down the hallway my mom and dad came with a bound.

Mom was dressed all in red, from her feet to her yoke,
And her clothes were all blemished with Jell-O and smoke;
A trayful of food she had spilled on her lace,
And she looked like a toddler just feeding her face.

My dad—how he hugged us! His laughing how jolly!
My kids jumped on his back, and called him a trolley!
My tight little mouth was drawn up like a bow,
And I shot words off my lips like darts at a foe;

"Children be careful, Papa's back is quite bad!
If he throws a spinal disk, you'll make Grandma mad!"
The plates were set and the dinner was ready
My son gave the prayer that included his teddy,

The room was jammed with people, tables and chairs,
My nephew threw stuffing into his dad's hairs;
A flash of Gram's eyes and a shake of her head,
Soon gave him to know he had something to dread;

We spoke many words and went straight to our meals,
And ate all the fixings despite how we'd feel,
Then sometime around twelve we expressed our last joys,
And returned back home to assemble the toys.

We placed the last gifts, and I gave a tired yawn,
I made a silent prayer, to sleep hopefully past dawn.
But my son did exclaim, as I walked past his door,
"Happy Christmas, dear Dad, I'll wake you 'round four."

Ken Swarner

The Aroma of Christmas

Sometimes I tried to recall the first Christmas. Most of it was a blank. The fragment I could remember included forced laughter, fake smiles and trying desperately to have a good time.

Christmas had come right on schedule, only three months after my husband's untimely death. There were no tears or discussion of his absence, only empty festivities. Occasionally I'm glad I don't remember more. Widow's shock, someone had called it, and they told me I would heal.

Twelve months later that healing was evidenced by the excitement welling up within me as I prepared for a grand and glorious holiday. The kids were coming! Two daughters, a son-in-law and two grandchildren had all agreed to spend Christmas at my home.

I decorated everything I could reach. Glass balls of many colors hung from the leaves of the rubber plant in the entryway and tinsel icicles waved lazily to and fro from branches of the weeping fig tree. Christmas cassettes filled the air with "Joy to the World" and "O Little Town of Bethlehem."

Poinsettias, holly and mistletoe decorated bedrooms, the

living room and over the bathtub. Even the dog diligently guarded the gingerbread boys hanging on the Christmas tree and growled each time the cat walked near. The aroma of Christmas was the best part because it deliciously replaced the aroma of death that had hung heavily in my home for so long. Spicy snickerdoodles and chewy lemon sugar cookies produced a spirit-lifting, pungent fragrance.

Sticky cinnamon rolls, butter-filled bread twists and golden-brown pumpkin pies found their way out of the busy kitchen of spicy holiday scents and into the freezer to await a celebration of our savior's birthday and a reunion of family and friends.

The aroma of Christmas was free to soar to the rafters, unhampered this year by an estate to settle, a business to close down, and clothes and tools to dispose of. This year, I could hardly wait to have the family gather for Christmas in my home.

But at 7:00 A.M. three days before Christmas, the first telephone call came. "Mom, I hope you'll understand. The weather here is below zero, and I've been up all night with freezing, bursting water pipes. There's no way I can leave this mobile home to the elements and come for Christmas. Are you going to be okay with that?"

"Of course!" I knew the weather in Portland had been record-breaking cold, and Jeri's mobile home was old and not well insulated. Jeri was still single, and to go off and leave could cost her so much in storm-damage repairs. "We'll have Christmas later," I told her. "You take care of that home."

The second call came only twenty minutes later. "Mom, with the windchill factor, it's forty-five below. We can't leave the sheep and the water pipes to come home for Christmas. Is there any way you can come here?"

"I don't see how I can get away, honey. That's all right. You and Gregg and the kids have a good Christmas, and I'll put your packages on the bus to you."

As I hung up, I felt very, very alone. I lived only 135 miles away from this daughter and my only grandchildren, but I couldn't go there for Christmas because I was committed to some people here in town.

I had invited my brother-in-law, who was a widower, and his eighty-four-year-old mother to come for Christmas dinner, and a young man from the singles group at church had already accepted, too. *I sure wouldn't have invited them if I had known my family wasn't going to be here,* I thought.

And I had told the old man across the street that I would bring him a plate of dinner at two o'clock on Christmas Day. He was a blunt old codger in his eighties. He always smelled like stale cigars and had brown goo running down his chin, matting his unkempt beard. I hadn't wanted to invite him over, so I offered to bring his dinner to him. "Me and Tish [his dog] don't need anything," he had told me. But it soothed my conscience to promise him dinner.

And I had invited a single lady friend with an eight-year-old boy to spend Christmas Eve with me and my family. And now my family wouldn't be here.

"Why, Lord?" I protested aloud. "Why can't I be with my family on Christmas? You knew they weren't going to be able to come; why didn't you stop me from becoming committed to all these others?"

The widow next door had come home from the hospital recently, and her family had left to have Christmas out of town because I had promised to check on her, get her mail and feed the dog. *Boy, am I stuck here!*

I would miss seeing my grandchildren open their beautiful packages and hearing their gleeful cries. And my daughter wanted a food dehydrator so badly. "Lord, you know I got her one; why don't I get to see her open the box and hear her squeal? Lord, it's Christmas!"

Unexpectedly an awesome humility silenced my

complaining heart. Without utterance or movement, the Lord began to answer me: "I know it's Christmas, Barbara; it's my birthday. What did you get me?"

"What do you mean, what did I get you, Lord?"

"Whose birthday is it?" he insisted. "What did you get me?"

It was at that moment that the expensive gifts around the Christmas tree didn't seem to matter anymore.

"What shall I get you, Lord?" There was only silence. "Could I start by inviting more folks to your birthday party? Perhaps I could take care of my neighbor lady a bit more willingly? I could even invite the old guy from across the street to bring his dog and sit down to the dinner table with us."

My heart began to flutter with anticipation. "There's that man from the gospel mission who I fired last summer while he was trimming my trees because I didn't like his attitude." I began to laugh. "Wouldn't it blow his mind if I called and invited him to dinner?

"And the checker from the grocery store who shoveled my driveway out the last time it snowed—he's alone now and will probably eat in a restaurant."

My joy soared! *What a menagerie of misplaced mortals, an ingenious assembly of aristocrats and renegades!*

The list began to grow as I telephoned people who would be alone for Christmas. Soon my table was filled, but not as full as my heart.

The old man across the street could hardly talk, he was so choked with emotion when I invited him to come over and join the crowd for dinner.

"Oh, come all ye faithful," I sang at the top of my lungs. "Come, even if you're not faithful! Y'all come!" And I punched down the last of the bread dough.

I do not remember ever having so much fun preparing Christmas dinner as the day I gave my Christmas to Jesus as a birthday gift. The aroma of the holiday filled my home as I'd planned. And the meaning of Christmas penetrated my heart in a way I'd not anticipated.

Never have I received such a precious gift as when I watched the man from the gospel mission fill his plate five times, and I sensed the Lord's nod of approval.

"Alone at Christmas? Never! It's Jesus' birthday, and I'm having a party. You want to come?"

Barbara Baumgardner

Charity's Gift

Every Christmas we hear a poem, *The Night Before Christmas*, but not many of us know that it was a special gift for a special child. During the fall of 1822, Dr. Clement Clarke Moore learned that his six-year-old daughter, Charity, might not recover from tuberculosis.

Charity knew that she was very ill. She said, "Father, please make a special present for me at Christmas."

He said, "Of course, but what would you like?"

She sighed. "I don't know. I am too tired to pick up toys. Maybe a story."

Dr. Moore turned and stared out the window so Charity could not see the tear in his eye. A verse came to him as he watched the wind whip up the fallen leaves.

> *As dry leaves that before the wild hurricane fly,*
> *When they meet with an obstacle, mount to the sky,*
> *So up to the house-top the coursers they flew,*
> *With the sleigh full of toys, and St. Nicholas too.*

He felt better because he knew that Charity's gift would be a poem—a very special poem.

Dr. Moore taught Bible studies, Greek and Hebrew at Columbia University in New York. Even so, he had a hard time finding just the right words for Charity's poem. Sometimes he thought she felt a little better, but most of the time she seemed to get weaker.

He became so busy thinking about the poem and worrying about Charity that he forgot to buy the goose for Christmas dinner. He knew how disappointed everyone would be if they did not have a Christmas goose so he put on his overcoat and hitched up his courser (or team) of horses.

In his poem, Moore hitched up a "courser of eight tiny reindeer" to Santa's sleigh because horses cannot easily travel over snow. The stars danced brightly and the moon gleamed full against the dark sky. Dr. Moore gazed on the sparkling Hudson River. In the deep quiet he added more lines to Charity's poem.

The moon on the breast of the new-fallen snow
which gave the lustre of mid-day to objects below.

Moore had learned about the Dutch Christmas traditions from his friend Washington Irving who had written *A History of New York* in 1809. Most of the people in his book were Dutch pioneers, who believed in a special magic. If a Dutchman wanted to go through keyholes or down a chimney he would just put his finger on his nose.

He spoke not a word but went straight to his work,
And filled all the stockings; then turned with a jerk,
And laying his finger aside of his nose
And giving a nod, up the chimney he rose;

In Holland on December 5, Sinter Klaas, Black Peter, and eight goats travel on a boat along the canals. At each town Sinter Klaas gives oranges to nice Dutch children, while Black Peter leaves lumps of coal or paddles in naughty children's shoes. Moore took his reindeer names from Sinter Klaas's goats.

> *Now, Dasher! Now, Dancer! Now Prancer and Vixen!*
> *On Comet! On Cupid, on Donder and Blitzen!*
> *To the top of the porch! To the top of the wall!*
> *Now dash away! Dash away! Dash away all!*

From Moore's childhood home in Manhattan came his memory of Jan Duyckinck, "chubby and plump, a right jolly old elf." The bearded Dutchman, who worked for Moore's father, smoked a "stump of a pipe." Pulling a sleigh full of wood, he often gave poor children wood so that they would not be cold.

Most people had only one pair of stockings that they washed out at night and hung "by the chimney with care." Moore did not want his children to wish for too much at Christmas so they hung up only one stocking. Poor children got prunes, also known as sugar plums, as a special treat.

> *The children were nestled all snug in their beds*
> *While visions of sugar plums danced in their heads;*

Everyone wore warm nightclothes during the cold winter. Their clothes gave him new words.

> *Mamma in her 'kerchief, and I in my cap,*
> *had just settled down for a long winter's nap.*

Although "more rapid than eagles his coursers they came," the problem of Santa delivering gifts around the world in one night has always been a real nuisance. Santa starts his journey at the East Coast, and by moving west, he keeps gaining time.

Just in time for Christmas Eve in 1822, Moore had all his words put together in his head, not on paper. The whole family gathered around Charity's bed. Moore took her hands in his. He felt nervous while he recited his poem. Would she like his poem? Would she rather have a real toy?

An Account of a Visit by St. Nicholas

'Twas the night before Christmas when all through the house
Not a creature was stirring, not even a mouse;
The stockings were hung by the chimney with care
In hopes that St. Nicholas soon would be there.

The children were nestled all snug in their beds
While visions of sugar plums danced in their heads;
And mamma in her 'kerchief, and I in my cap,
Had just settled down for a long winter's nap,

When out on the lawn there arose such a clatter
I sprang from the bed to see what was the matter.
Away to the window I flew like a flash,
Tore open the shutters and threw up the sash.

The moon on the breast of the new-fallen snow
Gave the lustre of mid-day to objects below,
When what to my wondering eyes should appear
But a miniature sleigh and eight tiny reindeer,

With a little old driver so lively and quick,
I knew in a moment it must be St. Nick.
More rapid than eagles his coursers they came,
And he whistled, and shouted and called them by name;

"Now, Dasher! Now, Dancer! Now Prancer and Vixen!
On, Comet! On Cupid! On Donder and Blitzen!
To the top of the porch! To the top of the wall!
Now dash away! Dash away! Dash away all."

As dry leaves that before the wild hurricane fly,
When they meet with an obstacle, mount to the sky,
So up to the house-top the coursers they flew,
With the sleigh full of toys, and St. Nicholas too.

And then, in a twinkling, I heard on the roof
The prancing and pawing of each little hoof,
As I drew in my hand, and was turning around
Down the chimney St. Nicholas came with a bound.

He was dressed all in fur, from his head to his foot,
And his clothes were all tarnished with ashes and soot;
A bundle of toys he had flung on his back,
And he looked like a peddler just opening his pack.

His eyes—how they twinkled! His dimples how merry!
His cheeks were like roses, his nose like a cherry!
His droll little mouth was drawn up like a bow,
And the beard of his chin was as white as the snow.

The stump of a pipe he held tight in his teeth
And the smoke it encircled his head like a wreath;
He had a broad face and a little round belly,
That shook, when he laughed like a bowlful of jelly.

He was chubby and plump, a right jolly old elf,
And I laughed when I saw him, in spite of myself
A wink of his eye and a twist of his head,
Soon gave me to know I had nothing to dread.

He spoke not a word but went straight to his work,
And filled all the stockings; then turned with a jerk,
And laying his finger aside of his nose
And giving a nod, up the chimney he rose.

He sprang to his sleigh, to his team gave a whistle,
And away they all flew like the down of a thistle.
But I heard him exclaim, ere he drove out of sight,
"HAPPY CHRISTMAS TO ALL, AND TO ALL A GOOD-NIGHT!"

When he finished Charity smiled and said, "Thank you, Papa. It is perfect." Then she fell asleep. From that day forward she got stronger and recovered from tuberculosis.

Dr. Moore never intended to publish the poem, but a relative sent it, without his knowledge, to the *New York Troy Sentinel.* The newspaper published "An Account of a Visit by St. Nicholas" on December 23, 1823. It became an instant hit with its special American Santa Claus.

Jane Eppinga

Bringing Christmas

Some of life's events make permanent etchings on your soul.

Like the Christmas our family spent volunteering with the people of Santisimo Sacramento. Situated in the heart of Piura, Peru, this church was the lifeblood of the thirty-three thousand citizens it served. We spent long, hot days sorting and distributing clothes, tearing down and rebuilding a house, fixing donated bikes and becoming part of the community.

I don't even have to close my eyes to remember endless sand dotted with scraggly trees, the truck's horn competing with mangy, barking dogs, the smell of heat and sweat, and the gritty taste of dirt roads. And the children. Hundreds of big-eyed, bronze-skinned, dark-haired children chasing after us with the hope of youth.

Several times a day, bouncing along sand and gravel, we all struggled to hold on to the sides of the white pickup truck, laughing so hard that our smiles petrified above our wind-dried teeth. Ginet, our driver, laid on the horn with the jubilation of Robin Hood delivering goods to the poor, while villagers ran from all corners of the surrounding pueblos.

Our three children—Clare, Bridget and Michael—helped prepare barrels of chocolate milk and hundreds of buttered rolls for distribution in the villages and the prison.

One afternoon, we pulled up to a small, dusty church, skirted the ever-present dogs and rearranged rickety wooden benches on the cement floor. One hundred fifty children sat patiently, each with a cup brought from home, to receive the coveted treat. Mothers remained in the doorway, watching as their children participated in prayer and songs before they were served chocolate milk and a buttered roll.

Finally, each child received a token toy. In less than twenty minutes, their Christmas had come . . . and gone.

We trucked through the pueblo, distributing more toys. One tiny girl ran after us for a good two hundred yards. When she finally reached the driver's side door, she was ecstatic to receive a small toy. As we drove on, an older girl grabbed the gift and left her sobbing among the crowd.

Distressed, at the next stop we explained what had happened and asked Ginet to drive back and search the village. At last, Clare and Bridget spotted the child outside her shack, still crying. When we replaced the toy, her smile was jubilant.

Naturally, questions haunted us during our stay:

How should we handle Christmas with our own children?

Would they expect gifts on Christmas morning?

Surrounded by such poverty, could we justify our giving and receiving?

As Steve and I pondered the situation and faced our choices, we couldn't help making comparisons between these different cultural traditions.

We saw Christmas in Peru celebrated so simply—with *Las Posadas* to commemorate the journey of Mary and

Joseph, bonfires, *panettone* (Italian bread) and *leche de choco-late* (hot cocoa). There were no Christmas trees, no gifts exchanged and no Santa Claus. The *only* reason for the season was the Holy Family and Christ's birth. The focus was clearly on people, relationships and doing for others.

What greater gift could we give our own children?

In the end, we presented each with a tiny finger harp from Kenya and a small token from Santa. As a family, we spent Christmas morning writing down what we hoped for each other. Those scraps of paper and their thoughtful words remain priceless to this day, and our children still revel in the memory of that humble celebration.

We had gone to volunteer and bring Christmas to the poor. Instead, the villagers of Piura brought a richer, deeper sense of Christmas to *us*—Christmas without the trappings.

Toby Abraham-Rhine

A Hush in the Rush

I always began December with Big Plans: baking ten kinds of cookies, decorating the house creatively and entertaining lavishly.

One bright morning in early December, while butter softened for the press cookies and yeast grew in sugar and water, the telephone rang. My recently widowed friend needed to talk. An hour passed. The butter melted; the yeast spilled over the bowl. And the clock was ticking. We chatted a bit longer, and her mood lightened as we made plans to meet.

A voice inside reminded me, *Christmas is, after all, about generosity.*

Our lunch the next day lasted longer than I anticipated, and snail-paced traffic slowed my trip home. When a car cut into my lane, a flash of anger almost kept me from seeing the old man waiting to cross the street. I braked to a stop and motioned him on.

Patience, whispered the inner voice, *allow time for kindness.*

While I rushed to wash my front windows before decorating them, an elderly neighbor threw a sweater over her shoulders and came over to pass the time. It got lonely, she confided, with her son and his wife at work all day. Reluctantly, I set aside the spray cleaner and the rags.

"Would you like to come in for a cup of tea?" I heard myself asking.

Ah, I heard the voice say, *you're getting the idea.*

Armed with a lengthy master list, I hurried off on the grim task of shopping. After an exhausting battle with crowds in overheated stores, I emerged triumphant and smug. Outside the mall, bell ringers shivered in the blowing snow, and I felt compelled to pull out my last bill for their plump kettle.

"Thank you, ma'am! Merry Christmas!"

I see you're learning sacrifice, too, the voice praised.

Later in the week, my daughter called long-distance, desperate for a heart-to-heart talk. I glanced at the unwrapped presents strewn across the floor. I looked at my watch. And back at the piles. Then I remembered the loneliness and isolation and frustration of young motherhood—and settled in the overstuffed chair for a long, leisurely chat.

"Check back with me again this afternoon," I said, "so I'll know how you're getting along." I tossed another look at the presents and shrugged.

The gift of your time, I heard, *is the best gift of all.*

The Sunday before Christmas, our still-bare tree leaned against one corner of the living room.

"We should've bought a new tree stand. The tree is top heavy, and this one won't hold it," my husband groaned. Ignored in my holiday rush, he looked tired and lonely with his rumpled gray hair, worn jeans and untucked shirttail—this man who was as much a part of my life as my own body.

I reached out and touched his rough cheek. "I'll help with the tree."

Good, said the inner voice, *you've remembered the love.*

Throughout the afternoon, we pruned and sawed. We got out ornaments accumulated and treasured throughout the long years of our marriage. And when the tree was trimmed, I made hot chocolate and served it in the little pot we first used so many Christmases ago.

On Christmas day, our children arrived, and the house rocked with laughter, conversation, grandbabies and music.

No one noticed the smears on the window where decorations hung askew or the branches missing from one side of the tree. No one cared that dinner was a potluck affair. No one commented on the lack of variety on the cookie tray.

But when I brought out a simple cake with one glowing white candle, the room hushed. Every one of us—wide-eyed children and solemn adults—held hands while we sang "Happy Birthday" to Jesus.

A feeling of contentment welled up inside me that had nothing to do with cookies, clean windows or fancy wrappings.

And that still, small voice said, *Yes!*

Ann K. Brandt

Bottomed Out

It was a difficult week.

He had completed some work in exchange for the promise that "the check is in the mail." *Not*. Only bills appeared in his mailbox and never a check to pay them.

It was the holiday season—with its own slew of stressors—and the car was on the fritz again, the larder was frightfully empty, and his regular payday wasn't until the end of the month. No food. No money. No hope.

For certain, he'd hit the bottom of the barrel.

What was he going to do? Teetering on the brink of despair, he took three deep breaths, reached for his overcoat, scarf and gloves, and headed toward the woods. Nature had always been the sanctuary he sought when he felt hopeless or depressed.

Accommodating his stride to the snow-covered ground, he crunched through the forest of regal pines and snow-flocked blue spruce. He shaded his eyes against brilliant sunlight where it mirrored the diamond-bright snow. The tip of his nose reddened, and his cheeks burned from the crisp air.

As he headed toward the pond backing his property, a deer bounded across the path. A more timid tufted titmouse followed from a distance.

And he felt his breathing gentle and his gait slow.

"Chickadee-dee-dee!" A vigilant warbler sounded its alarm. A crow flitted from treetop to fence post and back again with only an occasional, *"Caw, caaaw."* A red-winged blackbird answered from the rushes fringing the pond and flew past in a swooping arc.

As he witnessed the song and dance of these feathered companions, he let go of his cares and felt satisfied as a kind of peace replaced them. Once again, nature had worked its magic—a major spiritual reconstruction on his soul. Satisfied, he turned toward the house while full-throated birdsong echoed an affirmation.

He paused at the backyard barrel to see if any bird food remained to reward his friends for their uplifting music and pleasant company. Under the seed sack he lifted from the barrel, he was startled to discover an unopened bag of flour. Ah, food for the birds . . . and food for him.

A rummage through the kitchen cupboard turned up enough ingredients for two fragrant loaves of yeasty bread. A few handfuls of assorted dried beans, a can of tomatoes and *presto:* Rhode Island chili with freshly baked bread! Plenty for him *and* his landlady. Perhaps things were not as bad as they'd seemed.

Just as the two sat down to dine, the postman delivered a parcel from a friend: jam-and-honey spread. Suddenly, the meal became even more interesting!

He gazed at the feast spread before him and the friend-seated beside him and marveled at the gratitude he felt within.

Sometimes, he decided, *life's richest gifts are found at the bottom of the barrel.*

Margaret Kirk

St. Nick's Note

As the weatherman promised, the temperature climbs to ninety-eight by midafternoon. I waste no time retrieving the mail from our box.

"Whew! The humidity must be 102." I collapse into a kitchen chair.

"You know it!" My husband agrees. He sits with both hands wrapped around a large glass of iced tea, still sweating after mowing the lawn.

"It's only July. Aren't you rushing the season a bit, Santa?" I tease.

"Are you referring to my red nose and cheeks?" He wiggles his bushy eyebrows. "Just getting a headstart on Christmas this year."

My jolly old St. Nick delights hundreds of children—of all ages—each December. Whether he's appearing at schools or in parades, he spreads his special Santa brand of love and kindness.

"Anything important?" He points at the mail on the table.

Fanning the pile, I hand him a farming magazine, a soil-and-water conservation newsletter and this month's electric bill. Toward the bottom of the stack, I pause to inspect a small white envelope.

"You're not going to believe this." I turn the letter toward Alan. "It's addressed to Santa Claus."

"Well, maybe I'm not so early after all," he chuckles. But instead of a wish list, he pulls out a hand-decorated card. "Thank You" is scrawled across the front. A trace of moisture washes his eyes.

"Remember these little guys, Mrs. Claus?" He hands me the card.

Oh, yes, I remember.

Each year I help Santa make "special deliveries"—for organizations, church groups or even concerned individuals—to single-parent families, the newly widowed, recently divorced, unemployed or those whose income barely covers essentials. These anonymous deliveries from Santa mean more than gifts under their trees or dinner on their tables: These deliveries express love and concern.

And this card comes from one of those single parents.

A month before last Christmas, this young mother found herself single and the sole provider for her seven-year-old twins. When she'd escaped her abusive situation, she was forced to leave behind most personal items, including her sons' bikes. According to a caring counselor at the "safe house," the distressed woman dreaded explaining to her sons that Santa couldn't bring new bikes this year. She'd accepted all the help she felt she was entitled to and wouldn't ask for more. Besides, bikes were a luxury.

Her friends didn't agree.

Because of those friends, Santa and Mrs. Claus delivered quite a load of groceries, gaily wrapped presents—and two new bikes to the grateful mother. Identical blue-eyed, freckle-nosed faces burst into jack-o'lantern smiles a mile wide as they peeked around her skirt.

"Oh, my goodness . . . we can't . . . who are you?" she stammered.

"Santa, of course! And this is Mrs. Claus," my husband boomed with a wink at the boys. "You made a very special list this year, and we wanted to deliver these early."

Santa's parting, "Ho, ho, ho," still echoed on the porch when a small, excited voice reached us, "Mama, I told you Santa would find us, even if we have to hide from Daddy."

Opening the card that jolted my memory, I read aloud to Santa. "It took me seven long months to discover how to reach you. I was so surprised that morning you came, I'm not sure I remembered to thank you. You helped the healing process begin and gave us back faith and hope."

Twin smiley faces followed the mother's signature at the bottom.

They were identical to our own.

Pamela Bumpus

Angels and Angst

Another dull church meeting. I muffled my third yawn. The old geezer was *still* droning on about church involvement. Same-old same-old. I was taking notes, substituting for my mom, the group secretary. But I had other things to do. Important, sixteen-year-old stuff. I doodled on the edges of the pad.

Deep in daydreams, I nearly missed the good-lookin' guy who walked in late and sat across from me. Tucking a wisp of hair behind my ear, I straightened in my chair and cocked a suddenly interested, furrowed brow toward Gramps, but sneaked a look from the corner of my eye when Mr. Cute raised his hand and took the floor.

I flashed him my most intelligent smile.

"I think more young people should be teaching in our Sunday schools," he was saying. "Don't you?"

I nodded wholeheartedly.

He continued, "It would be a good way for teens to feel like they're part of the church. All we'd need are volunteers."

Suddenly, with no direct input from me, mine was the first hand to shoot into the air. I hoped he noticed. A second-grade Sunday school class was assigned to me. On the spot.

Oops.

For endless months of Sundays, I forfeited sleeping late to serve my "term" with a rambunctious bunch of seven-year-olds. *Term*, I decided, was synonymous with *serving a sentence.*

Skimping lesson preparation, I taught *my* way. I marched them around the room tooting pretend trumpets until the walls of Jericho collapsed—thankfully, just before I did. I awarded tiny gold stars for memorized Bible verses. I celebrated birthdays by counting out a penny per year to give to the poor. But, mostly, I got headaches from their unbridled enthusiasm and off-key renditions of "Jesus Loves Me."

The weeks plodded on, and so did I.

"Miss Whitley," the minister asked, "would you direct the Christmas program this year?"

I would, I agreed. It would be my final sacrifice. Then— quite firmly—I would quit. Hand in my resignation. I'd be outta there.

On Saturday morning, mothers deposited angels, wise men, shepherds and donkeys. The dress rehearsal went poorly. The donkey girl got a sliver in her knee, an angel wept over a broken halo, and the shepherds engaged in an unholy brawl. I popped two more aspirin and shouted directions across the noisy room.

That night, my stomach churned. From backstage I spotted . . . *him* . . . the cute guy, in the front row. And I . . . . very deliberately . . . stuck out my tongue. He didn't see me—but the minister did.

The minute the curtain opened, my seven-year-olds were magically transformed. Shepherds, heads swathed in terry towels, stood ramrod straight. Mary and Joseph knelt; angels heralded; wise men worshipped; donkeys . . . well, *everything* couldn't be perfect.

Except, maybe their voices.

"Si-i-lent night," the little ones serenaded.

"Ho-o-ly night," their sweet voices floated and filled the room.

"All is calm . . ." Sweeping the stage with a glance, I nodded in agreement. All *was* calm. And perfect.

Just like them.

By the end of the performance, I figured the gigantic lump in my throat might disfigure me for life. But, hey, I would learn to deal with it.

"Miss Whitley! Miss Whitley!" Matthew held onto his lopsided crown with one hand and a shoebox with the other. "My mom and dad came to see me! *Both* of them!"

"Both of them?" I marveled. I knew a neighbor brought lonely little Matthew to Sunday school each week. His divorced parents didn't have time.

"Miss Whitley," he tugged my arm for attention, "can I be in your class again next year?"

Ahhh, what a cute little fella.

And I agreed. On the spot.

"And, uh . . . Miss Whitley . . . thanks." He shoved the shoebox toward me. "For you." He ran to join his parents while I lifted the lid.

Oops.

But even as I stared at the ugly gift inside—aren't all grasshoppers ugly?—I recognized the love in a little boy's gratitude.

Someone walked near me and whispered, "God bless you, Miss Whitley, and thank you."

I glanced up at Mr. Cute and shot him a foolish smile.

"Thank *you*," I said. And meant it.

Sharon Whitley Larsen

A Place of Honor

"Package for you, ma'am."

The postman left a plain box. It bore no printing, no hint as to the contents. Our overwhelming urge to shake the box produced only a slight shift in the load. Carefully cutting around the top, we removed the lid and peered inside.

With a questioning look on his face, my husband slowly unpacked six chubby figures and stood them on the table. When he placed a small, triangular bundle at their feet, I couldn't suppress a broad grin. Black, beady eyes, looking slightly myopic and a bit crossed, stared at us from under snatches of acrylic hair. With no noticeable change in their expressions, they stood quietly awaiting our inspection and approval.

Some months earlier I had mentioned to our daughter Kaye Lynn my desire to have a set of heavy-duty, child-proof nativity dolls for our grandchildren to enjoy. I wanted peace of mind when inquisitive little fingers felt a need to hold or examine one.

I also thought their own private collection would distract them from the stunning crèche ensemble I hoped to acquire. I dreamed of a lavish array of ceramic or porcelain, perhaps even crystal, to occupy a place of honor in our home—a spot where Mary and Joseph could display their precious babe undisturbed. Each piece would stand amid ripples of gold lamé fabric, the bright glow of carefully directed lights reflecting off polished surfaces.

My husband and I giggled as we examined each little guest. A more comical group of adoring subjects I had never imagined! They had been crafted with a wild sense of humor and a practical streak as well. For instance, contrary to popular belief, a blonde Mary wore crisp, pink-and-white gingham—easy to launder, cool in a desert climate and ultrafeminine. Joseph, on the other hand, appeared dapper in his brown plaid—ideal for traveling the dusty roads of Judea. His flowing auburn hair and full beard lent an air of sophistication.

I imagined an audible sigh of relief as we unfurled the angel's white felt wings that had been tucked tightly around her body. Her embroidered eyes were stitched closed, either in reverence or perhaps fatigue after her busy night proclaiming the wondrous news. And baby Jesus slept through it all, an odd little three-inch package swaddled in blue felt, glued atop a pile of old-fashioned excelsior packing.

There were no shepherds. No doubt they left early, anxious to spread the joyous word; besides, they had sheep to tend. Robed in plush fabric, three wise men wore identical silver hats. No knees bent in adoration; their fat little bodies were not designed for that.

The unexpected gift became a cherished possession.

Our grandchildren love those little people. Each doll has been hugged and kissed and taken on walking tours throughout the house. Secrets have been whispered and bruised feelings healed as they rocked together.

Baby Jesus has enjoyed many a quiet nap under the sofa, in a drawer or on someone's bed. Joseph never complains when his long hair is brushed and braided, parted and ponytailed as little girls practice their tonsorial skills. To our delight, one of the grandchildren recently dubbed the wise men "those three old guys in the shower caps."

The dolls survive all this affection remarkably well. Their wire arms assume astonishing positions, but they're still flexible. The excelsior hay dried and broke off, but a handful of pale yarn works just fine—and baby Jesus slept right through the regluing. The angel's droopy wings need to be replaced with new white felt. At this rate, the set will be in fine shape for our great-grandchildren.

And my burning desire for an impressive crèche subsided. Our daughter Barbara displayed hers atop the piano while they lived with us—gold lamé, bright lights and all. When she moved, she not only took her porcelain figurines, but five grandchildren and the piano as well.

We were left with only our little stuffed dolls, and it was okay.

Recently, the delivery service left another brown cardboard box. It was huge and much too big to shake. How exciting to remove packing by the yard, boxes inside boxes, with Bubble-Pak® and cotton batting stuffed everywhere.

This time we unwrapped ceramic sheep and shepherds, cows and camels, donkeys and wise men (some of which *are* kneeling), and the holy family. Kaye Lynn had hand-painted them all, and they are beautiful.

Now, I must give some thought as to where I can best display the cast and characters of my new crèche. I want them to represent the peace of the season and the richness of its message—but with a bit of flair. And I also want them to be safe from curious little fingers. Which location will I designate as the "place of honor"?

On second thought, maybe that spot has already been chosen.

Is there a lovelier place than in the chubby arms of a child? Can gold lamé shine as brightly as the eyes of a toddler as he sings to his "baby"—even if it is a wise man? Do spotlights and crystal compare to the light of Christmas shining in the face of innocence as a granddaughter and Mary share a moment in deep discussion about parenting skills?

Those first fat, little dolls with their fake hair and poor eyesight have been in the place of honor all this time, and I never realized it.

Now if I can just remember to buy some new white felt!

Mary Kerr Danielson

The Lone Caroler

The mall's parking garage was so packed that we had to drive around and around, up and down several levels, before we found a space. Of course, I should have expected as much. After all, this was the week before Christmas at the busiest shopping mall in the county.

Jumping out of the car, I held tight to my purse in one hand and my shopping list in the other. Screeching brakes, tooting horns, shouting customers, banging trunk lids, gunning motors, blaring loudspeaker music—what clamor! I could hardly think. And I certainly needed to think straight to plan my mad dashes from store to store. So much to do and so little time in which to do it.

As I rushed to the garage elevator, somehow through all that noise I heard a strange *chrrr, chrrr*. It almost had a rhythm to it. But where was the sound coming from?

Looking up, I saw a hole in the garage wall. Nestled inside was a small brown bird, shaped like a chickadee, but more sparrowlike in color. In fact, contrasted against all the red and green and gold of the season, the bird was absolutely dull and ordinary. To look at, that is, but not to listen to. The tiny creature was singing its heart out.

Chrrr, chrrr . . .

There, among the jarring sounds of racing cars and people, I realized it was responding to music on the loud-speaker. A Christmas carol? Why, yes—"Silent Night."

Though I was very close to him now, he didn't try to fly, but kept pouring out his heart with complete abandon. Perfect in rhythm and pitch, he syncopated each measure of the three-quarter-time melody, coming in only on the last two beats. As in, "Si- *(chrrr, chrrr)*, night *(chrrr, chrrr)*, ho- *(chrrr, chrrr)*, night *(chrrr, chrrr)*." Almost calypso style.

I didn't recognize his species. Many kinds of birds winter here in Southern California, and I'm not a "birder." But in the crowded parking garage that day, he alone took time to rejoice in and praise the reason for the season.

So I stopped and joined him.

He didn't seem to mind the cars whizzing by us or that my voice was cracked and weak and off-key. Never had "sleep in heavenly peace" seemed so out of place; it was neither night nor silent.

Only when the carol ended did we both hurry off to our respective duties. But as I headed into the jam-packed mall, I, too, had wings. And a glowing smile. "Christ our savior is born." Hallelujah!

Bonnie Compton Hanson

Troubled

A song sung by Faith Hill in the blockbuster movie *The Grinch* asks: "Where are you, Christmas? Why can't I find you?" Well, sometimes the Christmas spirit is like a misplaced sock—you find it when you aren't looking and where you'd least expect it to show up.

I found it at a quarter past one in the morning.

On my way home from work, I stopped at the neighborhood doughnut shop. After parking in its ghost town of a parking lot, I was headed toward the door when I spotted trouble.

What lit a warning light on my intuition radar was a group of teenagers—three boys and a girl. Understand, I wasn't alarmed by their tattoos (the girl included) or their earrings (boys included—eyebrows as well as each of their ears). Rather, it was the extremely late hour and the fact they loitered on the sidewalk in a semicircle around an elderly man sitting in a chair. Wearing a tattered flannel shirt and barefoot, the man looked positively cold and probably homeless.

And in trouble with a capital T.

Against my better judgment, I went inside the store and ordered three doughnuts—while keeping a worried eye on the group outside. Nothing seemed to be happening.

Until I headed toward my car.

Something was indeed "going down." As ominously as a pirate ordering a prisoner to the plank, the teens told the old man to stand up and walk.

Oh, no, I thought. *Capital tee-are-oh-you-bee-el-ee.*

But wait. I had misjudged the situation. And I had misjudged the teens.

"How do those feel?" one of the boys asked. "Do they fit?"

The cold man took a few steps—maybe a dozen. He stopped, looked at his feet, turned around and walked back. "Yeah, they'z about my size," he answered, flashing a smile that, despite needing a dentist's attention, was friendly and warm on this cold night.

The teens, all four, grinned back.

"Keep them. They're yours," one of the boys replied. "I want you to have them."

I looked down. The teen was barefoot. The kid had just given the cold-and-probably-homeless man his expensive skateboarding sneakers—and, apparently, his socks, as well.

The other two boys sat on their skateboards by the curb, retying their shoelaces. Apparently, they, too, had let the man try on their sneakers to find which pair fit the best. The girl, meanwhile, gave the cold man her oversized sweatshirt.

With my heart warmed by the unfolding drama, I went back into the shop.

"Could I trouble you for another dozen doughnuts?" I asked, then told the clerk what I had witnessed.

Christmas spirit, it seemed, was more contagious than flu or chicken pox. Indeed, the cold night got even warmer when the woman not only wouldn't let me pay for the doughnuts, but added a large coffee, too.

"These are from the lady inside. Have a nice night," I

said as I delivered the warm doughnuts and piping-hot cup. The old man smiled appreciatively.

"You have a nice night, too," the teens said.

I already had.

Woody Woodburn

The Bicycle

He did it with all his heart and prospered.

2 Chronicles 31:21

When I was nine, I needed to earn money, so I asked Mr. Miceli, the *Herald-American*'s man in my Chicago neighborhood, about an after-school paper route. He said if I had a bicycle, he'd give me a route. My dad was working four jobs then. He built neon signs in a sheet metal shop during the day, delivered flowers until eight in the evening, drove a cab till midnight, and on weekends sold insurance door-to-door. He bought me a used bike, but right after that he was hospitalized with pneumonia and couldn't teach me how to ride it.

But Mr. Miceli hadn't asked to see me ride. He merely asked to see the bike. So I walked it down to his garage, showed it to him and got the job.

At first, I slung my delivery sack filled with rolled papers over the handlebars and walked my bike down the sidewalks. But pushing a bike with a load of paper was awkward. After a few days I left the bike at home and borrowed Mom's two-wheeled steel-mesh shopping cart.

Delivering papers from a bike is tricky. You get one chance to throw each paper, and if it misses the porch or stoop, too bad. So I left Mom's cart at the sidewalk and carried each paper to its proper destination. If it was a second-floor porch, and I missed the first throw, I retrieved the paper and threw again. On Sundays, when the papers were big and heavy, I carried each one up the stairs. If it was raining, I put my papers inside the screen doors or, at apartment buildings, in the entrance halls. In rain or snow I put Dad's old raincoat over the cart to keep the papers dry.

It took me longer to make my deliveries by cart than if I were on a bike, but I didn't mind. I got to meet everyone in the neighborhood, working-class people of Italian, German or Polish descent, who were invariably kind to me. If I saw something interesting while walking my route, such as a dog with puppies or a rainbow of oil on wet asphalt, I could stop to watch for a while.

When Dad returned from the hospital, he resumed his day job, but he was too weak to work the others and had to give them up. Now we needed every dime we could raise to pay bills, so we sold my bike. Since I still didn't know how to ride it, I didn't object.

Mr. Miceli must have known I wasn't using a bike, but he said nothing about it to me. In fact, he rarely spoke to any of us boys, unless it was to give us a hard time for missing a customer or leaving a paper in a puddle.

In eight months, I built my route from thirty-six subscribers to fifty-nine, mostly because customers sent me to their neighbors, who said they wanted to take the paper. Sometimes people stopped me on the street to tell me to add them to my list. I collected every Thursday evening, and since most customers gave me a little extra money, soon I was making almost as much in tips as I got in pay from Mr. Miceli. That was good, because Dad still couldn't work much and I had to give most of my wages to Mom.

On the Thursday evening before Christmas, I rang my first customer's doorbell. Even though the lights were on, nobody answered the door so I went on to the next house. No answer. The same thing happened at the next family's house and the one after that. Soon I had knocked and rung at most of my subscribers' doors, but not one appeared to be home. I was very worried; I had to pay for my papers every Friday. And while it was almost Christmas, I'd never thought everyone would be out shopping. So I was very happy when, going up the walkway to the Gordons' house, I heard music and voices. I rang the bell.

Instantly the door was flung open, and Mr. Gordon all but dragged me inside. Jammed into his living room were almost all my fifty-nine subscribers. In the middle of the room was a brand-new Schwinn bicycle. It was candy-apple red, and it had a generator-powered headlight and a bell. A canvas bag bulging with colorful envelopes hung from the handlebars.

"This is for you," Mrs. Gordon said. "We all chipped in." The envelopes held Christmas cards, along with the weekly subscription fees. Most also included a generous tip. I was dumbstruck. I didn't know what to say. Finally, one of the women called for quiet and gently led me to the center of the room.

"You are the best paperboy we've ever had," she said. "There's never been a day when a paper was missing or late, never a day when it got wet. We've all seen you out there in the rain and snow with that little shopping cart. And so we thought you ought to have a bicycle."

All I could say was "thank you." I said it over and over.

When I got home, I counted more than one hundred dollars in tips, a windfall that made me a family hero and brought our household a wonderful holiday season. My subscribers must have called Mr. Miceli, because when I got to his garage the next day to pick up my papers, he was waiting outside.

"Bring your bike tomorrow at ten, and I'll teach you how to ride," he said. And I did.

My subscribers gave me another gift that season: a shining lesson about taking pride in even the humblest work, a Christmas present I try to use often, as I remember the kind Chicagoans who gave it to me.

Marvin J. Wolf

Hot Christmas

Effort only fully releases its reward after a person refuses to quit.

Napoleon Hill

Enticed by the smells of turkey, green-bean casserole, cranberry sauce, fresh-baked rolls and assorted pies, my guests waited for their call to the Christmas dinner table. The newest member of our family, baby Kirtley, had been fed before everyone else. We were all impressed when she said "more" to get more mashed potatoes and "hot" when we blew on them to cool them down.

As the time neared for eating, I added a paper Christmas napkin to each place setting and even lined the roll basket with one. I then lit the candles and called the group to be seated. Kirtley's mom placed her back in her high chair and put some dry cereal on her tray for a snack. We then sat down.

After we said grace and passed the food around the table, all of us tucked our heads and began to shovel food into our mouths. Silence reigned in the dining room except for the few chewing noises.

Out of the blue, a teeny voice said, "Hot."

Kirtley's mom said to her baby, "Yes, candles are hot. Good girl. That's right. You're doing a good job of using your words."

Kirtley clapped her little hands and said, "Hot," in a louder voice.

Her mother began eating again after simply saying, "Yes, those candles are hot."

Now, Kirtley thrust her body around in the chair, pointed toward the candles and shouted a giant, loud, "HOT!"

With this, we all looked up to see the roll basket on fire! Flames licked high in the air above and around the basket. Kirtley pointed to me as I ran for the kitchen with the flaming basket, saying, "Hot," one more time. And then she sighed and went back to eating her pieces of dry cereal.

After a few minutes of panic, we managed to finish eating, safely and happily, pausing often to thank our young rescuer who, with just one word, had saved our Christmas dinner.

Dottie Smith

More Chicken Soup?

Many of the stories you have read in this book were submitted by readers like you who had read earlier Chicken Soup for the Soul books. We publish eight Chicken Soup for the Soul books every year. We invite you to contribute a story to one of these future volumes.

Stories may be up to twelve hundred words and must uplift or inspire. You may submit an original piece, something you have read or your favorite quotation on your refrigerator door.

To obtain a copy of our submission guidelines and a listing of upcoming Chicken Soup books, please write, fax or submit your story through our website.

Please send your submissions to:

www.chickensoup.com
or
Chicken Soup for the Soul
P.O. Box 30880
Santa Barbara, CA 93130
fax: 805-563-2945

Just send a copy of your stories and other pieces to any of the above addresses.

We will be sure that both you and the author are credited for your submission. We pay authors to reprint their stories.

For information about speaking engagements, other books, audiotapes, workshops and training programs, please contact any of our authors directly.

Who Is Jack Canfield?

Jack Canfield is the cocreator and editor of the Chicken Soup for the Soul series, which *Time* magazine has called "the publishing phenomenon of the decade." The series now has 105 titles with over 100 million copies in print in forty-one languages. Jack is also the co-author of eight other bestselling books including *The Success Principles: How to Get from Where You Are to Where You Want to Be, Dare to Win, The Aladdin Factor, You've Got to Read This Book,* and *The Power of Focus: How to Hit Your Business and Personal and Financial Targets with Absolute Certainty.*

Jack has recently developed a telephone coaching program and an online coaching program based on his most recent book *The Success Principles.* He also offers a seven-day Breakthrough to Success seminar every summer, which attracts 400 people from fifteen countries around the world.

Jack has conducted intensive personal and professional development seminars on the principles of success for over 900,000 people in twenty-one countries around the world. He has spoken to hundreds of thousands of others at numerous conferences and conventions and has been seen by millions of viewers on national television shows such as *The Today Show, Fox and Friends, Inside Edition, Hard Copy,* CNN's *Talk Back Live, 20/20, Eye to Eye,* the NBC *Nightly News,* and the CBS *Evening News.*

Jack is the recipient of many awards and honors, including three honorary doctorates and a Guinness World Records Certificate for having seven books from the Chicken Soup for the Soul series appearing on the *New York Times* bestseller list on May 24, 1998.

To write to Jack or for inquiries about Jack as a speaker, his coaching programs, or his seminars, use the following contact information:

The Canfield Companies
P.O. Box 30880 • Santa Barbara, CA 93130
phone: 805-563-2935 • fax: 805-563-2945
E-mail: info@jackcanfield.com or
visit his website at www.jackcanfield.com

Who Is Mark Victor Hansen?

In the area of human potential, no one is more respected than Mark Victor Hansen. For more than thirty years, Mark has focused solely on helping people from all walks of life reshape their personal vision of what's possible. His powerful messages of possibility, opportunity, and action have created powerful change in thousands of organizations and millions of individuals worldwide.

He is a sought-after keynote speaker, bestselling author, and marketing maven. Mark's credentials include a lifetime of entrepreneurial success and an extensive academic background. He is a prolific writer with many bestselling books, such as *The One Minute Millionaire, Cracking the Millionaire Code, How to Make the Rest of Your Life the Best of Your Life, The Power of Focus, The Aladdin Factor,* and *Dare to Win,* in addition to the Chicken Soup for the Soul series. Mark has made a profound influence through his library of audios, videos, and articles in the areas of big thinking, sales achievement, wealth building, publishing success, and personal and professional development.

Mark is the founder of the MEGA Seminar Series. MEGA Book Marketing University and Building Your MEGA Speaking Empire are annual conferences where Mark coaches and teaches new and aspiring authors, speakers, and experts on building lucrative publishing and speaking careers. Other MEGA events include MEGA Info-Marketing and My MEGA Life.

As a philanthropist and humanitarian, Mark works tirelessly for organizations such as Habitat for Humanity, American Red Cross, March of Dimes, Childhelp USA, and many others. He is the recipient of numerous awards that honor his entrepreneurial spirit, philanthropic heart, and business acumen. He is a lifetime member of the Horatio Alger Association of Distinguished Americans, an organization that honored Mark with the prestigious Horatio Alger Award for his extraordinary life achievements.

Mark Victor Hansen is an enthusiastic crusader of what's possible and is driven to make the world a better place.

Mark Victor Hansen & Associates, Inc.
P.O. Box 7665 • Newport Beach, CA 92658
phone: 949-764-2640 • fax: 949-722-6912
www.markvictorhansen.com

Contributors

Several of the stories in this book were taken from previously published sources, such as books, magazines and newspapers. These sources are acknowledged in the permissions section. If you would like to contact any of the contributors for information about their writing, or would like to invite them to speak in your community, look for their contact information included in their biography.

The remainder of the stories were submitted by readers of our previous Chicken Soup for the Soul books who responded to our requests for stories. We have also included information about them.

Toby Abraham-Rhine is a part-time counselor, teacher and performing artist. She and her husband choose to live very simply in order to travel. They saved for years, sold all they had and went around the world with their three children. Readers may enjoy the journey through *A Brilliant Teacher* from Sawtooth Press.

Joan Wester Anderson has authored hundreds of magazine articles and fourteen books, including an angel-and-miracle series, which has sold over two million copies. Her latest book is titled *Forever Young,* the authorized biography of actress Loretta Young. Joan can be reached at P.O. Box 127, Prospect Heights IL 60070.

Terry Andrews is a writer who lives on the Oregon coast. This story is based on memories of a family Christmas when she was growing up in Iowa. She is the author and illustrator of *The Spiritual Cat* and *The Spiritual Dog.* You can reach her by e-mail at *25terrya@seasurf.com.*

Mickey Bambrick is a freelance writer and entertaining public speaker. She has written a collection of inspirational stories on how God has "worked things to the good," and she's happy to share them in word or in speech. She can be contacted at 17612 Valentine Rd., Mount Vernon, WA 98273.

Barbara Baumgardner is an inspirational author who drives a motor home cross-country accompanied by her golden retriever, Molly. She is the author of three books, numerous articles and is a columnist for *RV Companion Magazine.* When not traveling, she nests in central Oregon and can be reached at *barbarab@bendcable.com.*

Kathryn Beisner is a writer and motivational storyteller. Her love of history and family traditions are celebrated in her popular audio book *Ordinary Women* *with Extraordinary Spirit!* and an by essay in *Chili Today, Hot Tamale.* Kathryn lives by the motto, "No Guts, No Story!" For more adventures visit *www.kbsproductions.com.*

Robert H. Bickmeyer is retired from General Motors. He writes for the Olive Branch Press, the Think Club and *Military Magazine*, as well as guest columns for newspapers in southeast Michigan. He is now writing a book, *Laughter in Real Life.* Bob plays senior citizen softball, volleyball and golf. He can be reached at (248) 879-0207.

Ann K. Brandt writes magazine articles and essays. Her first book, *Learning to Walk Again,* tells of her experience with Guillain-Barré. She is working on *Facing Brain Cancer with Hope,* a book for anyone affected by cancer. Please e-mail her at *AnnGeoB@msn.com.*

Marion Brenish works part time for the Department of Labor and is a freelance writer. When not traveling, Marion can be found sailing her thirty-two-foot ketch, "Gypsy," in San Diego Bay, with her husband, Randy. Marion may be reached at *catexrandy@aol.com.*

Isabel Bearman Bucher, a retired teacher, has been writing, with no training, since 1984. She was raising teenagers, and saying it on paper with words seemed better than committing murder. She's published dozens of articles in many genres and has completed two books: *Nonno's Monkey: An Italian American Memoir,* and *Tweet Irene,* the story of a little house sparrow that lived with her family loosely for three years. She was a miracle. She and her husband, Robert, continue their honeymoon with life, changing homes throughout the world, walking mountains, finding adventures.

Pam Bumpus and husband, Alan, live near Charleston, Illinois. They have two wonderful daughters, a beautiful granddaughter and a brand new grandson. Pam writes as a hobby and enjoys sharing her stories. She can be contacted at *plbump@yahoo.com.*

Steve Burt's inspirational bestsellers include *A Christmas Dozen* and *Unk's Fiddle.* The Ray Bradbury winner *Odd Lot* won a Benjamin Franklin Award; *Even Odder* was runner-up to *Harry Potter* for the 2003 Bram Stoker Award (horror's top prize); *Oddest Yet* was a 2004 Stoker Finalist; *Wicked Odd* is his newest book. *www.burtcreations.com.*

Kristine Byron is a decorator and writer of children's stories and rhymes. Kristine enjoys cooking, skiing and entertaining friends. She is hoping to have her books published in the near future. Please reach her at: *rbyron14@aol.com.*

Michele Wallace Campanelli is a national bestselling author. She lives in Florida with her husband, Louis, and pet iguana, Jamison. She is author of several nationally distributed books including: *Margarita: The Case of the Numbers Kidnapper, Keeper of the Shroud, Hero of Her Heart* and many short-story anthologies. Contact her at: *www.michelecampanelli.com.*

Jeanne Williams Carey raised eight children and numerous foster children.

This has kept her happily busy. She ventured into education and took delight in teaching as well. Jeanne now writes stories about the vivid courage, bright hopes and faith of people who know it's a great life. Her e-mail is: *JNNCARB@aol.com.*

Melody Carlson has worn many hats over the years, from preschool teacher to senior editor. But most of all, she loves to write! Currently she freelances from her home. In the past few years, she has published over sixty books for children, teens, and adults. Several of her books have been finalists for, and winners of, various writing awards. She has two grown sons and lives in Sisters, Oregon, with her husband and chocolate Lab. They enjoy skiing, hiking, gardening and biking in the beautiful Cascade Mountains.

Lt. Colonel Marlene Chase has served forty years as an officer in The Salvation Army and has been the editor of its national magazine, *The War Cry,* since 1995. She has three adult children all serving in the Army's ranks.

David R. Collins combined two careers, teaching English in Moline, Illinois, for thirty-five years and writing books for young readers. Many of his articles and stories sprang from his classroom experiences, as did "A Silent Voice." Named "Outstanding Illinois Educator," Collins has won recognition from the American Legion, the Veterans of Foreign Wars, the PTA and the Junior Literary Guild.

Tanja Crouch is a former music business vice president, having worked with Roy Orbison, Vince Gill, Randy Travis, and others. She authored *100 Careers in the Music Business* and *100 Careers in Film and Television,* and created/wrote/produced This Joint is Jumpin' and The Girls in the Band. A motivational speaker, Crouch teaches Sunday school and works in the LDS Nashville Tennessee Temple. Conhtact her at *www.crouchbooks.com.* E-mail: *thisjoint@aol.com.*

James Daigh has a bachelor's in creative writing/poetry. His careers have been in documentary and feature film production and publishing. His loves are: 1. his fantastic wife and inspiration, Marla; 2. poetry; 3. drawing and painting; 4. fine-art photography and this big, wide, beautiful world.

Mary Kerr Danielson began her writing career by joining a local writer's group at age fifty-something. (Known within a small circle of family and friends as the "Ditty Lady"—original verses for any and all obscure occasions—she's positive Hallmark isn't worried!) She and her husband, Kay, are parents of six daughters, one of whom is deceased. (After they all "left the nest," the nest was recently moved from Loveland, Colorado, to Riverdale, Utah.) Writing mainly about her life experiences, she also does poetry, plays and children's stories. E-mail her at *danielson_l@msn.com.*

John W. Doll began writing lyrics in Chicago for Lawrence Welk. He continued writing after moving to California. He is a regular contributor to the very successful *Chicken Soup for the Soul* series. He lives on an orange grove with his wife, Lanie. John recently completed a book titled *Autumn Leaves Around the World.* To order, contact him at 2377 Grand Ave., Fillmore, CA 93015 or fax 805-524-3821.

Barbara "Binkie" Dussalt is a retired grandmother who enjoys her family, which includes her children Trudy, Susie and Jeff, her granddaughters, Aubrey Jessica and Michelle, and her great-grandchildren, Morgan, Troy and Max. She loves crafts, sewing and making her own expression cards.

Jane Eppinga's writing credentials include more than 200 articles for both popular and professional publications. Her biography, *Henry Ossian Flipper: West Point's First Black Graduate*, was part of a package presented to President W. J. Clinton as a successful appeal to have Henry Ossian Flipper posthumously pardoned. Two of her books: *Arizona Twilight Tales: Good Ghosts, Evil Spirits, and Blue Ladies* and *Images of America: Tucson, Arizona* were recently released.

Ellen Hamilton Fenter is a pastor, writer, counselor, community activist and blogger who currently enjoys life and ministry in El Paso, Texas. She is a mother and grandmother whose heart always longs for the serenity of her native land, New Mexico. Pastor Ellen's enduring passion is for "the least of these."

Nancy B. Gibbs is a pastor's wife, the mother of three grown children, Chad, Brad and Becky, and the grandmother of a precious little girl, Hannah. She and her husband, Roy, live in Georgia with three dogs, Snowball, Benjamin Franklin and Daisey, and one yellow cat, Sunshine. Nancy may be reached at P.O. Box 53, Cordele, GA 31010 or by e-mail at *Daiseydood@aol.com.*

Joseph J. Gurneak has lived in New Jersey his entire life and is currently the police commissioner for his community. During his fifty-seven years, he has met many interesting and wonderful people who have enriched his life. Through his writing, he loves sharing those "slices of life" for others to experience and enjoy. You can reach Joseph at 110 Kennedy Mill Rd., Stewartsville, NJ 08886; 908-479-6020; or via e-mail at *Jgurneak@spragueEnergy.com.*

Angela Hall has been publisher/editor of a newspaper in Canada for twenty years. She has also edited several books, three of which were on the bestseller list. Angela is now retired and looking forward to devoting more time to writing letters of encouragement to sick and needy children as well as to survivors of cancer. You can reach her at *angel@belco.bc.ca.*

Rita Hampton is an assistant manager at the Bank of Montreal in British Columbia, Canada. She has been married for twenty-eight years and is the mother of four and grandmother to her newest angel, Michaela. She enjoys dancing, singing, cake decorating, photography, and reading and writing. She'd like to dedicate this story to all the angels who have helped her and her family through a difficult time. Contact Rita at 27057—28th Ave., Aldergrove, B.C., Canada V4W 3A3.

A lover of animals, both wild and tame, **Bonnie Compton Hanson** has authored or coauthored over twenty books, plus hundreds of poems and articles—including those in twelve *Chicken Soup* books.

Emily Sue Harvey's upbeat stories appear in women's magazines, *The Compassionate Friends* magazine, the *Chocolate* series, *Chicken Soup, From Eulogy* *to Joy* and *Caution: Children Praying*. Her two current completed novels are *God Only Knows* and *Sunny Flavors*. She writes to make a difference. Contact her at *emilysue1@aol.com.*

Dawn Holt is currently a school counselor at Westover High School in Fayetteville, North Carolina, fulfilling her son, Cameron's, last wishes that he not be forgotten, and that she come back to his high school to make a difference. She still makes the box of chocolate-covered cherries her annual gift to friends and family. She can be reached at *dawnholt@yahoo.com.*

Armené Humber is a career coach who helps low-income clients recognize their potential and find their places in today's challenging workplace. She lives in Southern California, has a master's degree in Christian leadership from Fuller Theological Seminary and enjoys writing inspirational stories. Contact her at *armhumber@aol.com.*

Linda DeMers Hummel writes about issues concerning women, children and families. She can be reached at *LindaDHummel@aol.com.*

Harrison Kelly is a freelance Christian writer living in Bartlett, Tennessee. He has two children, Brad, thirteen, and Kristina, nine. He and his wife, Lucretia, have been married for twenty years. Some of Harrison's works have been published in the *A Second Chicken Soup for the Woman's Soul* and *Chicken Soup for the Golfer's Soul.* He has compiled a collection of his true-life stories in a series, *Stories from a Loving Father.* You may contact him at *HK@harrisonkelly.com.*

Crystal Ward Kent is a lifelong animal lover who currently resides with two former shelter cats in Eliot, Maine. She is a writer by profession and has written for newspapers, magazines and books, including *Yankee Magazine* and Guidepost Books' *Listening to the Animals* series. She owns Kent Communications, which provides writing, design and marketing services, and currently is working on a book. Contact Crystal at 46 State Rd., Eliot, ME 03903; 207-439-1235.

Barbara King and her husband of thirty-five years have three children and two grandchildren. She teaches fifth grade on the Menominee Indian Reservation. She has had two short stories published in national magazines and relaxes by making "pique-assiette" mosaics. You can e-mail her at *mhoc@frontiernet.net.*

Margaret Kirk has a master's from Gaddard College with graduate work in heart-centered counseling from the University of Santa Monica. She is currently a fiber artist, doll maker and the executive director of the Four Corners Child Advocacy Center in Colorado. Please e-mail her at *eurydice4@yahoo.com.*

Vickie Ryan Koehler received her bachelor of arts from Sam Houston State University in Huntsville, Texas, in 1979, and then studied for her master's degree in Spanish at the University of Kentucky. She presently resides in Liverpool, Texas, with her family and teaches in the Alvin Independent School District.

Laura Lagana is an author, professional speaker and registered nurse. She is author of an inspirational anthology, *Touched by Angels of Mercy*, a coauthor of *Chicken Soup for the Volunteer's Soul*, as well as a frequent contributor to the *Chicken Soup for the Soul* series. She may be reached at Success Solutions, P.O. Box 7816, Wilmington, DE 19803; e-mail: *NurseAngel@LauraLagana.com*; Web site: *http://www.LauraLagana.com*.

Jessica Lamb is a freshman at Memorial High School. She enjoys volleyball, soccer, swimming and spending time with friends. Her favorite activity is being on the dance team at school. She has had a few of her poems published in the past. This is her first story to be published, and she dedicates it to her dad because he is always there for her.

Margaret Lang received her bachelor of arts from Brown University in 1963. She teaches women and children's groups in California. Margaret has three published stories, two in *Chicken Soup for the Father and Daughter Soul*. Her daughter is a physician/missionary, her son a youth pastor, and she has two granddaughters.

Charlotte A. Lanham is a retired teacher and columnist. She is a frequent contributor to *Chicken Soup for the Soul*. Charlotte and her husband, Ray, cofounded a nonprofit organization called Abbi's Room Foundation, providing beds and bedding for children of Habitat for Humanity families. E-mail her at *charlotte.lanham@sbcglobal.net*.

Sharon Whitley Larsen, a former special-education teacher, has contributed previously to *Chicken Soup* books (4th, 5th, Teenage and Golden editions). Her work has also appeared in *Reader's Digest, Los Angeles Times Magazine* and other publications. She currently writes travel stories for Copley News Service and can be reached at *SWhittles@aol.com*.

Veneta Leonard resides in Crown Point, a quaint, historic town in northwest Indiana where she enjoys reading spiritual and inspirational writings. With an associate degree in business management, she hopes to return to school someday. Right now, she enjoys the most important job she will ever have—being a mom!

Maddy Lincoln is thirteen years old and the second of four girls. She loves gymnastics, skiing, singing and writing. She hopes to become a famous author some day. Maddy would like to thank her English teacher, Mrs. Adler, and her family for all their help and support.

Jane and Michael Maas coauthored *Christmas in Wales: A Homecoming* and Michael, an architect, contributed the delightful drawings. Jane is an advertising executive. Despite this collaboration, their marriage remains intact. You can reach Jane at: *janemaas@worldnet.att.net*.

Mary Marcdante is an inspiring and dynamic professional speaker and author whose mission is to help people appreciate themselves and life. She is the author of *My Mother, My Friend: The Ten Most Important Things to Talk About with Your Mother* (Simon & Schuster/Fireside). Reach Mary at P.O. Box 2529, Del

Mar, CA 92014 or *www.marymarcdante.com* for her speaking topics, books and more inspiration.

Megan McKeown is a seventh-grader who lives in Olean, New York, with her mom, dad and three sisters, Molly, Kelly and Kaitlyn. She likes to play soccer and basketball. She also takes tap and jazz lessons and helps teach a class of younger children. Her favorite subject in school is language because she loves to express herself through writing.

W. W. Meade started writing at the age of fourteen. When he was twenty-two, his first short story was published in *Colliers Magazine*. He wrote fiction for the *Saturday Evening Post, Gentleman's Quarterly,* the *Ladies' Home Journal* and *Seventeen* among others. He then turned to writing nonfiction for magazines such as *Cosmopolitan, Redbook* and *Reader's Digest*. Later he became managing editor of Cosmopolitan and then managing editor of *Reader's Digest* Book Club. His last position in publishing was president and editor in chief of Avon books. Today, Walter lives in Florida and his first novel, *Unspeakable Acts,* was published in August 2001 by Upstart Press in New York City and can be purchased on *Amazon.com*.

Margaret Middleton has experienced miracles and unhappiness in her seventy-five years of life. God has been her foundation. She has written fifteen episodes of her childhood and, as an adult, a biography that readers will perceive as an adventurous experience of her life.

Cathy Miller is a Canadian teacher and freelance writer. "Delayed Delivery" first won a short story contest in her hometown of Sudbury, Ontario in 1992. The following year it was published in *Christmas in My Heart 2*, edited by Joe Wheeler, Review & Herald Publishing. It has been reprinted in several anthologies and magazines. She can be reached at *millerc@scdsb.edu.on.ca*.

Debby Mongeau graduated from the University of Montana in 1980 and moved to Alaska the following spring for a summer job. She stayed seventeen years. Debby, her husband and their five children, currently reside in Couer d'Alene, Idaho. She enjoys gardening, skiing, camping with her family and photography.

Nick Montavon, age thirteen, likes learning to skateboard and hanging out with his friends. Nick enjoyed being in Mrs. Beth Bennett's reading class this year because of her ability to teach great lessons and her dedication to her work. He thanks his parents for always keeping him on track in his early life.

Nancy Mueller is a professional speaker, trainer and coach in communication and people skills. She is a specialist in working globally, diversity, and cross-cultural relationships. Nancy is the author of *Work Worldwide: International Career Strategies for the Adventurous Job Seeker* (*www.AboutWorkWorldwide.com*). You can reach her at *NTMueller@aol.com* or (206) 784-8277.

Cathy Novakovich is a proud mother and grandmother. Currently employed as the administrative manager for a firm in Chicago she is eagerly anticipating an early retirement which will allow her more time for the things she loves, her growing family, reading, writing, and the great outdoors of camping and fishing. Please reach her at *luckynovas@aol.com*.

Sandra J. Payne has written several episodes of the television show, *Barney & Friends*, as well as the video, *Be My Valentine, Love, Barney*, and a book called, *Barney, I Did It Myself*. When she's not writing, Sandra travels as much as possible. She's happy to live with her husband, Perry, in Southern California as winters in Alaska are mighty chilly! Sandra can be reached at 11271 Ventura Blvd., Suite 317, Studio City, CA 91604 or e-mail her at *SJPwriter@aol.com*.

Denise Peebles is married and a mother of two children, Ashley, seventeen, and Jonathan, seven. She has been published in different e-zines and in her local newspaper. She has a story featured in the *Lauderdale County Book of History*. Her favorite topic to write about is her life and her family. It has been her dream to be a nationally published author, and now she is! You can contact her at *Speeb47489@aol.com*.

Shawn Pittman was born January 4, 1974, in a rare snowstorm in Las Vegas, Nevada. In 1993, he met Melissa Jordan in an online chat-room. They met face-to-face on November 10. It was true love. Since then they have been inseparable and got married February 29th, 2000. They wrote this story in loving memory of Shawn's mother, Jackie Pittman. Please contact them at *viirusandvelvet@hotmail.com*.

Penny Porter is the wife of a retired rancher, Bill, mother of six, grandmother of eight, and has always been in love with life and family. She is "one of the most successful freelancers ever to hit *Reader's Digest*," and has published in a wide range of national magazines, including *Arizona Highways, Catholic Digest* and *Guideposts*. She is the current president of The Society of Southwestern Authors, and her work has appeared in seven of the *Chicken Soup for the Soul* books. Signed copies of her fourth book, *Heartstrings and Tail-Tuggers*, are available through *wporter202@aol.com*.

Carrie Powell-Davidson, a music therapist by trade, spends her time instructing professional bartending at the University College, freelance writing for newspapers and magazines, and raising two young children with her husband, Mike. She operates a small retail business in bar supplies, sings in the choir, freelances as a bartender and catering assistant. A recent encounter with acting has opened many opportunities and Carrie hopes to someday host and write for her own TV show on entertaining—Vancouver Island style.

Linda C. Raybern is a lay minister, and ministers to the ill, the elderly and disabled. She enjoys writing fiction, nonfiction and inspirational articles. She has a husband, a grown son and four dogs that she rescued from the humane society. Her family, animals and her ministry all contribute to an enriching life.

Brittany Anne Reese is a sophomore in high school whose favorite class is English. She enjoys dancing and hopes to get a dance scholarship and pursue a career in dancing. She'd like to thank her family for their support and putting up with her prancing around the house for hours at a time.

Kristina Richardson is a wife, mother of two and an adventurer. She is also an amateur writer and a photographer. You can e-mail her at *Krissi6363@aol.com*.

Nancy Rue is the bestselling author of over sixty books for children and young people, including the current top-selling Lily series. She is a former high school teacher and theatre director, and she now teaches workshops for young writers nationwide. Nancy lives in Lebanon, Tennessee.

Karen M. Sackett's education included graduation from Idaho State University with a B.A. in education, graduate work at the University of Arizona and "being raised" by two active sons. She worked at a nursing center and continues to be involved in hospice. She loves writing, music and golfing with her husband.

David Scott is a sixteen-year-old whose hobbies include skating, fishing, skim boarding and surfing. He learned how to write and gained writing experience in his writing classes at school.

Annette Seaver's greatest passion is mothering. She currently has eleven children: seven biological, four adopted and two "on hold." She's been to China and Saoma, and anticipates traveling to Mongolia soon. She mentors unwed mothers, organizes a variety of teen activities, volunteers at school and church, and enjoys writing.

Dottie Smith is a real turkey. She was born on a snowy Thanksgiving Day. When she grew up she became a nurse, but also longed to do something creative. So she began to write for children. Her stories and articles have been published in numerous children's magazines. She lives in a noisy house with an African gray parrot, a cat named PK, a dog named Taylor and her husband, Bob. She has two grown children and four grandchildren. She can be reached at 708 Calvert Ave., Clinton SC 29325 or via e-mail at *dmdsmith@hotmail.com*.

Elaine C. Smothers is a former police officer turned freelance writer. She dedicates this story to her late mother, Joyce Carter, a woman of strong character and indomitable spirit. She lives in eastern North Carolina with her police-officer husband, stepson and their menagerie of animals, and enjoys sea kayaking, camping and reading. She can be reached via e-mail at *SeaDream91@aol.com*.

Linda Snelson mainly writes stories about personal experiences to share with friends and family members. A single mom, Linda stays busy with a full-time job as an executive assistant, does face-painting, and shares her leisure time with two daughters, two step daughters, and three grandchildren. She credits her daughter, Gina for inspiring her to write.

Rand Souden is a graduate of Drury College and Vanderbilt University School of Law. An attorney, writer and lecturer now residing in Los Angeles, California, he is involved in the rescue of abandoned and unwanted dogs and is completing a book of stories about animal rescue. Reach him at *Rsouden@aol.com*.

Linda Stafford lives in Hawaii and enjoys writing inspirational books. She teaches a writing class at the University of Hawaii at Hilo. She has four children who make her life sparkle.

Storm Stafford is a student at the University of Hawaii Manoa. She plans to teach Women's Studies when she graduates.

Robin Clephane Steward is a stay-at-home mother of three. She lives in Indianapolis with her husband, Brian, two sons, a daughter and a lovable mutt named Boots. She enjoys Anne Perry novels, John Wayne movies and performing taxi service between her home and her local middle and high schools.

Gary Swanson received his Bachelor's degree in English from Pacific Union College in 1968; and a master's degree in English and education from Loma Linda University in 1979. He has taught high school English, journalism, and creative writing, and is presently editor of *CQ*, a religious education periodical for young adults.

Ken Swarner writes the syndicated humor column, "Family Man," for newspapers in the U.S. and Canada. He can be seen at *www.kenswarner.bigstep.com*.

Martha Pendergrass Templeton is a writer, teacher and storyteller who lives in Mentone, Alabama with her husband, Tony, and her son, Rayfe. She is beginning her first year as an instructional coach at Summerville Middle School in Summerville, Georgia. This is the fourth publication of the story from her childhood, "Simple Wooden Boxes." She still owns the box that her father made for her so many years ago; it is among her most precious possessions.

Stephanie Welcher Thompson married her sweetheart, Michael, on February 14, 2002. These days, they enjoy family life in an Oklahoma City suburb with their darling two-and-a-half-year-old daughter, Micah. Reach them at P.O. Box 1502, Edmond, OK 73083, or *stephanie@stateofchange.net*.

Quynh Thuc Tran is a ten-year-old who lives in a small city in California where she attends elementary school. She likes to draw and read during her free time and loves to write mysterious stories. Living in California has inspired her to write stories and poems about all there is to do.

Whitney Von Lake Hopler is the author of the new book, *A Creative Life: God's Design for You* (Xulon Press, 2002) and serves as an editor for *Crosswalk.com*, the largest Christian site on the Internet. She lives in Virginia with her husband, Russ, daughter, Honor, and cat, Milkshake. She can be reached via e-mail at *WhitneyVLH@aol.com*.

Molly Walden is an eighth-grade honor-roll student in Orlando, Florida. She enjoys writing poetry and stories, acting, rowing (crew) and swimming. Her academic goal is to get her master's degree in biology/animal technology. Molly's story, *The Christmas Care Bear*, was inspired by her ninety-four-year-old great-grandmother, whose lessons of love, support and compassion have been instilled in yet another generation.

Jim West is one of the most sought after cruise professionals in the travel industry. He is the author of four travel books and a contributing author in *Chicken Soup for the Traveler's Soul.* He was a professional cruise director for ten years; has sailed on over 850 cruises, including a cruise to Antarctica with Sir Edmund Hillary; visited over 72 countries around the world and is a popular international speaker. He has received his certification in Youth Ministry from the University in Stubenville, Ohio, and continues to minister to teens through a travel ministry. You can reach Jim at *www.TravelWest.com* or by calling (815) 878-3600.

Ernie Witham writes a humor column called "Ernie's World" for the Montecito Journal in Montecito, California. His humor has also been published in the *Los Angeles Times, The Santa Barbara News-Press,* and numerous magazines and anthologies, including five *Chicken Soup for the Soul* books. He is available to lead humor workshops for any age group and can be reached at *ernie@ernieswebsite.com.*

Marvin J. Wolf has written as a professional since 1965, and his byline has appeared in periodicals and bookstores in at least 132 nations. He is the author, coauthor or ghostwriter of a dozen books and hundreds of magazine and newspaper articles, as well as of marketing, advertising and business literature. The American Society of Journalists and Authors (ASJA) honored Wolf with their prestigious Robert C. Anderson lifetime achievement award in 1994. He was ASJA runner-up Author of the Year in 1995. He has also been honored by the Greater Los Angeles Area Press Club, the U.S. Marine Corps Combat Correspondents Association, the Orange County [California] Advertising Federation, the IABC, the Southern California Business Communicators and the Pacific Industrial Communicators Association. He can be e-mailed at *Marvwolf@attbi.com.*

Woody Woodburn is a sports columnist for the *Daily Breeze* in Torrance, California. He has been honored for column writing by the Associated Press Sports Editors, appeared in *The Best American Sports Writing* anthology, is a frequent contributor to the *Chicken Soup* series and authored two books. He can be reached at *Woodycolumn@aol.com.*

Jane Zaffino recently retired from Bell Canada after thirty years of dedicated service. She is now pursuing her lifelong dream of writing by taking courses at George Brown College. She currently lives in Toronto with her husband of thirty years and their two children. You can reach Jane at *janezaffino@yahoo.ca.*

Lynne Zielinski's articles, stories, essays and book reviews have appeared in national magazines and anthologies. Lynne believes life is a gift from God and what we do with it is our gift to God. She lives in Huntsville, Alabama, and can be reached at 256-883-1592, email: *ArisWay@aol.com.*

Permissions *(continued from page ii)*

Reptiles Reconciled. Reprinted by permission of Linda C. Raybern. ©1995 Linda C. Raybern.

Delayed Delivery. Reprinted by permission of Cathryn Miller. ©2001 Cathryn Miller.

'Twas the Night b4 Christmas. Reprinted by permission of Mary Marcdante. ©1995 Mary Marcdante.

The Santa Claus on I-40, Gold, Common Sense and Fur and *Deck the Halls.* Reprinted by permission of Linda Stafford. ©2000 Linda Stafford.

A Cat Named Christmas. Reprinted by permission of Rand Souden. ©1994 Rand Souden.

Blue Christmas. Reprinted by permission of Terry Andrews. ©1984 Terry Andrews.

Nickled and Dimed. Reprinted by permission of Barbara Dussalt. ©1985 Barbara Dussalt.

Charlie's Coat. Reprinted by permission of Robin Clephane Steward. ©2004 Robin Clephane Steward.

I'm Not Scrooge . . . I'm Just Broke! Reprinted by permission of Storm Stafford. ©2002 Storm Stafford.

Helping Lauren. Reprinted by permission of Maddy Lincoln and Debbie Lincoln. ©2002 Maddy Lincoln.

Many Times Over. Reprinted by permission of Nick Montavon and Deborah Montavon. ©2002 Nick Montavon.

A Warm Bed for Christmas. Reprinted by permission of Elaine C. Smothers. ©1998 Elaine C. Smothers.

Love Cannot Be Measured. Reprinted by permission of Quynh Thuc Tran and Hung Tran. ©2002 Quynh Thuc Tran.

Mason's Sacrifice. Reprinted by permission of Veneta Leonard. ©2002 Veneta Leonard.

An Inch of Kindness. Reprinted by permission of Jeanne Williams Carey. ©1989 Jeanne Williams Carey.

Simple Wooden Boxes. Reprinted by permission of Martha Pendergrass Templeton. ©1994 Martha Pendergrass Templeton.

Christmas in the Sticks. Reprinted by permission of Deborah L. Mongeau. ©2001 Deborah L. Mongeau.

An Unlikely Angel. Reprinted by permission of Crystal Ward Kent. ©2002 Crystal Ward Kent.

Double Angels. Reprinted by permission of David Scott and Renee Scott. ©2002 David Scott.

An Angel Among Us. Reprinted by permission of Rita Hampton. ©2002 Rita Hampton.

From the Heart. Reprinted by permission of Jessica Lamb and Larry J. Lamb. ©2002 Jessica Lamb.

A Timeless Gift. Reprinted by permission of Harrison Kelly. ©2001 Harrison Kelly.

The Christmas Cookie Can. Reprinted by permission of Joseph J. Gurneak. ©2002 Joseph J. Gurneak.

The Unusual Package. Reprinted by permission of Barbara King. ©2002 Barbara King.

The Christmas Care Bear. Reprinted by permission of Molly Walden and Jane S. Walden. ©2002 Molly Walden.

Truly Cool. Reprinted by permission of Brittany Anne Reese and Beverly Jo Bierstedt. ©2002 Brittany Anne Reese.

Christmas Mother. Reprinted by permission of John W. Doll. ©1990 John W. Doll.

Kevin and the Saint. Reprinted by permission of Michele Wallace Campanelli. ©1998 Michele Wallace Campanelli.

Heaven-Sent. Reprinted by permission of Mickey Bambrick. ©1997 Mickey Bambrick.

Secret Santa. Reprinted by permission of Tanja Crouch. ©1997 Tanja Crouch.

An Angel in Chains. Reprinted by permission of Penny Porter. ©2001 Penny Porter. Originally appeared in *Arizona Highways.*

Timber! and *Sugarplums.* Reprinted by permission of Ken Swarner. ©2000 Ken Swarner.

Christmas in the Country of Miracles. Reprinted by permission of Jane and Michael Maas. ©1994 Jane and Michael Maas.

The Heavenly Salesman and *Blessed Bounty.* Reprinted by permission of Joan Wester Anderson. ©1992, 1996 Joan Wester Anderson.

A Christmas Gift I'll Never Forget. Reprinted by permission of Linda DeMers Hummel. ©1992 Linda DeMers Hummel.

The Other Reindeer. Reprinted by permission of Carrie Powell-Davidson. ©1999 Carrie Powell-Davidson.